Money, Power, and Print

Money, Power, and Print

Interdisciplinary Studies on the Financial Revolution in the British Isles

Edited by
Charles Ivar McGrath
and Chris Fauske

DELAWARE

Newark: University of Delaware Press

Associated University Presses
2010 Eastpark Boulevard
Cranbury, NJ 08512

The paper used in this publication meets the requirements of the American National Standard for Permanence of Paper for Printed Library Materials Z39.48-1984.

Library of Congress Cataloging-in-Publication Data

Money, power, and print : interdisciplinary studies on the financial revolution in the British Isles / edited by Charles Ivar McGrath and Chris Fauske.
p. cm.
Includes bibliographical references and index.
ISBN 978-0-87413-027-0 (alk. paper)
1. Finance—Great Britain—History. 2. Economics literature—Great Britain—History. I. McGrath, Charles Ivar. II. Fauske, Christopher J., 1963-
HG186.G7M583 2008
332.0941'09032—dc22
2007051015

PRINTED IN THE UNITED STATES OF AMERICA

Contents

Acknowledgments

MONEY, POWER, AND PRINT: INTERDISCIPLINARY STUDIES ON THE FINANCIAL Revolution in the British Isles grew out of what has become a biennial colloquium of almost the same name. The colloquium, initially held in 2004 at the University of Regina, Saskatchewan, reconvened at the Public Library of Armagh in 2006 and at The Rooms in St John's, Newfoundland, in 2008. As this collection went to press, it was hoped to hold a fourth colloquium in 2010 in Scotland before returning to Regina in 2012 and beginning the cycle again. The Web site of the colloquium can be viewed at www.moneypowerandprint.org.

The colloquia, this collection, and the Web site would not have been possible without the active involvement from the very beginning of our colleague, friend, and web master, Rick Kleer, at the University of Regina. Our sincere thanks and appreciation go to him.

We also gratefully acknowledge the on-going support of the School of Arts and Sciences at Salem State College in Salem, Massachusetts, and of the Graduate School at Salem State College.

Abbreviations

B.L.	British Library
Cal. S.P. Dom.	*Calendar of State Papers, Domestic Series, 1660–1704,* 42 vols. (London: HMSO, 1860–1972)
Cal. Treas. Bks.	*Calendar of Treasury Books, 1660–1718,* 32 vols. (London: HMSO, 1904–62)
H.M.C.	Historical Manuscripts Commission
Nat. Arch.	National Arhives, London (formerly the Public Record Office)

Money, Power, and Print

Money, Power, and Print: Interdisciplinary Studies on the Financial Revolution in the British Isles

Charles Ivar McGrath
and Chris Fauske

THE PUBLICATION IN 1989 OF JOHN BREWER'S BOOK, *THE SINEWS OF Power: War, Money and the English State, 1688–1783,* played a significant role in refocusing attention on a subject that, if measured in terms of publications only, has not received as much notice as it warrants.[1] The financial revolution, and its importance in the emergence of the English fiscal-military state, the English or British nation, or the "first" or "old" British empire (depending on emphasis), was a crucial and complex phenomenon in English history.[2] Yet it also had an importance for other countries in the British Isles and further afield, and has a significance that reaches beyond the realms of academia.

The centrality of economic concerns to the financial revolution jostle side by side for attention with the writings of the likes of John Locke, Charles Davenant, Joseph Addison, Richard Steele, Jonathan Swift, Daniel Defoe, and George Berkeley, the prints, paintings, and engravings of William Hogarth, the plays and drama of John Gay, Thomas Shadwell, Colley Cibber, George Farquhar, and Susanna Centlivre, the extremities of projecting, speculation, privateering, and piracy, the later reflections of David Hume and Adam Smith, and the pleas from the geographical and political peripheries for some consideration within the grand scheme of things.

Thus, as the title of this book implies, the English financial revolution should rightly be called the British financial revolution. What commenced in England took hold elsewhere in the British Isles. In 1967 P. G. M. Dickson explained that the use of "English" and "England" throughout his book *The Financial Revolution in England. A Study in the Development of Public Credit, 1688–1756* was a deliberate action on the grounds that "English historians' perennial ignorance of Irish and Scottish developments, and of the reaction of these developments on English ones, cannot, respectably, be redeemed by substituting 'British' for 'English' and then continuing to ignore Ireland and Scotland."[3]

Since that time, redress has been made in many areas of early modern historical writing that focuses upon one or other parts of the British Isles within the broader context of the islands as a whole, most usually under the heading of "new British history." However, while such work has included integrated studies of religious practice, economies, societies, and politics, the financial revolution has been noticeable by its absence, despite being a topic that lends itself readily to comparative and interdisciplinary study and that is of such central importance to our understanding of much of the early modern and modern world. The reality was that British military and economic growth and global expansion in the eighteenth century was "to a very large degree . . . accompanied by and depended upon a number of altogether less dramatic developments. Victory in battle relied in the first place upon an adequate supply of men and munitions, which, in turn, depended upon sufficient money and proper organisation."[4] Thus, the financial revolution is deserving of further study not least because "of its importance in financing the capture of empire and in stimulating growth of the internal capital market."[5]

The importance of the financial revolution is evidenced by the fact that the attention that has been paid to the subject has, at least in recent times, had a greater influence on scholarship than such a small number of works might otherwise imply. This influence, and importance, was acknowledged by Brewer when he prefaced *The Sinews of Power* with the statement that "Much of this book is . . . concerned with such technical matters as military and civilian administration, taxation and public finances. These are topics with which readers are often unfamiliar and which, despite some outstanding detailed studies, are rarely incorporated into histories of the Stuarts and Hanoverians. My aim is to remedy this omission: to put finance, administration and war at the centre stage of the drama—where they rightly belong."[6]

Possibly the first serious engagement with the topic, beyond the realms of contemporary pamphleteering, was by David Hume, in his essay "Of Public Credit." This was followed later in the eighteenth century by Adam Smith's more substantive consideration, "Of Public Debts," at the end of *The Wealth of Nations.* However, these initial attempts at retrospective consideration were significantly influenced by the fact that both authors were still close in time to the phenomenon they were writing about, and by the fact that both feared that what we now refer to as the financial revolution was possibly the beginning of the end for government, and society, in Britain as they knew it.[7]

That fear was reflective of the writing that had preceded both Hume and Smith. From the outset of the financial revolution most of the contemporary published literature addressing the phenomenon did so from a hostile perspective. As Dickson put it,

> The main reaction of contemporaries to the rapid changes in public and private finance in the six decades after 1688 . . . were essentially ones of alarm and disapproval. They were based on fear of dislocation of the social order by the rise of new economic interests, and dislike of commercial and financial manipulation of all kinds, and had roots going back into the Middle Ages. They were to be much in evidence again during the early stages of industrialism, which also seemed to threaten "traditional" society. Neither alarm nor disapproval were precise; indeed each put a premium on blurring or misstating facts in order to make a case. Neither was truly historical though both depended on appeals to a largely unhistorical past.[8]

In the twentieth century, the subject received its most detailed consideration in Dickson's previously mentioned work, *The Financial Revolution in England.* Dickson's motivation stemmed in part from the fact that he believed that the financial revolution had been "virtually neglected by historians."[9] Prior to that time, the early modern taxation system in England had been considered by William Kennedy, and later, in 1975, by C. D. Chandaman.[10] Since the 1970s others have, to varying degrees, endeavored to add to our understanding of the financial revolution: J. G. A. Pocock has, in passing, addressed the subject on a number of occasions.[11] In a series of important articles, Patrick O'Brien and P. A. Hunt have opened up the world of innovation in indirect taxation in the seventeenth and eighteenth centuries.[12] Within a more focused timeframe, D. W. Jones has examined war finance in the time of William III and John Churchill, duke of Marlborough.[13] Michael Braddick has added greatly to our understanding of seventeenth-century taxation.[14] And David Stasavage has brought the political economist's gaze to bear on the subject, in a work that examines the role of financial innovation in relation to the emergence of democracy in Britain.[15]

A particular debt is owed to the work of Henry Roseveare. Having uncovered the mysteries of the English treasury in the early modern period, in 1991 Roseveare provided one of the most useful, and concise, studies of the financial revolution, a study which should remain the first port of call for the uninitiated and a place to revisit on a regular basis for the more seasoned traveler.[16] In entitling his book *The Financial Revolution, 1660–1760,* Roseveare explicitly argued for a greater consideration and appreciation of the Restoration period with regard to the origins of many of the factors that facilitated the financial innovations of the 1690s and the early eighteenth century.[17] In so doing, he gave a cohesion and sense of unity to the separate works of Dickson, Brewer, Jones, and O'Brien and Hunt, among others.

This current collection of essays, while owing a debt to all the works mentioned above, seeks nonetheless to redress the financial emphasis in published output on this seminal period through an interdisciplinary approach aimed at the nonspecialist reader. The essays in this volume cannot answer all of the questions about the cultural, social, and literary aspects of the financial revolution, but they answer some of those questions and may prompt others to search out answers to further questions raised in the reading of them.

That there was an evolutionary move toward what in retrospect can be recognized as something akin to a financial revolution is evident from the material gathered and assessed in these essays. But if the "revolution" was more a case of evolution, then it must have developed from preexisting practices and ideas. In considering from whence the changes in the British fiscal state came, and how and when such changes were observed by contemporaries, there is, of course, no single approach that is definitively appropriate. A chronological examination might seem, at first, to offer a logical guide to considering the topic, but such chronological arrangement sets aside the fact that some aspects of the financial revolution proceeded in fits and starts and that others are better understood through the commentaries they provoked, commentaries that tended to look back to earlier conditions. To attempt to follow the progress from evolution to revolution in a straight historical line turns out not to work so well in practice.

Starting with some broader sweeps of the contemporary pen before focusing retrospectively on specific technical matters offers a means to arrive, albeit with some diversions and detours, at something approaching a coherent picture. So it is that this collection opens with a consideration of the voluminous output of one particular author who in almost every way represents the opportunity and uncertainty of the times. It was not just the liberalizing of the printing presses that encouraged the explosion of pamphlets that marked the years immediately following the accession of William III and Mary II, but also the existence of an audience eager for advice, comment, and insight. One man, perhaps more than any other, did his best to meet the needs of every section of that audience. James Hartley, in "The Chameleon Daniel Defoe: Public Writing in the Age before Economic Theory," argues that "If we take Defoe as emblematic of his age, and the popularity of his writings would suggest that this is not an unreasonable thing to do, then we can see in his writings the state of thought about economic matters at the time." This is an approach that reveals one certainty: there is no single truth guiding Defoe's truly vast body of economic literature.

On the basis of this premise, Hartley argues that "if Defoe is a window on the contemporary public mind, then it is apparent that the public was neither for nor against the financial revolution. It simply did not understand what was going on. . . . There was no conscious decision here, no long-fought battle where the proponents of change won out. Instead, there was a stumbling toward modernity in an age before the theories explaining it had been discovered." Thus, as Hartley concludes, "the miracle of the financial revolution in the early eighteenth century becomes even more stunning . . . [because it] was not the result of a well-conceived vision of the future, but rather it was simply the stumbling workings of an economy populated by people holding a mass of contradictory beliefs." From which insight, grounded in a reading of the most prolific author of his time, it follows that we should look not for method and inevitability in the march toward the making of a modern economic system, but, rather, for luck, experiment, happenstance, and intuition, together with some rather optimistic cobbling together of existing ways of doing business with new-fangled ideas.

Just how dependent the new was upon the old, and why it was that the old had to go, is made clear by Stephen Timmons in his discussion of "The Hearth Tax and Finance in the West Country, 1662–92." Timmons identifies the network of personal and professional relationships throughout the southwestern-most English counties of Devon and Cornwall that grew up during the years when the hearth tax was one of the main revenue streams for the Crown, and argues that "despite the fact that the most problematic of the five branches of revenue in the Restoration period was the hearth tax, the example of the West Country also illustrates that collection of the hearth tax laid the groundwork for post-1688 revenue collection practices in the same region." The relationships that underpinned the collection of the hearth tax, relationships that were often transient and driven at least as much by business as by personal or political ties, helped establish the idea that tax was a business proposition. While local collection of the hearth tax was a function that fell, more often than not, to local residents, management of the collection was overseen by constantly shifting consortia of regional brokers with mercantile connections in London. Indeed, writes Timmons, "a number of people seem to have recognized in the newly implemented methods for collecting hearth tax revenue opportunities for personal advancement previously unavailable to them, opportunities that required the development of financial networks stretching beyond traditional familial and geographic boundaries."

These networks would later expand to offer opportunities for those in the regions to participate for the first time, relatively easily, in the financial schemes of the City of London. Backing the collection of the hearth tax was also a system in which, as Timmons demonstrates, "the receivers and collectors [of the tax] relied on local networks of financiers to provide bonds (and share profits)." In many ways, the collection of the hearth tax had developed by the time of the invasion of William of Orange into a miniature version of future financial schemes, in which bonds and other sureties were staked against the potential for future income sufficient not only to pay off the bonds but also to turn a profit.

Administration of the hearth tax turned out to be no less fraught with personal risk, untrustworthy middlemen, and complicated legal cases, than later speculative ventures based upon the pursuit of wealth either located in distant and in exotic locales such as Madagascar, or to be found in the growth of the stock market and facilitated by the creation of a permanent national debt complete with tradable promissory notes. The outlines of future financial disputes, involving in later years not so much the government as various groupings of financiers, speculators, and hopeful individuals, can be found in pre-1688 governmental practices, practices that also show that when one consortium failed there was always another ready to take its place.

Competing consortia not only sought to build personal gain on existing structures, even if for the public good; they also challenged each other for the opportunity to launch new and imaginative schemes designed, whether carefully or optimistically, to enrich their members while also addressing the increasingly desperate needs of the government treasury. Yet needy although the treasury might have been, its overseers were not rash enough to fall for many of the less well-conceived schemes that appeared at first glance to offer a solution to their problems. In fact, they also resisted for some time plans that in retrospect turned out to work quite well.

The treasury lords demanded, and received, changes in proposals for the Bank of England and a National Land Bank that owed more to a concern with fiscal propriety than to financial recklessness, as Richard Kleer demonstrates in "'Fictitious Cash': English Public Finance and Paper Money, 1689–97." Ultimately, Kleer determines, "resistance to the Bank of England came from within the government administration itself," which is hardly a ringing endorsement of the idea of a great revolution in finance that swept the land at the same time as William and Mary began their reign as England's only comonarchs. Kleer details the debates that occupied three years of the Westminster parliament's time before the Bank of England proposal finally passed. Much of that debate was taken up with the seemingly arcane matter of interest rates and just how securely "paper money" had to be tied to available specie. A significant ancillary debate was waged around the question of whether promises of future earnings through rents on land could or should be used to secure liquidity for the proposed National Land Bank, various forms of which were offered as alternatives to the Bank of England. The lines of the debate certainly appeared to contemporaries to reflect other partisan political concerns, and public commentators indeed took this approach, but this did not mean that the managers of the state's financial condition saw the debate in the same terms. In fact, as Kleer points out, "sensible administrative conservatism does not make for nearly so interesting a story as a struggle between parliament and Crown for control of the purse."

Just as a consortium of publicly minded investors willing to make money off the state's fiscal needs could be found ready to replace another consortium that had failed at the same task, so conversely, the failure of one group of potential investors to deliver funding for a scheme did not always stop that scheme in its tracks. Arne Bialuschewski, in "Greed, Fraud, and Popular Culture: John Breholt's Madagascar Schemes of the Early Eighteenth Century," examines Breholt's several-year campaign to fund an expedition to Madagascar to recover supposed caches of pirate treasure. Bialuschewski demonstrates the degree to which speculative enthusiasm penetrated the geographic regions of the newly formed united kingdom of England and Scotland. It was a time when privateering was only just going out of fashion as a policy of state, a fall from favor driven, Bialuschewski reminds us, in part by the problem that English chartered privateers in the Indian Ocean had an uncomfortable habit "upon receiving their commissions . . . of . . . promptly sailing to the Arabian Sea, where they turned pirate and preyed upon the richly loaded pilgrim fleets that sailed annually from Surat to Mocha and Jeddah on the Red Sea." Such activity threatened the burgeoning trade with India. It also led to stories reaching Britain of great wealth and fabulous prospects awaiting those who could recover the pirates' treasures. The plausibility of these stories was enhanced by the growth of a popular press quite happy to reprint gossip, innuendo, and sheer invention as reportable fact.

Bialuschewski observes that Breholt knew, also, how to work a crowd and "organized a series of public meetings to promote his Madagascar scheme." It appears, he writes, that "Breholt was a charismatic speaker, for witnesses praised his rhetorical skills. The gatherings were also well prepared public-relations events," designed to work in conjunction with a media campaign that enlisted Daniel Defoe among others. Bialuschewski suggests that Defoe was quite happy to overlook various moral objections to Breholt's scheme because, after all, "all respected founders of great empires were in fact robbers."

Given so much information, misinformation, and opportunistic engagement with the economic debates of the day, writers with an acerbic turn of phrase and an eye for the moment had plenty of opportunity to demonstrate their skills without necessarily having to worry about the validity of their point. Just as Defoe could be almost all things to all people, so another writer who had his own moments of great prolixity was Jonathan Swift—who at times worked for the same paymaster as Defoe but refused even to use his fellow author's name, referring to him on one of the two occasions he mentioned him as "the 'Fellow' that was *pilloryed,* I have forgot his Name."[18] If Defoe's great strength was his ability to adjust his analysis for his audience, Swift's was to adjust his audience for his analysis. Swift's writings represent an emerging sense that the political sphere was the economic sphere and that both were, in some important if ill-definable sense, the public sphere, as Alan Downie points out in "*Gulliver's Travels,* the Contemporary Debate on the Financial Revolution, and the Bourgeois Public Sphere." In book two of *Gulliver's Travels,* Swift encapsulates his long-standing objection to changing financial realities by conflating the economic with the personal when he has the king of Brobdingnag "ask . . . who were our Creditors? And, where we found Money to pay them? He wondered to hear me talk of such chargeable and extensive Wars . . . He asked what Business we had out of our own Island, unless upon the Score of Trade or Treaty, or to defend our Coasts with our Fleet. Above all, he was amazed to hear me talk of a mercenary standing Army in the midst of Peace, and among a free People."[19] Writing in the mid-1720s, Swift appears to consider that the simple expedient of dismissing the army and circumscribing the powers of banks and merchants would be sufficient to restore a mythical *status quo ante* to a nation gone astray.

That Swift's own writings elsewhere demonstrate that this solution could not possibly work bothered him not one iota, as Chris Fauske argues in "Misunderstanding what Swift Misunderstood, or, the Economy of a Province." It helped Swift not to bother himself particularly with the causes of events, or even with the motives behind the causes, but rather to look simply at specifically chosen effects and to make his case from there. So it was that Swift's contribution to the debate over the Wood's halfpence affair in Ireland in 1724–25 conveniently ignored the fact that the coin was to be offered at something close to its actual metal value.[20] Rather, by suggesting that shopkeepers and other small merchants refuse to accept the coin at all, Swift was playing on fears based on ignorance of coinage and invoking memories of the plight of the Irish Protestant merchants and small landholders in the years between 1688, when William of Orange landed in England, and 1691, when his forces finally secured

Ireland.[21] That Swift was not in the business of making economic arguments helps explain why four years later, in 1728, he was complaining that "within three Years past, the running Cash of the Nation, which was about five Hundred Thousand Pounds, is now less than two; and must daily diminish, unless we have Liberty to coin, as well as that important Kingdom the Isle of *Man*; and the meanest Prince in the *German* Empire."[22]

It is true that the scheme that granted William Wood the right to mint coin for Ireland in England had upsetting political implications for Ireland's constitutional status *viz à viz* Britain, but Swift's manipulation of those constitutional questions had very little, if anything, to do with the subject he claimed to be so concerned about: the plight of Ireland's impoverished mercantile and artisan classes. So it is that while Swift's work should be considered in context it should not be considered as providing a context.

Understanding context is a tricky matter, for what a contemporary considers contextual, retrospective analysis might suggest is either extraneous or misunderstood. And as the cases of Defoe and Swift indicate, professional authors pick and choose as they wish, or as they think their audience would wish them to choose, so that contextualizing their works is fraught with difficulty. Nonetheless, a careful reading of contemporary debate and correspondence that was not always available to the broader population should allow us to construct a template from which to understand a debate that was always partially filtered by those conducting it or influenced by its results.

While the struggle between parliament and Crown too often becomes the lens through which the British past is observed, Irish history has frequently been viewed through an entirely different lens, and one that is often as disruptive to the original image as that used to reflect upon British history of the period. However, events in England and, later, Britain, necessarily affected what happened in Ireland, though both the cause and the effect were frequently complicated by the relevant people in Ireland and the relevant people in England not being fully cognizant of what the other party or group was doing. Additional complications were caused by contemporary inabilities to understand the end point of ideas and actions being introduced at that time, which naturally has an impact upon later historical interpretation.

Taking such considerations on board, Charles Ivar McGrath, in "The Irish Experience of 'Financial Revolution,' 1660–1760," argues that in Ireland, as in Britain, the financial revolution was not marked by a specific event that signalled a new period in public finance, but by a slow, inexorable creeping toward a system more recognizably modern than not. From such a perspective, 1688 becomes a marker for the point in time when the various separate components came together, constituting a cumulative revolution in financial practice with the Glorious Revolution serving as a catalyst.

Just as in Britain, where the immediate effects of long-term structural readjustments are often best understood by looking at a smaller sample, so in Ireland the fluctuations in the pace of change can be seen by examining the state of private sector banking in the 1730s. The changes that did come to Ireland were, ironically, both accelerated and postponed by an often overlooked period of "economic growth [which] began in the middle of the 1730s and [which] may be a striking period of expansion when looked at in the long run," as Eoin Magennis reminds us in "Whither the Irish Financial Revolution? Money, Banks, and Politics in Ireland in the 1730s." Magennis considers how this period in Irish history offers an opportunity to understand better the nuances of contemporary responses to events that could not be fully understood as they unfolded. One inevitable result of this was that "Pamphlets upon pamphlets must be wrote to explain the causes and effects of things; the money'd interest against the landed, the landed interest ever jealous of the money'd; the whole world must know all our reasons for every act of prudence or of state."[23] And who was to say which pamphlets were more honest in their appraisal of the situation? Who can say today with any certainty which authors knew of what they wrote, even if we can better determine which of them happened to have history on their side? The failure of the apparently sound Burton and Falkiner's bank in June 1733 did little to help clarify matters and nothing at all to help either the public or the political classes distinguish private-purpose banks from public-service banks.

Changes in public financing in the late seventeenth and early eighteenth centuries, however incidental and haphazard their implementation, ultimately did produce a system of government substantively different to any that had gone before. Yet it is no easy thing to assess those changes or their impact. The new system of finance shaped many more public and private actions than even the most prolific of commentators could address. So it is that to attempt to understand the rhetoric that underpinned the intersection of money, power, and print as it related to the financial revolution in the British Isles one must pay attention to more than just the money, or the power, or the print.

Notes

1. John Brewer, *The Sinews of Power: War, Money and the English State, 1688–1783* (London: Unwin Hyman, 1989), xi.

2. For some of the arguments put forward for the emergence of the fiscal-military state, the nation and the empire in this context, see ibid; P. G. M. Dickson, *The Financial Revolution in England: A Study in the Development of Public Credit, 1688–1756* (London: Macmillan, 1967), xxi; Linda Colley, *Britons: Forging the Nation, 1707–1837* (New Haven, CT: Yale University Press, 1992), 56–71; J. G. A. Pocock, *The Machiavellian Moment: Florentine Political Thought and the Atlantic Republican Tradition* (Princeton, NJ: Princeton University Press, 1975), 423–61; J. G. A. Pocock, *Virtue, Commerce, and History: Essays on Political Thought and History, Chiefly in the Eighteenth Century* (Cambridge: Cambridge University Press, 1985), 98–102, 108–23; M. J. Braddick, *The Nerves of State: Taxation and the Financing of the English State, 1558–1714* (Manchester: Manchester University Press, 1996); Henry Roseveare, *The Financial Revolution, 1660–1760* (London: Longman, 1991).

3. Dickson, *Financial Revolution*, xvii.

4. Brewer, *Sinews of Power*, xv.

5. Dickson, *Financial Revolution*, 12.

6. Brewer, *Sinews of Power*, xi.

7. David Hume, "Of Public Credit," in *David Hume: Political Essays*, ed. Knud Haakonssen (Cambridge: Cambridge University Press, 1994), 166–78; Adam Smith, "Of Public Debts," in Adam Smith, *An Inquiry into the Nature and Causes of the Wealth of Nations*, ed. Edwin Cannan, pref. George J. Stigler (Chicago: University of Chicago Press, 1976), 441–86.

8. Dickson, *Financial Revolution*, 35.

9. Ibid., 12.

10. William Kennedy, *English Taxation, 1640–1799* (London: London School of Economics, 1913); C. D. Chandaman, *The English Public Revenue, 1660–1688* (Oxford: Clarendon, 1975).

11. Pocock, *Machiavellian Moment*, 423–61; Pocock, *Virtue, Commerce, and History*, 98–102, 108–23.

12. P. K. O'Brien, "The Political Economy of British Taxation, 1660–1815," *Economic History Review* 41, no. 1 (Feb. 1988): 1–32; Patrick K. O'Brien and P. A. Hunt, "The Rise of a Fiscal State in England, 1485–1815," *Historical Research* 66, no. 160 (June 1993): 129–76; Patrick K. O'Brien and P. A. Hunt, "The Emergence and Consolidation of Excises in the English Fiscal System before the Glorious Revolution," *British Tax Review* no. 1 (1997): 35–58.

13. D. W. Jones, *War and Economy in the Age of William III and Marlborough* (Oxford: Blackwell, 1988).

14. M. J. Braddick, *Parliamentary Taxation in Seventeenth-Century England: Local Administration and Response* (Woodbridge: Royal Historical Society, 1994); Braddick, *Nerves of State.*

15. David Stasavage, *Public Credit and the Birth of the Democratic State: France and Great Britain, 1688–1789* (Cambridge: Cambridge University Press, 2003).

16. Henry Roseveare, *The Treasury: The Evolution of a British Institution* (London: Allen Lane, 1969); Henry Roseveare, *The Treasury, 1660–1870: The Foundation of Control* (London: Allen & Unwin, 1973).

17. Roseveare, *Financial Revolution*, vi.

18. [Jonathan Swift], *A Letter from a Member of the House of Commons in Ireland to a Member of the House of Commons in England Concerning the Sacramental Test* (London, 1708), in *The Prose Writings of Jonathan Swift*, volume 2, *Bickerstaff Papers and Pamphlets on the Church*, ed. Herbert Davis (Oxford: Blackwell, 1957), 113.

19. Jonathan Swift, *Gulliver's Travels* (London, 1726), in *The Prose Writings of Jonathan Swift*, volume 11, *Gulliver's Travels*, ed. Herbert Davis (Oxford: Blackwell, 1959), 180–1.

20. For the Wood's halfpence affair, see Albert Goodwin, "Wood's Halfpence," *English Historical Review* 51, no. 204 (Oct. 1936): 647–74; Patrick McNally, "Wood's Halfpence, Carteret, and the Government of Ireland, 1723–6," *Irish Historical Studies* 30, no. 119 (May 1997): 354–76; Sabine Baltes, *The Pamphlet Controversy about Wood's Halfpence (1722–25) and the Tradition of Irish Constitutional Nationalism* (Frankfurt: Peter Lang, 2002).

21. For Ireland in the years 1688–91, see J. G. Simms, *Jacobite Ireland, 1685–91* (London: Routledge & K. Paul, 1969; repr., Dublin: Four Courts Press, 2000).

22. [Jonathan Swift], *A Short View of the State of Ireland* (Dublin, 1728), in *The Prose Writings of Jonathan Swift*, volume 12, *Irish Tracts, 1728–1733*, ed. Herbert Davis (Oxford: Blackwell, 1971), 11.

23. Daniel Webb, *An Enquiry into the Reasons of the Decay of Credit, Trade and Manufactures in Ireland* (Dublin, 1735), 15.

The Chameleon Daniel Defoe: Public Writing in the Age before Economic Theory

James E. Hartley

> Of children's books, any more than of playthings, I had scarcely any, except an occasional gift from a relation or acquaintance: among those I had, *Robinson Crusoe* was preeminent, and continued to delight me through all my boyhood.
>
> —J. S. Mill, *Autobiography of John Stuart Mill* (1873)[1]

> Since we must have books, there is one book which, to my thinking, supplies the best treatise on an education according to nature. This is the first book Emile will read; for a long time it will form his whole library, and it will always retain an honored place. It will be the text to which all our talks about natural science are but the commentary. It will serve to test our progress towards a right judgment, and it will always be read with delight, so long as our taste is unspoilt. What is this wonderful book? Is it Aristotle? Pliny? Buffon? No; it is *Robinson Crusoe.*
>
> —J.-J. Rousseau, *Emile, or Education* (1911)[2]

In 1719 Daniel Defoe first published *The Life and Strange Surprising Adventures of Robinson Crusoe, of York, Mariner,* an account purporting to be written by Crusoe himself of his abandonment by pirates on a deserted island and the life he lived there for twenty-eight years. The book was, like much of Defoe's work, a tremendous commercial success. In retrospect, it seems to have tapped into the aspirations of a generation filled with images of colorful pirates and the hardships of colonizing a new continent.

But the novel is much more than a morality tale for children. In the economics literature, *Robinson Crusoe* has become a metaphor for the workings of a market economy. A particular example gives an appreciation of the economic sophistication of this novel. When Crusoe finds a chest full of money on board his shipwrecked vessel, he exclaims, "I smiled to myself at the sight of the money. 'O drug!' said I aloud, 'what are thou good for? Thou are not worth to me, no, not the taking off the ground; one of those knives is worth all this heap; I have no manner of use for thee, even remain where thou art, and go to the bottom as a creature whose life is not worth saving.' However, upon second thoughts, I took it away."[3] To the modern economist, that passage is astute twice over. First it shows a recognition that money has no intrinsic value and thus is literally worthless on a deserted island. But, second, and even more interestingly, in the fact that Crusoe realizes the worthlessness of money and yet takes it anyway, Defoe is showing the strange allure of money over the minds of rational people. In a mercantilist age, in which nations often confused the hoarding of gold with the generation of wealth, Crusoe is showing himself a man of the times and Defoe is asking us to laugh at him.

While Defoe is now best known for this particular novel, it was not how Defoe first came to the attention of the English public. Indeed, *Robinson Crusoe* was not even published until Defoe was around sixty years old. His first major book, *An Essay upon Projects,* had been published in 1687, and he wrote continuously for the rest of his life. The sheer volume of material written by Defoe is staggering. While nobody seems to doubt that the number of publications is large, there is extensive debate over just how large.[4] Peter Earle summed up the matter nicely when he observed that after he had signed a contract to write a book on Defoe, "To my horror I discovered that Defoe was probably the most prolific writer in the English language, a writer moreover who wrote on every conceivable topic from angels to annuities and from adultery to agriculture. But it was too late to back out."[5] The variety of material is immense; the formats varied. As was customary in the day, much of the writing was anonymous, but less customary was the fact that Defoe was writing multiple anonymous journals, including anonymous commentaries on his own anonymously published works.

So great was Defoe's presence on the English scene in the early eighteenth century that Earle would write, "It is possible to base a study of English society in the early eighteenth century almost entirely on the writings of Daniel Defoe."[6] One of the dominant events of that time was the financial revolution, which was part of the larger movement toward the industrial revolution. Defoe wrote extensively on all aspects of these economics changes. To understand Defoe's thoughts on the changes in finance, it is necessary to understand first Defoe's thoughts on the broader economic changes that form the background for the changes in finance. England in the early eighteenth century was poised between the world of the mercantilists and the world of free trade, between the world of a rigid social and economic structure and the world of high economic mobility, between a feudal society and a capitalist society. If we take Defoe as emblematic of his age, and the popularity of his writings would suggest that this is not an unreasonable thing to do, then we can see in his writings the state of thought about economic matters at the time.

Defoe and the Changing Economic World

Defoe as vanguard

Adam Smith's monumental 1776 tome *An Inquiry into the Nature and Causes of The Wealth of Nations* begins with a brief "introduction and plan of the work," outlining his overall argument.[7] This introduction is important because the book itself covers such a host of matters, it is often easy to lose the forest for the trees. Smith's outline makes it very clear that his book is intended to be a primer on economic development, an explanation of how societies move from their primitive agricultural origins to civilized, thriving states. The principle cause of this change is the division of labor, and the principle cause of the division of labor is the tendency of man to want to exchange in trade. The end result of this process is the development of industry, which increases the wealth of the country. This has the remarkable result that "a workman, even of the lowest and poorest order, if he is frugal and industrious, may enjoy a greater share of the necessaries and conveniences of life than it is possible for any savage to acquire."[8] Societies that are developed in this manner have thriving towns and large revenues for the sovereign to spend.

The general theme of *The Wealth of Nations* can also be summarized thus:

> [I]n all the manufacturing countries in *Europe* the case is the same in degree; as trade has increased, the miseries of the people have abated, the poor being employed by manufacture, by navigation, and the ordi-

> nary labors which trade furnishes for their hands; they have accordingly lived better, their poverty has been less, and they have been able to feed, who before might be said only to starve; and in those countries 'tis observable, that where trade is most effectually extended, and has the greatest influence, there the poor live best, their wages are highest; and where wages are highest, the consumption of provisions increases most; where the consumption of provision is most increased, the rate of provision is highest; and where provisions are dearest, the rents of lands are advanced most.
>
> Again, *for the climax does not end here*; where the rents of lands are advanced, the taxes and payments to the governor are the larger; and where the larger taxes are levied, the revenue being increased, that prince or governor is the richer; and where nations grow richer, they in proportion grow more powerful.
>
> Thus trade is the foundation of wealth, and wealth of power.[9]

What is remarkable about this summary of *The Wealth of Nations* is that it was not written by Smith. Instead, it was written by Defoe in *A Plan of the English Commerce,* published almost fifty years before Smith's work. Of particular interest is Defoe's argument that wages should be kept high. In a precursor to the efficiency wage literature, Defoe argues that higher wages lead to fitter and more productive workers. Thus, while England's wages are higher than those of many of her trading partners, both her productivity and the quality of her goods are also higher. It would thus be counterproductive, Defoe argues, to seek to lower the wages of laborers and the price of the manufactured goods; the end result would be lower-quality goods produced by less efficient workers.

Moreover, Defoe notes approvingly that the general course of trade leads to a remarkable degree of social mobility. Traders and merchants by their efforts and frugality acquire wealth, which raises them up to the point where their children can marry into the best of families; meanwhile the older gentry, through declining fortunes, often see their children becoming traders. There is, similarly, such an extensive web of relationships between the gentry and traders of all sorts that "they that learn thus to despise trading people as such, must either be entirely ignorant of the world, or perfectly incapable of the just impression of these things."[10]

This idea that the class distinctions in English society must give way to the dynamic changes occurring in the early eighteenth century was the theme of one of Defoe's earliest published works, *The*

True-Born Englishman, a poetic satire "pointed at the vanity of those who talk of their antiquity and value themselves upon their pedigree."[11] The poem concludes: "For fame of families is all a cheat, / 'Tis personal virtue only makes us great."[12] The occasion of the poem was a defense of William III against charges that because he was not a "true-born Englishman" his claim to the throne was suspect. Defoe's counter to this charge was enormously popular, earning him quite a sizeable sum. The argument of the poem is that England is a race of mongrels,

> From whose mixed relics our compounded breed
> By spurious generation does succeed,
> Making a race uncertain and uneven,
> Derived from all the nations under Heaven.[13]

The similarity of the argument here to that with respect to professional classes in *A Plan of the English Commerce* is striking. In both cases, Defoe approvingly notes that ancestry is not decisive, that the changes in English society are a sign of progress and are simply continuations of the dynamic nature of English society since its founding.

Defoe as rearguard

Under the pseudonym of "Andrew Moreton," Defoe published a series of pamphlets advocating social reform. The most ambitious of these pamphlets, *Augusta Triumphans,* advocated such things as establishing a university in London and an academy of music, the suppression of prostitution and gambling, and an expansion of the police force to help stop street crime.[14] Another of the Moreton pamphlets advocated the creation of *The Protestant Monastery,* a place where the elderly who were neglected by their children could live in ease.[15] The general thrust of the Moreton pamphlets is clear; they are designed to advocate for serious social reform to help eliminate some of the problems of the age.

It is in this spirit that the most popular of the Moreton pamphlets, *Every-Body's Business is No-Body's Business,* set out to reform one of the great problems of the day. The title is suggestive of what would later come to be known as the problem of providing public goods, goods which are beneficial for society as a whole but which cannot be provided by any individual acting alone. It is exactly this sort of problem Moreton discusses, an increasingly severe problem that people felt helpless to solve. What was this problem? It was, as the subtitle stated, "the Pride, Insolence, and Exorbitant Wages of our Women-Servants, Footman, &c."

The problems being caused by servants were twofold, both exemplified in the difficulties Moreton's sister had recently had in hiring a housemaid. The first was the fact that the prospective employee demanded an extraordinarily high wage for her services. Moreton complains that the wages of servants have risen from 30*s.* a year to £8 per year. These increasing wages place real hardship on those desiring to hire servants, so much so that many people are forced to go without. The problem of high wages further disturbs the country because the servants now demand silk and satin clothing, much to the detriment of the manufacturers of woolen clothing.

However, an even greater problem than the high wages being demanded by the servants is their refusal to do the work expected of them. As Moreton's sister gradually discovers the list of things her prospective employee would not do, she at last exclaimed

> "For God's sake, what can you do?"
>
> "Madam," reply'd she pertly, "I know my business, and don't fear a service; there are more places than parish churches; if you wash at home, you should have a laundry-maid; if you give entertainments, you must have a cook-maid; if you have any needle-work, you should have a chamber-maid; and such a house as this is enough for a house-maid in all conscience."[16]

Similarly, Moreton later complains that "a gentleman keeps a servant, who, among other things, is to clean his master's shoes; but our gentlemen's gentlemen are above it now a-days, and your man's man performs the office; for which piece of service you pay double and treble."[17] The problem, in other words, is the division of labor.

Moreton does not hesitate to offer a series of wide-ranging reforms to correct this growing problem. He advocates a limit of the wages that can be paid to servants; they should start at 40*s.* per year, which would rise to £5 per year after seven years of service at the same place. The clothing of servants, and in particular women servants, should be regulated to ensure that they no longer dress above their station. Servants should be prohibited from leaving their place of employment until a time agreed upon in advance.

The Moreton pamphlets as a whole are tapping into the uncertainties of the age; the disruptions caused by the changing economic situation had altered a great many of the previously established relations, such as those between parents and children and those between masters and servants. In these pamphlets, Defoe puts himself squarely on the side of those resisting the changes. Wages must be kept down; the division of labor must be retarded; economic relations must be heavily regulated by the state and not left up to the market.

It is not simply the change in the status of servants that concerns Defoe about the economic changes in England. As Defoe surveys the landscape of England, he sees that production is a zero-sum game: "Nothing obeys the course of nature more exactly than trade, causes and consequences follow as directly as day and night; if one man can do two men's work, one of the two must stand still; if a manufacture grows in one place, that or another will sink somewhere else; and I wonder from what weak thoughts in trade any man could form a notion that vast quantities of goods shall be made in one place and not the less either of them, or some other sort, be made in another place."[18] Here, there is no notion of economic progress in which new wealth is generated by an increasing amount of production. For every new manufacturer of cloth that springs up, another must fall. For every mechanical improvement that doubles productivity, someone must necessarily become unemployed.

Defoe's views on the zero-sum nature of production led him into some strange contortions in the essay *Giving Alms No Charity*.[19] The essay is an argument against a proposal to set up workhouses throughout the country to reduce the number of beggars and other poor people. Defoe argues as above that for every poor person hired in one of these new workhouses to manufacture goods, there will be another poor person formerly employed elsewhere who will lose his job. The net result, Defoe argues, will be an increase in the numbers of the poor. However, Defoe's solution to the problem of the poor is simply to have them work in the manufacturing firms that already exist. As Defoe puts it, "There is in England more labor than hands to perform it, and consequently a want of people, not of employment."[20] Indeed, England could easily absorb two million immigrants without harm. The problem of beggars is a problem not of a lack of places to work, but rather a lack of willingness to work. Defoe's problems grow even greater when he discusses the results of technological change: "All methods to bring our trade to be managed by fewer hands than it was before are in themselves pernicious to *England* in general, as it lessens the employment of the poor, unhinges their hands from the labor, and tends to bring our hands to be superior to our employ, which as yet it is not."[21]

Giving Alms No Charity thus presents us with the following argument: there are already more job openings than people to fill them (labor demand is greater than labor supply); if an old firm hires a new employee there is no loss to society, but if a new firm hires a new employee then an employee of an older firm will lose his job. There would seem to be no difference between these two cases, and yet Defoe offers one as the solution to the problem and the other as a cause of even greater problems. Similarly, Defoe notes that firms suffer from a lack of workers and thus increasing the number of workers in a given firm is both possible and profitable; however, while adding another worker would not hurt the current workers, adding a new technology that will allow a given worker to produce more will cause some workers to lose their jobs. Again, if the firm could hire another worker with no loss to the first worker, then it should be able to hire a machine to do the same work with no loss to the first worker, yet Defoe offers one as the solution to the problem and the other as "pernicious." Economic theory gives us no means of reconciling this difference. However, a general resistance to change perfectly explains it: if one is resistant to the changes brought about by factories arising in some places and declining in others or to the effects of technological change, then there is a very real difference between the otherwise parallel cases.

An illustrative example?

The previous section makes it clear that Defoe can not be easily pinned down either as a forerunner of modern times or as a relic of an earlier age. Thus, it is helpful to look more closely at the economic issue that was perhaps most dear to Defoe's heart—that of trade. As Defoe wrote in the final issue of the *Review*, "Writing upon trade was the whore I really doted upon."[22] And we can find the key to understanding Defoe's thoughts on the financial and economic changes of the eighteenth century in his thoughts on international trade, the subject of one of the greatest debates of his day.

Defoe on trade

There is perhaps no better indication of Defoe's emphasis on trade in his writings than the two-volume work, *The Complete English Trades-*

man. The work is a sort of "How to Succeed in Business" for the eighteenth century, containing advice on everything from how to keep good records to how to deal with customers to how to avoid bankruptcy. Indeed, there is no better way to grasp the ambitious nature of the work than to read the complete title of it: *The Complete English Tradesman: Directing him in the several Parts and Progressions of Trade, From his First Entering upon Business, to his Leaving off. Particularly with Regard to Diligence, Over-trading, Diversions, Expensive Living, Suretiship, Early Marrying, Compositions, Partnership, Trading Frauds, Fine Shops, Credit, Punctuality, Borrowing Money, Discounting, Book-keeping, Monopolies, Combinations, Under-selling, Engrossing, Litigiousness, Projects, &c. With Useful Generals in Trade, Describing The Principles and Foundations of the Home Trade of Great Britain: With Tables of the British Manufactures, Product, Shipping, Land-Carriage, Importation, Home-Consumption, &c. Calculated for the Use of all our Inland Tradesman, as well in the City as Country.*

In addition to being a guidebook, the work serves as a great encomium to the institution of trade itself. Defoe lists three things in which England exceeds all nations in the world, the first of which is: "That we are the greatest trading country in the world, because we have the greatest exportation of the growth and product of our land, and of the manufacture and labor of our people; and the greatest importation and consumption of the growth, product, and manufactures of other countries from abroad, of any nation in the world."[23] Note that the emphasis in this passage is on both exports and imports. Coupled with the aforementioned recognition of the sterility of money itself, Defoe is advancing a serious argument against mercantilist polices of trade restrictions. It is trade that makes England great, and thus it would seem that anything that would tend to restrict that trade would limit the very thing that enables England to triumph. "The benefits of trade are greater than simply the increase in consumption: These things prove abundantly that the greatness of the British nation is not owing to war and conquests; to enlarging its dominions by the sword, or subjecting the people of other countries to our power; but it is all owing to trade, to the increase of our commerce at home, and the extending it abroad."[24] Tradesmen are the true gentlemen and leading citizens of England; ladies should not hesitate to marry tradesmen; it was tradesmen who made such excellent officers in the armed forces during the wars with France; it is owing to the work of tradesmen that new lands have been found and settled, extending the wealth of the nation.

The discovery of new lands simply furthered the most remarkable advantage of international trade:

> The different climates and soil in the world have by the wisdom and direction of *nature naturing*, which I call God, produced such differing species of things, all of them in their kind equally necessary, or at least useful and desirable, as insensibly preserves the dependence of the most remote parts of the world upon one another, and at least makes them useful to each other and contributing to one another's convenience, necessity, or delight. . . . The generations of the world could not subsist in the manner prescribed without the mutual assistance and concurrence of one another. . . . The merchant by his correspondence reconciles the infinite variety which, as I noted, has by the infinite wisdom of Providence been scattered over the face of the world.[25]

As a result, the propensity to trade across borders is a strong one, and the state can do little to prevent it from occurring: "It is evident, prohibition of trade is only transposing trade and resolving to trade at second and third hand; for both we and the Dutch must and always do trade with France: when the Dutch trade was open and ours prohibited, we traded through their hands . . . the prohibition serves only to make our trade more difficult and less profitable; and we take a great deal of pains to perplex our trade and rob ourselves of the just advantages of general commerce."[26] In other words, things designed to hinder trade end up hurting the country itself: "Heavy duties . . . burden our Commerce, and the rigorous exacting of those duties ruins not the merchant only, but the duties themselves and the trade that should raise them."[27]

The ultimate consequences of preventing international trade are spelled out in a seemingly unlikely place, Defoe's work of fiction *A Journal of the Plague Year.* Maximillian Novak, for example, in his work *Economics and the Fiction of Daniel Defoe*, refers to this book only to note that it shows Defoe's concern for the poor.[28] But scattered among the sundry anecdotes and tables in the *Journal* is an economic argument relevant to the trade disputes at the time of its writing. The work was published in 1722 and purports to be the journal of someone identified only by the initials H. F. The journal recounts the author's experience living through the outbreak of the bubonic plague in London in 1665. The putative author was a merchant who decided to stay in town during the plague, and his journal recounts the rumors and stories he heard and reproduces extensive facts and figures from an assortment of publications.

The importance of economic matters to the work is signaled quite early. In discussing why he decided to stay in London, the author notes: "I had two important things before me: the one was the carrying on of my business and shop, which was considerable, and in which was embarked all my effects in the world; and the other was the preservation of my life in so dismal a calamity as I saw apparently was coming upon the whole city."[29] The author decides to stay; his business, particularly his overseas trade in the Americas, was too important for consideration of his life to trump.

The narration continues with the plague growing gradually worse as the weeks pass, until, at the last, the narrative closes with an account of the end of the plague. Until the end, things in London are looking bleaker and bleaker as the death toll rises and the situation gets ever more difficult to control. The end of the plague comes as a "merciful" surprise. The narrative thus has the structure of an increasing disaster that is ended only by the mercy of God. Situated immediately before the surprise abatement of the plague, in other words situated exactly where the structure of the narrative would require the worst consequences of the plague to be discussed, the narrator states, "It must not be forgot here to take some notice of the state of trade during the time of this common calamity, and this with respect to foreign trade, as also to our home trade."[30] There follows an extended discussion of the calamity of a lack of trade brought about by the calamity of the plague itself.

The author notes that foreign trade almost completely ceased as foreign nations became afraid to trade with a city in the midst of a plague. Domestic trade also stopped as other parts of the country tried to contain the spread of the disease. The results of this cessation of trade were not trivial, and it is worth quoting Defoe at length here:

> But to come to matters of trade. First, foreign exportation being stopped or at least very much interrupted and rendered difficult, a general stop of all those manufactures followed of course which were usually brought for exportation; and though sometimes merchants abroad were importunate for goods, yet little was sent, the passages being so generally stopped that the English ships would not be admitted, as is said already, into their port.
>
> This put a stop to the manufactures that were for exportation in most parts of England, except in some out–ports; and even that was

> soon stopped, for they all had the plague in their turn. But though this was felt all over England, yet, what was still worse, all intercourse of trade for home consumption of manufactures, especially those which usually circulated through the Londoner's hands, was stopped at once, the trade of the city being stopped.
>
> All kinds of handicrafts in the city, &c., tradesmen and mechanics, were, as I have said before, out of employ; and this occasioned the putting-off and dismissing an innumerable number of journeymen and workmen of all sorts, seeing nothing was done relating to such trades but what might be said to be absolutely necessary.
>
> This caused the multitude of single people in London to be unprovided for, as also families whose living depended upon the labor of the heads of those families; I say, this reduced them to extreme misery; and I must confess it is for the honor of the city of London, and will be for many ages, as long as this is to be spoken of, that they were able to supply with charitable provision the wants of so many thousands of those as afterwards fell sick and were distressed: so that it may be safely averred that nobody perished for want, at least that the magistrates had any notice given them of.
>
> This stagnation of our manufacturing trade in the country would have put the people there to much greater difficulties, but that the master-workmen, clothiers and others, to the uttermost of their stocks and strength, kept on making their goods to keep the poor at work, believing that soon as the sickness should abate they would have a quick demand in proportion to the decay of their trade at that time. But as none but those masters that were rich could do thus, and that many were poor and not able, the manufacturing trade in England suffered greatly, and the poor were pinched all over England by the calamity of the city of London only.[31]

It is *immediately* following that passage that the narrator begins the discussion of the end of the plague. The passage itself is as fine an example of a testimony to the benefits of trade in general, and international trade in specific, as could be imagined. It shows how the end of an ability to export gradually comes to destroy all commerce, not just in the exporting industries, but also in the other industries, and not just in London, but also in the surrounding area. The description of the spread of this economic calamity parallels the book-length description of the spread of the plague itself from a single house to the neighboring houses to those who interacted with those houses to other parts of the city to the surrounding countryside—the economic calamity and the plague form a remarkable parallel.

Written at a time when the question of the benefits of trade was an open debate, *A Journal of the Plague Year* leaves little doubt about the importance of continuing to trade both domestically and abroad. The plague had broken out again in continental Europe in 1721, giving Defoe's book an immediate topicality. But also in 1721, yet another piece of mercantilist legislation was passed, prohibiting the use of any printed calicos, an update of an act of 1700 that prohibited the import of such cloth.[32] The legislation was designed to help the domestic woolen industry in England, which was suffering from the competition of cheaper cloth imported from abroad. *A Journal of the Plague Year* thus carries a double warning to the people of England; not only is the spread of the bubonic plague something to fear, but so also is the spread of the plague of the cessation of commercial activity that would result from the cessation of international trade.

Defoe on trade (déjà vu?)

As noted above, Defoe's *A Plan of the English Commerce* contains a striking anticipation of Adam Smith's argument that it is through trade that a nation develops, and Smith's work itself contains an extended attack on mercantilist polices. Defoe, on the other hand, also wrote:

> Nor can we blame any foreign nation for prohibiting the use and wearing of our manufacture, if they can either make them at home, or make any which they can shift with in their stead.
>
> The reason is plan; 'tis the interest of every nation to encourage their own trade, to encourage those manufactures that will employ their own subjects, consume their own growth of provisions, as well as materials of commerce, and such as will keep their money or species at home.[33]

A Plan of the English Commerce was not the only piece in which Defoe made such a striking endorsement of mercantilist policies. In an early edition of the *Review*, he sets forth the reason that England should trade with France:

> Having therefore once but proved that our trade to France, if open, would be to our gain, I would be glad to have any man tell me, why it should be stopped? If it be to our gain, it must be to their loss; and if we are, as by the declaration of war, by all means to annoy them both by sea and land, let us trade with them. We shall beggar them by it, and all men will allow that's as quick a way of beating them as to fight them.

> We ought to trade with every nation we can bubble; I wish we traded with none that bubble us.[34]

That is again as concise a statement of mercantilist trade theory as can be made.

Above, we saw the paean to trade provided in *The Complete English Tradesman*. But, Defoe's encomium extended a bit further. Twice in the midst of the chapter devoted to the glory of the English tradesman in the world, Defoe gives biblical support to his argument. First, "so the English tradesman may be allowed to rank with the best gentleman in Europe; and as the prophet Isaiah said of the merchants of Tyre, that her traffickers were the honorable of the earth, Isa. xxiii. 8."[35] Later, the comparison to Tyre is extended:

> The whole glory and greatness of England then being thus raised by trade, it must be unaccountable folly and ignorance in us to lessen that one article in our own esteem, which is the only fountain from whence we all, take us as a nation, are raised, and by which we are enriched and maintained. The Scripture says, speaking of the riches and glory of the city of Tyre, which was indeed at that time the great port or emporium of the world for foreign commerce, from whence all the silks and fine manufactures of Persia and India were exported all over the western world, that her merchants were princes, and in another place, by thy traffic thou has increased thy riches, Ezek. xxviii. 5. Certain it is, that our traffic has increased our riches.[36]

Is Defoe hinting in these passages that all of this is merely his little joke on us? Take both of the biblical passages that Defoe uses. The passage from Ezekiel comes in the middle of an address to the prince of Tyre (the portion quoted by Defoe is in italics):

> Thus saith the Lord God; Because thine heart is lifted up, and thou hast said, I am a God, I sit in the seat of God, in the midst of the seas; yet thou art a man, and not God, though thou set thine heart as the heart of God. . . . By thy great wisdom and *by thy traffick hast thou increased thy riches*, and thine heart is lifted up because of thy riches: therefore thus saith the Lord God; Because thou hast set thine heart as the heart of God; Behold, therefore I will bring strangers upon thee, the terrible of the nations; and they shall draw their swords against the beauty of thy wisdom, and they shall defile thy brightness. They shall bring thee down to the pit, and thou shalt die the deaths of them that are slain in the midst of the seas.[37]

The passage from Isaiah quoted by Defoe is similarly in the midst of a chapter describing how God has destroyed Tyre for its sin of pride. Defoe, who had been raised in a religious household, and who, when young, had studied for the ministry, and whose earliest writings include a pamphlet on religion that earned him some time in prison, was surely not unaware of the context in which the half-verses he quoted above were located.

If we use these biblical references as a key to understanding the work as a whole, then, suddenly, *The English Tradesman* emerges as a sort of guide for the damned. Defoe is implicitly arguing in this work that the very practices of the English tradesmen are the source of a misbegotten pride, that the trade of England, the very thing that he adduces as the greatness of England, is nothing more than history repeating itself with England playing the role of the condemned nation of Tyre.

Similarly, I noted above that *A Journal of the Plague Year* can be read as an argument against the Calico Act of 1721. But, this was not Defoe's only comment on the purpose of that act. In *A Humble Proposal to the People of England, for the Increase of Their Trade, and Encouragement of their Manufactures,* Defoe argues for the importance of the woolen manufactures.

> I am for encouraging all manufactures that can be invented and set up among us, and that may tend to the employment of the poor and improvement of our produce; such things having a national tendency to raising the rent of our lands, assisting the consumption of our growth, and, in a word, increasing trade in general; I say I am for encouraging new manufactures of all sorts, with this one exception only, namely, that they do not interfere with, and tend to the prejudice of the woolen manufacture, which is the main and essential manufacture of England.
>
> But the woolen manufacture is the life and blood of the whole nation, the soul of our trade, the top of all manufactures, and nothing can be erected that either rivals it or any way lessens it or interferes with it, without wounding us in the more noble and vital part, and, in effect, endangering the whole.[38]

This passage exemplifies what is increasingly obvious as the confusion inherent in attempting to interpret Defoe. The first part of the passage is as forward-looking a statement about the importance of the growth of industries as anything that can be found in Smith, but the second part is as backward looking an argument for the importance of one particular industry as anything from the mercantilist age. And yet Defoe seems blithely unaware of the tension of those two parts. Is legislation preventing the trade of calico prints good for the country or not?

Making sense of Defoe

Faced with the assortment of views Defoe expressed on international trade, what have the commentators on his work concluded? Everything. William Lee calls him the "first and foremost advocate of 'Free Trade.'"[39] Novak has no hesitation in labeling him a mercantilist.[40] William Payne says he was both.[41] Paul Dottin says he was a protectionist who also opportunistically wrote against his own convictions.[42] John Moore argues Defoe was two centuries ahead of his time; that he is "a constructive thinker for our own time" from whom we can still learn economics.[43] William Minto argues that while he was in favor of prohibitions on trade, he often used the popular prejudices of the day to make an argument.[44] Paula Backscheider says that Defoe's writings on trade are "transparently mercenary."[45] Joseph Schumpeter says that while Defoe did not contribute anything new to economic analysis, he ranks high in the history of free-trade analysis.[46] And so on.

How then can we make sense of Defoe? Perhaps the place to start is with the words of one of his earlier biographers: "He was a great, a truly great liar, perhaps the greatest liar that ever lived."[47] In that case, it becomes impossible to determine what *Defoe* really thought about any particular issue. The commentators on his work divine his "true" thought by selecting a thread from among his writings and determining that his writings that contradict that thread were the ones in which he was lying. A typical discussion of Defoe's economic writings thus reads something akin to "Defoe argues in favor of mercantilist policies . . . except when he does not . . . but the latter (or the former) writings are not Defoe's true beliefs." It would seem to be difficult at this late date to offer any authoritative conclusions on which of the strands of Defoe's thought are most representative of Defoe's inner mind.

To find some cohesive economic theory in Defoe's writing is thus to impose order where there is none. In this respect, Defoe may have not only been a truly great liar, he may also have been the best representative of the age in which he lived. Regardless of whether he believed anything he wrote, Defoe certainly knew how to write works that would be popular. He had an uncanny ability to write exactly what his readers wanted to read; in so doing, he had a remarkable ability to tap into the prevailing doctrines of the day. While we cannot use Defoe's writings to determine what *Defoe* thought, they would seem to be good indicators of the thought of that broad, shifty beast called "Public Opinion."

Thus, when we turn to Defoe's remarks on the financial revolution, it comes as no surprise to find that deciphering his views on the changes in finance is problematic at best. This has not stopped others from trying. Perhaps the most indicative conclusion is offered up by John McVeagh in his introduction to an edited volume collecting some of Defoe's writings on finance: "If Defoe's pamphlets do not always strike the reader as internally consistent this is because they offer different analyses and urge different solutions for different occasions. For example he both harshly criticizes and backs the South Sea Company in different circumstances. But bedrock convictions show through, such as patriotism, loyalty to Harley and Harley's South Sea scheme and the characteristic insistences on fair-dealing, on self-interest driving the money-market, and on fraud not succeeding."[48] That "patriotism" is the first-listed *unifying* theme in Defoe's writings on finance is surely damning by faint praise. Perhaps Defoe's pamphlets do not always strike the reader as internally consistent because they are, in fact, internally inconsistent.

Even more curious, however, and perhaps indicative, is that many of the major pamphlets on finance written by Defoe are surprisingly vacuous. For example, the impressive-sounding 1710 pamphlet *An Essay upon Publick Credit* is primarily an argument that the new government should honor the debts of the old government.[49] *An Essay upon Loans* published that same year repeats the argument, adding that people should lend to the government regardless of who is in power.[50] For essays with such comprehensive titles, these arguments seem shockingly tame. The explanation is that the essays were not written to be explorations of finance at all; rather they were written for purely political reasons as an aid to Robert Harley and the Tories who had recently come to power. In essence, both of these essays were simply means of convincing the Whigs who had lost the election that they should not withhold financial support for the new government because the debts of the government transcend the debts of a particular party. Defoe is rather frank about all this in a letter to Harley:

> I am vain of saying Sir the first step I took has been successful and has done more service than I expected, in which the town does me too much honor, in supposing it well enough done to be your own. I mean the Essay Upon Credit.
>
> If you think it proper, I would offer another piece of the same kind; which I would call an Essay Upon Loans; in which I think it may be of some service, to take a certain people a little off of a notion, that they can bring the government to do what they please, by refusing to advance their money; laying no weight upon the advantages the lenders make, and what need they stand in of funds. This Sir I promise my self shall tend to lessen the vanity of some people, who still fancy the government must be obliged to change hands again merely to oblige them, if they do but exert themselves by keeping back their money.
>
> After this Sir, I would offer *An Essay upon Banks,* in which I would attempt to bring those men of paper to know themselves a little, by showing how well the government can do without the Bank, and how ill the Bank can do without the government.[51]

The promised *Essay on Banks* was either never written or it has been lost. But its function in this trilogy is interesting because Defoe had earlier written at length upon the Bank of England, and that earlier essay was hardly an argument that the government could do without the bank. Rather, in *An Essay upon Projects,* Defoe wrote that the Bank of England "is a very good fund, a very useful one, and a very profitable one: It has been useful to the government, and . . . [is] a particular glory to our nation. . . . Besides this, I believe the present Bank of *England* has been very useful to the Exchequer."[52]

Again to take another specific example, what did Defoe think about stockjobbers, members of the stock exchange who traded stocks on their own accounts? It would seem fairly straightforward to say that Defoe took a low view of these individuals. After all, one of Defoe's earliest publications was *The Villainy of Stock-Jobbers Detected.*[53] Defoe would repeat this same theme eighteen years later in *The Anatomy of Exchange Alley,* whose purpose was to prove "*that* Scandalous Trade, as it is now carry'd on, to be Knavish in its Private practice, and Treason in its Publick."[54] These stockjobbers, Defoe explains, are conspiring against the public to spread false news to cause stock prices to rise or fall, to join with traitors to spread rumors that will terrify and discourage the public, to destroy public credit, and to engage in a list of other such malicious practices. Indeed, the essay explains, the stockjobbers themselves know they are evil:

> Have I not heard T.W.B.O. and J.S. a thousand times say they know their employment was a branch of highway robbing, and only differed in two things, *First in Degree, (viz.)* that it was ten thousand times worse, committed upon fathers, brothers, widows, orphans, and intimate friends; in all which cases, highwaymen, generally touched with remorse and affected with principles of humanity and generosity, stop short and choose to prey upon strangers only. *Secondly in danger, (viz.)* that these rob securely; the other, with the utmost risque that the highwaymen run, at the hazard of their lives, being sure to be hanged first or last, whereas these rob only at the hazard of their reputation which is generally lost before they begin, and of their souls, which trifle is not worth the mentioning.[55]

What could be clearer? Can we at least be certain that Defoe saw stockjobbing as a public menace? In *The Director*, Defoe describes the effects of stockjobbers causing changes in the price of a stock: "For all this is nothing to the stock, any more than crying Fire to the city, when there is no fire; the fright burns no houses, the town is not the worse, only a few *Old Women*, perhaps, may go out of their wits for half an hour, and then, *as they were*, all is well again, and they laugh at one another; and so it is here, the company make the same dividends, have the same stock at bottom, nothing is hurt, nothing diminished, they *are as they were*, only the frightened *Old Women* are the losers, and so I think they ought to be."[56] Moreover not only do stockjobbers just hurt a few old women, who after all probably deserve their losses, but the value of the stock itself is completely unaffected by the working of the stockjobbers. "If this then is the case, what are we asking, and what need is there for all this fright? What is it to us what price the stock grew at among the jobbers, and in the Alley, what interest is established, and that it bears proportion to 400 *per cent*? Let want of money, or want of credit, or want of temper, or what want you will, cause men to run it down, and call it a hundred, or what they please, like lottery tickets, 'twill always be worth 400 to keep, whatever it is so to sell or no; and upon this foot the stock will always out-live the attacks upon it, and the price must at last come up to the value."[57]

Perhaps the clearest way to see the shifting nature of Defoe's writings on finance is to see what he had to say about credit itself. Calling it "the life of our inland trade," Defoe argues that without it, trade would fall to one-twentieth of its current level.[58] Credit similarly allows England to conduct trade with the rest of the world to a much greater extent than would otherwise be possible.[59] Not only does credit do these wonders for trade, but it is of immeasurable benefit to the government, allowing it, for example, to conduct wars that it otherwise could not afford.[60] But, in the same essay in which he lauds credit used by merchants, he condemns petty credit (that used by people in order to buy consumption goods) as "the shame of our Gentry, and the ruin of our trade."[61] In other words, credit is good for the merchant to be able to buy the goods to sell to the consumer but bad for the consumer to buy the goods from the merchant.

So, where does Defoe stand on the dramatic increase of the use of credit? What does Defoe think?

> That substantial non-entity called CREDIT seems to have a distinct essence (if nothing can be said to exist) from all the phenomena in nature. It is in itself the lightest and most volatile body in the world, movable beyond the swiftness of lightening; the greatest alchemists could never fix its mercury, or find out its quality; it is neither a soul or a body; it is neither visible or invisible; it is all consequence, and yet not the effect of a cause; it is being without matter, a substance without form. A perfect free agent acting by wheels and springs absolutely undiscovered, it comes without call, and goes away unsent; if it flees, the whole nation cannot stay it; if it stays away, no importunity can prevail for its return. No law can reach it, acts of Parliament cannot influence it; its motions are natural to itself, and never to be constrained; it is sullen and ill-neutered enough in its actings, and perfectly imperceptible in its moving; it comes to a man, or a body of men, or a nation, insensibly, as dust upon the cloths; it goes imperceptibly as light vanishes into darkness; it comes with surprise, and goes without notice.[62]

Perhaps the best summary of Defoe's views on the financial revolution is to simply substitute "Defoe's Thought" for "Credit" in that paragraph.

A PRETHEORETIC AGE?

Whatever are Defoe's other virtues as a public writer, consistency is clearly not one of them. In simultaneously anonymously published works, Defoe could write ably both in favor and against a bill before parliament.[63] However, all of the apparent contradictions in Defoe's thought discussed above do not fall so neatly into opposing arguments on particular legislative proposals.

Consider, for example, the *Review*, a periodical written by Defoe from 1704 through 1713—5,600 pages in all. It was for a time one of the most popular periodicals in London and thus makes a good barometer of the public mood. In the *Review*, Novak finds much of his evidence that Defoe was a mercantilist, which would suggest a receptiveness by the public to such views.[64] Moore, on the other hand, finds in the *Review* much of his evidence that Defoe was in advance of his time in rejecting mercantilist doctrines, again suggesting, given Defoe's commitment to writing for profit, that the public was receptive to such views.[65] So is the author of the *Review* a mercantilist or not? Payne, in his study of that periodical concludes thus:

> In his preoccupation with credit as a substitute for a bullion economy, his arguments for high wages, his disapproval of workhouses, his belief in competition, expansion of trade, and the free movement of labor [Defoe] foreshadowed the coming *laissez faire* philosophy. On the other hand, in his eagerness for a favorable balance of trade, his emphasis on the value of bullion and coin, his approval of chartered colonial companies, his insistence on the importance of colonial trade, and the need of fostering it; in his emphasis on a large population kept busily employed, in his contempt, even hatred, for speculation, he places himself directly in the stream of mercantilist philosophy, and might well be called a "thorough-going mercantilist."[66]

In Payne's summary, we may find why scholarly opinion on Defoe is so divided. Novak is focused on just one part of that list; Moore on the other.

Taking all the parts of the argument in the *Review* together, however, can we say that Defoe was contradicting himself? Not necessarily. Defoe may seem so full of contradictions to us in part because we are looking for structure, for a consistent economic theory. But the very idea of a modern economic theory had yet to be developed. And thus to try to understand the arguments about the financial revolution in terms of competing economic theories is inherently anachronistic.

While economists and historians are wont to find some order in the economic writings of the early eighteenth century, the orders so found are notoriously slippery.[67] Consider the case of tariffs. In contemporary economic theory, we write down models in order to determine whether and in which condition trade restrictions are beneficial or harmful; it is as close to a consensus as anything in modern economics that they are harmful. We tend thus to look back at the early eighteenth century and conclude that there was a grand debate between those who believed that trade restrictions were beneficial (the mercantilists) and those who opposed them (the forerunners of Adam Smith). But if we take Defoe as typical, the debate at that time was not framed in this manner. For Defoe, trade restrictions in general are not the issue at all. Instead, it is obvious that the nation needs increased trade, and that anything that hinders trade is bad for the nation. It is equally obvious that the woolen industry, for example, must be protected at all costs because given the size of the woolen trade to do otherwise is bad for the nation. These views seem contradictory to us because we realize that we cannot get both implications out of the same theory of the economy. But in an age before there was such a thing as economic theory, the contradictions may not have been obvious at all.

If Defoe is a window on the contemporary public mind, then it is apparent that the public was neither for nor against the financial revolution. It simply did not understand what was going on. Things were changing and some of the changes seemed good and others bad. There was no conscious decision here, no long-fought battle where the proponents of change won out. Instead, there was a stumbling toward modernity in an age before the theories explaining it had been discovered.

Thus, if we take Defoe as representative of the age in which he lived, then the miracle of the financial revolution in the early eighteenth century becomes even more stunning. It was not the result of a well-conceived vision of the future, but rather it was simply the stumbling workings of an economy populated by people holding a mass of contradictory beliefs. It was, in other words, the triumph not of the intellect, but of the market, that invisible, chaotic beast. Moreover, if this reading of the age is correct, it makes Adam Smith's *magnum opus* even that much greater; by deciphering and systemizing the nature of the market, Smith introduced an ability to understand the economy in a systematic way that had never before existed.

Notes

1. John Stuart Mill, *Autobiography of John Stuart Mill* (London, 1873), in *Essential Works of John Stuart Mill*, ed. Max Lerner (New York: Bantam Books, 1961), 15.

2. Jean Jacques Rousseau, *Emile, or Education*, trans. Barbara Foxley (New York: E. P. Dutton, 1911), 147.

3. Daniel Defoe, *The Life and Strange Surprising Adventures of Robinson Crusoe, of York, Mariner* (London, 1719; repr., Mineola: Dover, 1998), 41.

4. Maximillian Novak has a brief discussion of this debate (*Daniel Defoe: Master of Fictions* [Oxford: Oxford University Press, 2001], 3–5). The most inclusive list of publications, having 566 separate items, is found in John Robert Moore, *A Checklist of the Writings of Daniel Defoe*, 2d ed. (Hamden: Archon, 1971).

5. Peter Earle, *The World of Defoe* (New York: Atheneum, 1976), vii. Earle is not the only author of a work on Defoe who has had that experience.

6. Ibid., viii.

7. Adam Smith, *An Inquiry into the Nature and Causes of the Wealth of Nations*, ed. Edwin Cannan, pref. George J. Stigler (Chicago: University of Chicago Press, 1976).

8. Ibid., 2.

9. Daniel Defoe, *A Plan of the English Commerce* (London, 1728), in *Political and Economic Writings of Daniel Defoe*, vol. 7, *Trade*, ed. John McVeagh (London: Pickering & Chatto, 2000), 151–52.

10. Ibid., 133.

11. Daniel Defoe, "An Explanatory Preface," in *A True Collection of the Writings of the Author of the True Born Englishman* (London, 1703), in *The Earlier Life and The Chief Earlier Works of Daniel Defoe*, ed. Henry Morley (London, 1889), 178.

12. Daniel Defoe, "The True-Born Englishman," (London, 1700), in *The Earlier Life*, ed. Morley, 218.

13. Ibid., 189.

14. Daniel Defoe, *Augusta Triumphans* (London, 1728), in *Political and Economic Writings of Daniel Defoe*, vol. 8, *Social Reform*, ed. W. R. Owens (London: Pickering & Chatto, 2000).

15. Daniel Defoe, *The Protestant Monastery* (London, 1727), in *Political and Economic Writings . . .* vol. 8, ed. Owens.

16. Daniel Defoe, *Every-Body's Business is Nobody's Business* (London, 1725), in *Political and Economic Writings . . .*vol. 8, ed. Owens, 227.

17. Ibid., 230.

18. Daniel Defoe, *A Review of the Affairs of France* 2.7 (Mar. 20, 1705), in *Defoe's Review*, vol. 2, ed. Arthur Secord (New York: Columbia University Press, 1938), 26.

19. Daniel Defoe, *Giving Alms No Charity* (London, 1704), in *Political and Economic Writings . . . vol.* 8, ed. Owens.

20. Ibid., 174.

21. Ibid., 183.

22. Daniel Defoe, *Review* 1.106 (June 11, 1713), in *Defoe's Review*, vol. 9, ed. Arthur Secord (New York: Columbia University Press, 1938), 214.

23. Daniel Defoe, *The Complete English Tradesman*, 2 vols. (Oxford, 1841), 1:242. The other two reasons for the greatness of England are that "our climate is the

best and most agreeable to live in, because a man can be more out of doors in England than in other countries" and "our men are the stoutest and best, because, strip them naked from the waist upwards, and give them no weapons at all but their hands and heels, and turn them into a room or stage, and lock them in with the like number of other men of any nation, man for man, and they shall beat the best men you shall find in the world."

24. Ibid., 1:249.

25. Daniel Defoe, *A Review of the State of the English Nation* 3.2 (Jan. 3, 1706), in *Defoe's Review*, vol. 3, ed. Arthur Secord (New York: Columbia University Press, 1938), 5–7.

26. Daniel Defoe, *A Review of the State of the British Nation* 7.146 (Mar. 1, 1711), in *Defoe's Review*, vol. 7, ed. Arthur Secord (New York: Columbia University Press, 1938), 582.

27. Daniel Defoe, *A Review of the State of the British Nation* 8.81 (29 Sept. 1711), in *Defoe's Review*, vol. 8, ed. Arthur Secord (New York: Columbia University Press, 1938), 326.

28. Maximillian Novak, *Economics and the Fiction of Daniel Defoe* (Berkeley: University of California Press, 1962).

29. Daniel Defoe, *A Journal of the Plague Year: Being Observations or Memorials of the Most Remarkable Occurrences, as Well Public as Private, which Happened in London during the Last Great Visitation in 1665* (London, 1722), repr., ed. Christopher Bristow (London: Penguin, 1966), 30.

30. Ibid., 223.

31. Ibid., 232–33.

32. Eli F. Heckscher, *Mercantilism*, trans. Mendel Shapiro, 2 vols. (London: George Allen & Unwin, 1935), 1:174.

33. Defoe, *Plan of the English Commerce*, 154.

34. Daniel Defoe, *A Review of the Affairs of France* 88 (Jan. 6, 1705), in *Defoe's Review*, vol. 1, ed. Arthur Secord (New York: Columbia University Press, 1938), 366.

35. Defoe, *Complete English Tradesman*, 1:248.

36. Ibid., 1:253.

37. Ezekiel 28:1, 5–8, King James Version.

38. Daniel Defoe, *A Humble Proposal to the People of England, for the Increase of Their Trade, and Encouragement of their Manufactures, Whether the Present Uncertainty of Affairs Issues in Peace or War* (London, 1729), in Defoe, *Complete English Tradesman*, 1:50.

39. William Lee, *Daniel Defoe: His Life and Recently Discovered Writings* (London, 1869), 214.

40. Novak, *Economics*.

41. William Lytton Payne, *Mr Review: Daniel Defoe as Author of The Review* (Morningside Heights: King's Crown Press, 1947).

42. Paul Dottin, *The Life and Strange and Surprising Adventures of Daniel Defoe*, trans. Louise Ragan (London: Stanley Paul, 1928).

43. John Robert Moore, "Daniel Defoe and Modern Economic Theory," *Indiana University Studies* 21, no. 104 (June 1934): 3–28.

44. William Minto, *Daniel Defoe* (New York: Harper, 1901).

45. Paula Backscheider, *Daniel Defoe: Ambition and Innovation* (Lexington: University Presses of Kentucky, 1986).

46. Joseph Schumpeter, *History of Economic Analysis* (New York: Oxford University Press, 1954), 372.

47. Minto, *Defoe*, 165.

48. John McVeagh, "Introduction," in *Political and Economic Writings of Daniel Defoe*, vol. 6, *Finance*, ed. John McVeagh (London: Pickering & Chatto, 2000), 27.

49. Daniel Defoe, *An Essay upon Publick Credit* (London, 1710), in *Political and Economic Writings* . . . vol. 6, ed. McVeagh.

50. Daniel Defoe, *An Essay upon Loans* (London, 1710), in *Political and Economic Writing* . . . vol. 6, ed. McVeagh.

51. George Harris Healey, ed., *The Letters of Daniel Defoe* (Oxford: Clarendon, 1955), 277.

52. Daniel Defoe, *An Essay upon Projects* (London, 1687), in *Political and Economic Writings* . . . vol. 8, ed. Owens, 47.

53. Daniel Defoe, "The Villainy of Stock-Jobbers Detected," (London, 1701), in *Political and Economic Writings* . . . vol. 6, ed. McVeagh.

54. Daniel Defoe, "The Anatomy of Exchange Alley," (London, 1719), in *Political and Economic Writings* . . . vol. 6, ed. McVeagh, 127.

55. Ibid., 132.

56. Daniel Defoe, *The Director* 15 (Monday, Oct. 24, 1720), in *Political and Economic Writings* . . . vol. 6, ed. McVeagh, 251.

57. Daniel Defoe, *The Director* 17 (Monday, Nov. 21, 1720), in *Political and Economic Writings* . . . vol. 6, ed. McVeagh, 229.

58. Daniel Defoe, *A Review of the State of the British Nation* 5.131 (Jan. 27, 1709), in *Defoe's Review*, vol. 5, ed. Arthur Secord (New York: Columbia University Press, 1938), 523.

59. Defoe, *Complete English Tradesman*, 1:271.

60. Daniel Defoe, *A Review of the State of the British Nation* 6.31 (Jun. 14, 1709), in *Defoe's Review*, vol. 6, ed. Arthur Secord (New York: Columbia University Press, 1938).

61. Defoe, *Review of . . . the British Nation* 5.131, in *Review*, vol. 5, ed. Secord, 523.

62. Defoe, *Review of . . . the British Nation* 6.31, in *Review*, vol. 6, ed. Secord, 122.

63. Backscheider, *Daniel Defoe*, 65–67, discusses one such episode.

64. Novak, *Economics*.

65. Moore, "Defoe and Modern Economic Theory."

66. Payne, *Mr Review*, 92.

67. See, for example, the discussion in Mark Blaug, *Economic Theory in Retrospect*, 4th ed. (Cambridge: Cambridge University Press, 1985).

The Hearth Tax and Finance in the West Country, 1662–92

Stephen Timmons

RECENT SCHOLARSHIP CLAIMS THE SUCCESS OF THE ENGLISH FINANCIAL revolution depended upon a tight collaboration between central and local authorities forged during the last decades of the Restoration era.[1] If that argument is true, there should be evidence from the regions of England to demonstrate the development of local networks built around the taxation and levy structures of pre-1688 governments. Indeed (and perhaps ironically), given that the most problematic of the five branches of the public revenue in the Restoration period was the hearth tax, the example of the West Country does illustrate that collection of the hearth tax laid the groundwork for post-1688 revenue collection practices in the same region.

While historiography focuses upon popular resistance to the hearth tax as the ultimate reason for its demise after 1688, the cumbersome arrangement of responsibility and accountability hamstrung the levy from the outset. Whether the Crown appointed officials in counties such as Devon and Cornwall, or allowed tax farmers in London to choose their own agents, the receivers and collectors relied on local networks of financiers to provide bonds (and share profits) and on local justices of the peace and constables to ensure collection from reluctant ratepayers. This reliance on local networks was particularly significant in locales such as Devon and Cornwall where the proportion of the hearth tax as a part of royal revenue emanating from the region was higher than the national average of 10 percent.[2]

The collapse of the hearth tax, however, left intact the mechanisms for the creation of networks of regional financiers willing to risk their capital serving as receivers between the collectors of the

698 parishes in Devon and Cornwall and the treasury in Westminster. Thus the fiscal health of the nation continued to depend upon regional financiers ensuring there was an adequate flow of direct property taxes to back the government's increasing reliance on loans to finance its wars.

Devon was at the center of hearth tax debate from the outset. Sir Courtenay Pole, member for Honiton, introduced the first hearth tax bill into the English House of Commons in 1662 and subsequently carried it to the House of Lords. The Country party damned Pole as "Sir Chimney Poole," and disapproval of the hearth tax became the first of a series of planks in the platform of an emerging opposition party.[3] The provisions for collecting the hearth tax in the first two acts of 1662 and 1663, like other measures favored by the Cavalier parliament after the Restoration, such as reintroducing Latin for some government documents, harkened back to previous centuries with the appointment of the sheriff as the chief financial officer. However, by the late seventeenth century gathering taxes was the least of the sheriff's responsibilities and one for which many appointees were ill-equipped. The accounts of Oliver Sawle, sheriff of Cornwall from September 29, 1662 through 1663, totaled £3,208 2*s.* but still had not cleared the exchequer in 1676, some time after his death. Similarly, a list compiled at about the same time by the deputy auditor of the county, a Mr. Pollard, that enumerated sums claimed by individual constables and others, had been lost. The total figure outstanding was known (£670 10*s.*), but there was no exact accounting of this total. In light of such occurrences, a provision of the second act allowed the sheriff to appoint a deputy as collector in order to improve the collection process and record keeping.[4]

Additionally, both of the first two hearth tax acts stipulated that the sheriffs work with the constables and the high constables as the major agents for gathering the tax in the parishes and hundreds, rather than with their own subordinates, the undersheriffs and bailiffs. The compensation for this arrangement cost the Crown seven pence in every pound sterling of revenue collected: two pence for the constables, one for the high constables, three for the sheriffs, and one for the clerk of the peace (yet another instance of crossing lines of authority). This practice of rewarding regional officials for efficient collection of revenue would continue after 1688. The justices of the peace, who would usually appoint and oversee the activities of the constables, were relegated to a secondary activity of certifying exceptions to payment of the hearth tax because of poverty or other reasons. The second hearth tax act added a third layer of confusion when it mandated that two "substantial inhabitants" of the parish assist the constables, though without otherwise clarifying the nature of the appointment of such people.[5]

Whatever the discontent with the hearth tax, little active opposition appeared in Devon. No riots broke out, and the only person convicted by the quarter sessions for assaulting an officer was Elizabeth Codner, who was released after a day's imprisonment. Substantial passive disobedience developed almost immediately, however. Gilbert Burrington of Sampford in Crediton refused to allow the constables to enter his home; he later joined William, Prince of Orange, at Exeter in 1688 before any other of the county's gentlemen. More widely throughout the county, constables requested several extra months to file their accounts with the clerk of the peace, complaining that they had too little time to finish verifying the returns filed by individual householders, a complaint that was heard from other areas of the country as well.[6] Over the border, Sir Jonathan Trelawny was reporting by December 1663 that Cornish justices were acquiescing to the manner in which the county's inhabitants were walling up otherwise useful chimneys and reporting dilapidation of their property because they believed the current accounts would serve as the basis for future payments. Significantly, though, Trelawny attributed this "not so much [to] disaffection as [to] a numbness on their spirits."[7]

The most difficult part of the hearth tax for which to account is also the most incomplete. By the 1670s the exchequer was demanding a complete list of all who were exempt from the hearth tax because of poverty. During the 1660s some parishes had included the names and numbers of the poor in their returns but most had not, making a final count for the number of hearths in Devon and Cornwall during the earlier years an exercise in futility. The substantial decrease in the number of reported taxable hearths in Devon, from 77,940 in 1663 to 66,582 in 1665, may have resulted from deliberate misrepresentation by the inhabitants and constables, or it may have occurred because more people were claiming exemptions on the grounds of poverty, or there may have been a combination of both factors.[8]

Payment of the hearth tax fell most heavily on the lower ranks of the middling sort, rather than on the poor, who could claim exemption, or on the wealthy, such as Sir Courtenay Pole, the original sponsor of the hearth tax bill in the Commons, Edmund Prideaux of Padstow, or Sir William Morice of Stoke Damarel, all of whom could afford the relatively inexpensive payment of two shillings per year, and who had pushed the measure through parliament in the first place. The poor benefited particularly from the hearth tax. Not only did the first act exempt those who could not pay poor or church rates, but it also excepted those whose homes and land were each valued at less than a pound sterling a year, or who owned less than ten pounds sterling of possessions.

Whatever the successes or failures of the first two hearth tax acts, the third hearth tax act of 1664 added an entirely new financial infrastructure, further tapping into and relying upon regional networks of borrowing and lending that already existed in lieu of a formally established banking system. The act gave the king authority to appoint receivers in the counties and collectors in the parishes to levy the tax. Rather than establishing a fiscal bureaucracy from the ground up, however, the Crown interpreted the provisions of the third act in a manner that allowed for the creation of a for-profit business in which county receivers and their sureties were rewarded with any surplus money they gathered above and beyond the amount agreed with the Crown or its agents, and the collectors and their bondsmen were paid a portion of their intake rather than a set salary. The underlying assumption was that far more wealth existed in the country, at least as expressed in terms of usable hearths, than the inhabitants or local authorities were prepared to admit, and this assumption drove all further assessments of the hearth tax throughout the rest of its existence. In its own justification, the act cited "defects in the said [first two acts] and great negligence of the said officers . . . and . . . sundry fraudulent practices."[9]

The third act sought to end major evasions of payment of the tax, such as the walling up of hearths, the subdividing of houses or estates into smaller dwellings, or the certifying of houses with more than two hearths as poor and therefore exempt, a common practice in the town of Barnstaple, for example. The act also made the inhabitant then in residence liable for payment in order to discourage a high turnover rate of tenants, none of whom would have occupied the dwelling long enough to pay the tax. Sir Edmund Sawyer, senior auditor of the exchequer, issued printed instructions to the collectors that outlined not only a logical way to account for and record the names, households, and hearths in each parish, but that also summarized in four paragraphs the provisions of the three acts for exemptions for poverty in a very clear and practical manner.[10] The third act nonetheless compounded the administrative difficulties of the first two acts; it still expected the constables to accompany collectors (and to be reimbursed at the same rate as before—a definite blow to profits), and it mandated that local justices of the peace still certify exemptions, resolve all disputes, and quell opposition.

In November 1665, court officials undid all the potentially good work of the third act by sending a circular letter to the clerks and commissioners of the peace in each county which, while reiterating some of the more significant alterations in the third act, and judiciously interpreting other provisions, made fundamental changes that did not always have the backing of legal interpretations. For example, the insistence that smiths, braziers, and pewterers should provide payment for hearths fixed to their furnaces and forges would not receive definite confirmation from the court of king's bench until 1671–72. Additionally, requiring hearth duties from free schools and mills, and from royal lodgings leased to others, added new provisions to the act. Most importantly, the core of Sawyer's letter arbitrarily ended the ability of individual justices to exempt households at their discretion and informed the county benches that only their decisions on the subject during the quarter sessions would be honored. More than any other aspect of the letter, this decree set the gentry against the royal authority imbued in the new act: it not only severely restricted the traditional powers of individual justices, it also unilaterally overturned the provisions that the members of parliament had framed.[11]

The Crown's first attempt to collect the hearth tax through receivers it appointed ended in dismal failure. A royal proclamation was issued in December 1665 demanding that all arrears be paid immediately to the receivers and collectors, and blamed the justices for withholding support from hearth tax officers faced with intransigence.[12] In June 1667, the treasury finally lost patience with the receivers from Cornwall, Robert and William Scawen, and orders went out for their arrest so that they could give an accounting for Michaelmas 1664-Lady Day 1666, especially the last period. The Scawens's contact in London had neglected to pay £150 of the funds due. In January 1668, the Scawens took the precaution of securing a £400 bond from Robert Sawle, which covered levying and paying the tax and arrears, but excluded any legal charges their actions might accrue. And wisely so. In March 1668, the treasury disallowed certificates of exemption amounting to £360 from 7,200 of Cornwall's paupers and impressed mariners. The justices of the peace charged the deficit to the Scawens; the Scawens attempted to shift it back to the county. The case dragged on through 1677 without reaching any resolution.[13]

Collection of the hearth tax in Devon went even more poorly than in Cornwall. In 1668, William Harris signed on as receiver for the county's income, but the collectors he appointed could not deliver their monies. Harris, a Welshman, fled to Monmouthshire. Letters went out from the treasury to fifteen of Devon's justices of the peace asking them to inquire why such men as Edmund Hitchcock, who had charge of the parishes in Hayridge and Tiverton hundreds in north Devon, remained in arrears to Harris and could not even return the list of hearths. Sir Walter Yonge, a leading radical in Devon, filed his own complaint against a collector named Chilcott. In another instance, Samuel Lewis of Sheepwash had imprisoned for an alleged debt William Milton, the collector in north Devon for Shebbear and Black Torrington hundreds in which Lewis resided. Lewis then seized Milton's land, valued at £2,000. The case was eventually removed to the king's bench, but seven other cases went unresolved, and, according to the terms of their agreement, the treasury demanded that Walter and Thomas Pritchard, two of Harris's sureties, pay £500 and provide securities for another £1,500, and then called for another £500 when the case remained unresolved. The treasury also sequestered the estate of Cadwallader Jones, customer of Sandwich (a sinecure position in the customs service), who had provided additional surety for Harris. In order to regain his property, Jones asked for authorization from the treasury to go to Devon, inspect the books of Harris and his collectors, and return with the names of the people who still held the money. The treasury promised that "we will see that assistance is given you for recovery of the same from such persons." Jones's efforts availed him little. He was temporarily imprisoned until he could pay £300 of the £2,500 he had originally undertaken on Harris's behalf, but he eventually regained his freedom and his position as customer. Devon's justices did little, if anything, to help resolve the matter.[14] In retrospect, it was perhaps because of this somewhat ineffective approach to tax collection that Devon and Cornwall escaped the riots against the hearth tax during the winter of 1667–68 which hit the counties immediately to the east particularly hard.

Matters did not improve with the appointment of Edward Rutter as the new receiver. Unlike Harris, Rutter did not flee the county, but he did take strong legal action against six of his collectors for arrears totaling £8,932.[15] More tellingly, two collectors, Nicholas Webb and William Trevisa, took action against Rutter himself. Both cases had remarkable similarities. Rutter had assigned each man extensive tracts in Devon, far more extensive than those assigned to the high constables under the original act. Rutter paid all his collectors the standard rate of one shilling for every pound sterling collected and, as an added incentive, promised them half the income from taxes on all hearths discovered that were not included on the exchequer's existing rolls. Not surprisingly, both Webb and Trevisa made extensive discoveries in their territory, Webb 979 and Trevisa 2,595. Belatedly realizing the cost, Rutter tried to back out of the agreement; the exchequer forced him to pay. At the same time, in their eagerness to make more money from discovered hearths, both Webb and Trevisa fell behind in their collection for known hearths. Webb paid £1,505 7*s.* (with £86 11*s.* still owed by a subcollector), Trevisa £1,594, but both still owed substantial arrears, Webb £175 5*s.* and Trevisa £129 15*s.* The farmers in London started putting pressure on Rutter, and Rutter in turn sent letters to all his collectors to hasten the collection. Apparently, he made verbal promises to both Webb and Trevisa that if they hired additional assistants he would pay extra for them—according to Webb, the princely sum of £60 per year, three times that of a similar position in the customs service. Both hired four family members, friends, or neighbors, but Rutter apparently paid them the going rate of one shilling per pound and, much to Webb's and Trevisa's chagrin, took it out of his collectors' pay. Finally losing patience with both men, Rutter hired a total of nine new collectors for the same areas who assisted with the collections of 1669 but interfered dramatically with Webb's and Trevisa's attempts to gather their arrears. Disputes over the main facts of the cases, as well as quarreling over the amounts involved, identifying jurisdictions and times of the assignments, and hearings on other incidents involved in the case brought Rutter's farming of the hearth tax to a standstill.[16] North Devon proved to be an impossible place to work, despite the lack of physical opposition, violence, and riots, not only for the hearth tax collectors, but also for excise agents and customs officers.

Some obstacles were primarily the consequence of an emerging way of doing business, relying not only on local connections but, more importantly, on a relatively wide reaching web of financial and personal connections. A number of people seem to have recognized the opportunities for personal advancement in the new methods for collecting hearth tax revenue that had previously been unavailable to them, opportunities that required the development of financial networks stretching beyond traditional familial and geographic boundaries. Rutter can only be classified as a "new man." He claimed residence at Youlston in the parish of Shirwell, but the Chichester family owned that estate continuously during the century. Rutter was able to recruit two neighboring craftsmen to assist him, but other than John Gay of Frithelstock most of his recruits to gather the hearth tax in north and west Devon came from elsewhere. Six, including his accountant and clerk, came from Plymouth, and three worked as constables in places where the tax was collected. The Trevisas, a family of minor gentry who appear in the 1620 visitation to Cornwall but not in any lists of justices of the peace from later in the century, recruited eight people from four parishes surrounding their ancient seat of Crocadon. Rutter had borrowed £200 from the senior Trevisa at one point, and employment as a hearth tax collector for the son may have been a form of payback.

The Crown's second attempt to appoint its own officials failed as miserably as the first in the West Country. Two new royal agents, Richard Sherwyn, a treasury clerk, and William Webb, auditor to the former farmers, chose George Clerke of Tiverton as receiver for Devon and Cornwall.[17] Clerke and his backers, all from Devon, fared no better than the farmers in returning their due to the exchequer. Clerke, John Norman, and Thomas Prowse quarreled over the division of £3,588 10*s.* 6*d.* of profits. Norman, a surety and financier, still retained £2,291 3*s.* 4*d.* in March 1676 which he and Clerke had owed for Michaelmas 1671, leaving Clerke a further £1,200 in arrears for all the money he should have paid by Lady Day 1674. One of his collectors, Robert Wood, had died, still owing him £200. William Boggan, one of Clerke's sureties, claimed that he himself, Anthony Salter, Prowse, and John Brooke, had already taken possession of both Clerke's and Norman's lands and paid most of what was owed by the group to the Crown, with the exception of Clerke's own share. But in February 1677, Thomas Bere, leader of the second group of Clerke's sureties, maintained that he, Salter, and James Calwoodleigh had paid an additional £722 6*s.* 9*d.* for Clerke's remaining arrears, and only Prowse still owed £307 6*s.* 9*d.* Prowse himself later claimed to have remitted a total of £1,400, temporarily obtained an injunction against a Mr. Northcote who was receiving £1,800 from the Crown, but ignored Bere's claim that he had also received £400 of hearth money from Clerke. The proceedings began in December 1672 and had not ended by July 1680.[18]

To better enforce provisions of the hearth tax acts, successful assessments often depended more upon the efforts of outsiders as collectors, instead of locals who might side with their neighbors and underreport the number of chargeable hearths. One such collector, Robert Nailer of Surrey, "did behave himself very honestly and justly," "made a diligent friend," "and . . . had good relations and friends" when he resided with Bartholomew Gidley until early 1672 in Antony, across the sound from Plymouth. Nailer's employment in east Cornwall overlapped with Rutter's farm of the hearth tax and Clerke's appointment as receiver. Nailer kept an account book separate from official returns of moneys that he had received from his own men employed in the various parishes in Cornwall to which he was assigned, listing dates and amounts as he acquired them. In later years, Nailer kept his own strict account of receipts from payment of the hearth money. He also prepared a page of several notes that he could leave at the homes of absent owners and occupants, requiring them to report the number of hearths in their homes within a six-day period and threatening forcible entry if they did not. Nailer also submitted a much larger blank notice, dated 1666, to the parish as a whole, threatening the full weight of the law and the exchequer against home owners absent at the time of the inspection.[19] Conscientious collectors such as Nailer were aided by the 1668 publication *The Several Acts of Parliament Made for Establishing, Ordering, and Collecting of His Majesties Revenue Arising by Hearth Money*, prepared by John Bill and associates. This volume reprinted all three hearth tax acts in their entirety with full marginalia indicating major topics, an index of major headings (sixty-three pages), and a reprint of the 1665 proclamation (though it was misdated as 1666).[20]

Few collectors kept their employment as collectors as long as Nailer. The papers of the Hele family of Gnaton, Newton Ferrers, indicate that thirteen different men signed twenty surviving copies of hearth tax receipts from Lady Day 1673 through Michaelmas 1686. Some receipts do not survive from times of political upheaval, such as the Exclusion Crisis of 1679 to 1681, the Rye House plot of 1683, and Monmouth's rebellion in 1685.[21]

Whatever the problems facing hearth tax collectors, the practice of appointing individuals from Westminster to manage the collections continued. In December 1678, letters patent appointed a new group of farmers, and, as the political crisis worsened in 1679, a royal proclamation to that effect appeared in September when their commission first took effect.

Three of the West Country farmers were quiet financiers who apparently harbored no further political ambitions. One followed the prevailing court wind. The fifth, Anthony Rowe, supported the duke of Monmouth and would not waver in his political principles during the coming decade.[22] To better assist the collectors, John Bill and associates reprinted *The Several Acts of . . . Hearth Money* in 1678 and again in 1681 so that the technical provisions of the law remained in the public domain.[23]

The advent of the Exclusion Crisis in 1679, which centered on the attempt in parliament to debar Charles II's younger brother, James, duke of York, from the succession to the throne because of his Catholicism, breathed new life into political opposition to the hearth tax. Local objections to the hearth tax arose in Exeter during the elections for the first exclusion parliament in March 1679, when radicals disturbed the normally staid proceedings. While mayor in 1676, William Glyde had augmented the presence of the opposition in the city by allowing fifteen or sixteen nonconformist ministers to preach. During the elections, he promised the poorer masters and craftsmen that the power of the corporation would be decreased and the unpopular hearth tax removed. The day of the election he gathered a mob to disrupt the proceedings at the city guildhall. Endymion Walker, the city sheriff, attempted to expel them, but chanting "Down with the church, down with the chamber," the mob accosted the royalist electors. Glyde assaulted Walker when the sheriff adjourned the proceedings for the night, and then Glyde assailed his successor, William Sandford, and scattered the polling books. The mob prowled the city throughout the night. When the rioting continued the next day, the sheriff canceled the election for several days until passions could cool. Even so, the mob and haranguing ministers kept the city inflamed so that Glyde and Malachi Pyne, another radical, were returned over the vested interests of the bishop and the corporation.[24]

Opposition by local leaders to the hearth tax could take more subtle forms. When the farmers renegotiated their contract with the new lord treasurer, Laurence Hyde, earl of Rochester, in early 1681, they increased their bid by £17,600 in return for any expected surpluses, which amounted to £20,000 per year. Henry Pollexfen, a Lincoln's Inn lawyer who had a residence in Woodbury, just south of Exeter, challenged the alleged lack of disclosure before the treasury commissioners in late 1681. Pollexfen was an establishment Whig who would quickly join William of Orange's party in 1688. He opposed Monmouth's faction, however, and would obtain a notorious reputation in Devon for prosecuting captured rebels during Judge George Jeffreys's bloody assizes in 1685.[25]

Nor did the dissolution of the third and final exclusion parliament in 1681 end local attempts to evade the hearth tax. In July and August 1682, the treasury informed the mayor and town clerk of Bodmin that it would no longer allow their practice of preventing hearth tax collectors from securing payments due from newly constructed, or "discovered," hearths until the cumbersome process of certifying them in the exchequer had been completed. The attorney general had already issued an opinion stating that such distraints were perfectly legal. In January 1683, the treasury sent a similar notice to Devon's justices of the peace who were engaging in the same practice.[26] In 1683, the publication of a royal proclamation appointing a new hearth tax commission justified the new method of collection because "certain justices have refused to enforce the laws because the profits got to the farmers of the revenue."[27]

The decision to assign the hearth tax back to a royal commission was part of the Crown's general strategy of seeking to tighten its hold over the country after the debacle of the Exclusion Crisis, a strategy which also included the restructuring of parliamentary boroughs and the prosecution of Protestant dissenters. The new letters patent appointed two former associates of the old farmers, who were to assist seven officials experienced in royal finance. In effect, the commissioners of the excise were made the commissioners of the hearth tax, with the bonding of hearth tax collectors being handled through the administrative apparatus of the excise, thereby reducing the difficulties that had plagued Harris, Clerke, Rutter, and the Scawens in the West Country.[28] In October 1684, the treasury ordered the publication of a more complete set of instructions for receivers and collectors than that written two decades earlier by Sir Edmund Sawyer.

These instructions contained not only the provisions of the three acts but also reviewed judicial interpretations of how the acts should be applied, summarized administrative decisions on how to act in those grey areas not specifically covered by either legislation or rulings, and included advice gleaned from twenty years of practical experience about how to best collect the tax without antagonizing either inhabitants or local officials.[29]

Popular, passive resistance to the hearth tax actually expanded during the years when administration was supposedly strengthening. The inhabitants of 241 of 452 parishes in Devon (excluding Exeter and the county's other boroughs) attested to local justices that they had razed some of their hearths and so were exempt from part of their taxation.[30] The date is known for 289 of 542 certificates of razing; for 129 no date is listed; and 124 are undetermined from the available data. Mapping shows clearly defined areas of demolition occurring throughout the county where local justices cooperated with the inhabitants in certifying the destruction, or, just as clearly, indicates where in many isolated and small groups of parishes the authorities refused to recognize any legitimacy in dismantling hearths. At first, the entire process was led by Devon's radical gentry disgruntled by the Crown's policies before, during, and, most especially, after the Exclusion Crisis, but a sampling of the documentation indicates that by 1688 demolition had become the preserve of the plebeian element, either out of economic necessity or to help undermine the regime by withholding anticipated tax revenues.[31]

Despite its radical roots, Monmouth's rebellion had little impact on the existence of the hearth tax in the West Country, and efforts to collect the tax redoubled afterward. For example, Sampson Hele of Gnaton, Newton Ferrers, apparently paid the hearth tax for only one tenant from 1681 to 1683, but in 1686 paid for seventeen hearths in eleven different houses. Challenging the social and political prominence of the gentry who often owned such housing had always proved problematic for collectors from more humble backgrounds. Disaster invariably ensued. At the urging of his superior officer, William Clench, a subcollector, had forcibly distrained goods from a Cornish justice of the peace and "other persons of quality," to force them to pay the hearth tax for their poorer tenants. An altercation with one of the inhabitants of Penzance had already landed Clench before the mayor's court, and now both constables and high constables escorted the collectors through that part of Cornwall to ensure collection of the tax. Clench's final confrontation came in March 1687 against George Robinson, son of a distinguished royalist. In front of witnesses, Clench grabbed a waistcoat and tankard from Robinson, intending to distrain them, but fell to the ground after the waistcoat tore. The case landed before king's bench, with Robinson, supported by Sir Joseph Tredenham, one of the preeminent county gentry, offering an out-of-court settlement of £5, and Samuel Hardwick, the receiver-general for Cornwall and Devon—and another outsider—insisting upon his officer's probity.[32]

Initially, the Glorious Revolution of 1688 had no impact on the existence of the hearth tax. Nothing was said in William of Orange's *Declaration* or *Additional Declaration* concerning the status of the hearth tax or other revenues.[33] Indeed, after landing in Devon, William's financial commissioners, including James II's former commissioner Anthony Rowe, circulated a public announcement on November 13 notifying the populace that they would officially receive all the customs, excise, and hearth tax duties. The expedition had been seizing the royal revenue since landing, although some officials resisted their demands. The Penzance customs collector, Robert Manly, deserted his post shortly after hearing of the expedition's departure from the Netherlands. Francis Blight joined James's forces, taking with him almost £440 from diocesan tenths.[34] James's loyalists urged customs officers to keep as little money on hand as possible and to convey the surplus to the army at Salisbury. For its part, the Williamite council issued warrants to apprehend excise officers who had fled into the countryside.

Williamite efforts to reconstruct the mechanisms of revenue collection in some cases relied upon co-opting existing customs and excise officers, who, in turn, demanded their regular salary before they would cooperate. Elsewhere, new personnel replaced existing officers as part of the revolt. In some instances, William's council assigned dragoons to accompany revenue officials to help convince reluctant people to pay their taxes. Nonetheless, in comparison with the excise and the customs, the collection of the hearth tax almost entirely collapsed. As late as January 1689, the new regime issued a proclamation with orders for the continued payment of customs duty, the excise, the hearth tax, and other assessments, which many people had neglected or refused to pay since William's landing in November 1688.[35] Yet the hearth tax made an expedient concession that the new king and queen and parliament could make to people otherwise unaffected by the more grand provisions of the revolutionary settlement. The new government declared the hearth tax "not only a great oppression to the poorer sort, but a badge of slavery upon the whole people, exposing every man's house to be entered into and searched at pleasure by persons unknown to him. . . . Not only by restoring the rights and liberties which have been invaded contrary to law, but in desiring to make them happy and at ease by taking away such burdens as by law were fixed upon them."[36]

Even Tories could play to the crowd when it benefited their position. Sir Edward Seymour, of Totnes, representing Exeter, and a former speaker of the House of Commons, demanded that the government punish the officials who had devised the unpopular tax decades earlier. But the last hearth tax act provided for the continued payment through March 25, 1689, as well as for full payment of all arrears, and a royal proclamation of June 1689 reminded the country that despite its abolition, arrears of the hearth tax were still owed.[37]

Practicality infused principle. The commissioners of the excise reported in early February 1689 that supporters of James II's regime had effectively undermined further collection of the hearth tax at the revolution. The clerk of securities had made off with the collectors' bonds, and many of the collectors themselves had disappeared with both their books and their accounts. The whole tiresome process of enumerating the hearths in each parish would have had to be redone after it became apparent that the collection due in March 1689 was inadequate. As a case in point, Samuel Hardwick, receiver-general for Cornwall, Devon, Somerset, and Dorset had regularly entrusted the transfer of his funds to Westminster to Thomas Morris, a carrier based in Exeter. After Morris had been bankrupted by the arrival of the Anglo-Dutch army in November 1688, Hardwick had been able to recover only £110 of the £200 entered on his accounts. In September 1691 the commissioners of the excise recommended that due allowance be made and his accounts closed. Yet regional financial networks still provided the sinews of war. General Charles Trelawny received money from several sources in 1689 for his regiment stationed in Plymouth, including £1,750 from the hearth tax.[38]

The tax settlement upon which the financial revolution finally rested was a step back from the construction of fiscal bureaucracies such as the customs (1,313 officers in 1690) and the excise (1,211) that had been so successful in the reigns of Charles II and James II.

At the same time, the government abandoned the minimal debt characteristic of the 1680s and fueled the war effort of the 1690s and thereafter with budgets running to ten times the amount of income. Parliament reverted to a type of direct taxation employed during the interregnum, the first years of the restoration, and, sporadically, during the 1670s, with large commissions of unpaid county gentry—most of the justices of the peace, their sons and cousins, parish gentlemen, borough magistrates, and other worthies—overseeing assessors and collectors whom they appointed in each parish, in effect becoming similar to "Europe's quasi-autonomous fiscal estates."[39] The hearth tax, for all its shortcomings, had provided the middling sort who comprised low-ranking officers with more regular practice in that type of collection than had the eighteen subsidies and three poll taxes of the same era, and even if the collectors were now confined to their own parishes they had the experience of the hearth tax to fall back upon. Indeed, the most positive concession effected by the end of the hearth tax was that their pay increased tremendously, from one pence per pound sterling collected to three pence under the 1692 land tax.

The Bank of England and the East India Company became model institutions of the financial revolution; however, most of their directors, subscribers, and brokers came from London's environs, and provincial banks did not appear until the mid-eighteenth century.[40] While receivers of the land tax lost the independence they had enjoyed under the hearth tax, and men such as Scawen, Harris, Rutter, Clerke, Hardwick, and Webb, but not Trevisa or Sawle, were excluded from the commission lists, receiverships still remained a desirable option for local financiers, and receivers and their backers sought both employment and profits from the new taxation system.

Despite a lifetime of almost three decades, the hearth tax suffered from the same shortcomings at its demise that it had at its inception. The tax was, in effect, an attempt to combine positive elements of both indirect and direct taxes (independent collection agencies coupled with mandatory payment by all households) that ended with the worst aspects of each (periodic resistance on the part of taxpayers combined with the necessity for cooperation from local elites, who were then assigned a subordinate role in the process). The direct taxes passed after the Glorious Revolution, especially the land tax, returned more broadly to the principle that the county gentry would assist the central government in commissioning and collecting the duties—social and political responsibilities that became the enduring hallmark of the financial revolution.

The experience of the hearth tax (and poll taxes) had convinced the gentry and aristocracy in parliament that progressive taxes were the only means of ensuring adequate revenue for a national budget, which was dependant, to a substantial proportion, upon public credit, and were the only assessments acceptable to the middling sorts, who had an accepted political voice but often little in the way of effective political power. Making parish leaders responsible for the assessment and collection of the new direct taxes, instead of outsiders, bought off much of the local opposition that had plagued the hearth tax. Nevertheless, the hearth tax provided a valuable training ground for local financial networks in bonding, receiving, and profiting from tax gathering under difficult circumstances.

Appendix

Certificates of demolition of fire hearths, Devon, 1667–89

1667:	2	1675:	14	1683:	26
1668:	4	1676:	0	1684:	28
1669:	4	1677:	7	1685:	17
1670:	0	1678:	13	1686:	38
1671:	3	1679:	14	1687:	25
1672:	1	1680:	9	1688:	42
1673:	6	1681:	10	1689:	1
1674:	12	1682:	13		

Source: Certificates of Demolition of Fire Hearths, QS 79/3, Old A5/183/2, Hearth Tax Papers, Devon Record Office.

Notes

I would like to thank Nick Barratt for his work in the National Archives, and the staffs of the Devon Record Office, the North Devon Record Office, the Cornwall Record Office, the Cornish Studies Library, and the Royal Lemington Spa Library, Warwickshire.

1. Steve Pincus and Alan Houston, "Introduction," in *A Nation Transformed: England after the Restoration,* eds. Steve Pincus and Alan Houston (Cambridge: Cambridge University Press, 2001), 12; M. J. Braddick, *Parliamentary Taxation in Seventeenth-Century England: Local Administration and Response* (Woodbridge: Royal Historical Society, 1994), 289–96; Mark Goldie, "The Unacknowledged Republic: Office Holding in Early Modern England," in *The Politics of the Excluded, c. 1500–1850,* ed. Tim Harris (New York: Palgrave, 2001), 154–55; P. G. M. Dickson, *The Financial Revolution in England. A Study in the Development of Public Credit 1688–1756* (London: Macmillan, 1967), 43.

2. C. D. Chandaman, *The English Public Revenue, 1660–1688* (Oxford: Clarendon, 1975), 89 n.1, 306, 308, 313–16, 321–22, 326, 329. The fiscal year began at midsummer. Excise totals include the gross produce both of normal excise and of additional excise accounts. The hearth tax accounts for the period include a combination of gross and net returns, but not both for the same year. Customs, the direct taxes, and the small branches include just net returns.

3. Ibid., 77–81; Basil Duke Henning, ed., *The History of Parliament: The House of Commons, 1660–1690,* 3 vols. (London: Secker and Warburg, 1983), 3:253–55.

4. 14 Car. 2, c. 10, *The Statutes of the Realm,* 12 vols. (London, 1810–28), 5:390–93; 15 Car. 2, c. 13, *Statutes of the Realm,* 5:493–95; *Cal. Treas. Bks. 16767–9,* 279, 403.

5. 15 Car. 2, c. 13, *Statutes of the Realm,* 5:493–95; *Cal. Treas. Bks. 1676–79,* 279, 403.

6. *Bibliotheca Lindesiana (Volumes 5 and 6): A Bibliography of Royal Proclamations of the Tudor and Stuart Sovereigns, and of Others Published Under Authority, 1485–1714,* volume 1, *England and Wales,* ed. James Ludovic Lindsay, 26th earl of Crawford and 9th earl of Balcarres (Oxford: Clarendon, 1910), no. 3358, 404; Alexander Henry Abercromby Hamilton, *Quarter Sessions from Queen Elizabeth to Queen Anne* (London: Sampson Low, Marston, Searle, and Rivington, 1878), 203, 204; Stephen K. Roberts, *Recovery and Restoration in an English County: Devon Local Administration, 1646–1670* (Exeter: Exeter University Press, 1985), 124, 136 n.102; Gilbert Burnet, *The Expedition of his Highness the Prince of Orange for England, in A Collection of Scarce and Valuable Tracts [Somers' Tracts],* ed. Walter Scott (London, 1813), 9:276–80; Alexander Jenkins, *The History of the City of Exeter* (London, 1806), 185–86; Charles Dalton, ed., *English Army Lists and Commission Registers, 1661–1714,* 6 vols. (London: Eyre and Spottiswoode, 1892–1904; repr. London: Francis Edwards Ltd., 1960), 2:191.

7. *Cal. S.P. Dom. 1663–64,* 371.

8. C. A. F. Meekings, *Analysis of Hearth Tax Accounts, 1662–1665,* List and Index Society, vol. 153 (London: HMSO, 1979), 39–45, 57–70 (incomplete pagination); C. A. F. Meekings, *Analysis of Hearth Tax Accounts, 1666–1699,* List and Index Society, vol. 163 (London: HMSO, 1980), 27–9. T. L. Stoate, ed., *Cornwall Hearth and Poll Taxation, 1660–1664: Direct Taxation in Cornwall in the Reign of Charles II* (Bristol: Lower Court, Almondsbury, 1981), viii

9. 16 Charles II, c. 3, *Statutes of the Realm,* 5:514–16.

10. Ibid.; Chandaman, *English Public Revenue,* 86 and n.1; "Instructions to the Officers," reprinted in Tom Arkell, "Printed Instructions for administering the Hearth Tax," in *Surveying the People: The Interpretation and Use of Document Sources for the Study of Population in the Later Seventeenth Century,* eds. Kevin Schurer and Tom Arkell (Oxford: Local Population Studies, 1992), 56–64. Arkell believes that

Sawyer's efforts just led to further confusion (Arkell, "Printed Instructions," 54–55).

11. *Cal. Treas. Bks. 1660–67,* 689; *Cal. Treas. Bks. 1669–72,* 668, 800, 947, 1228; *Cal. Treas. Bks. 1676–79,* 466, 675; earl of Southampton and Lord Ashley to the justices of the peace of the county of Lancaster, Nov. 30, 1665, in H.M.C., *Kenyon MSS,* 76; H.M.C., *Earl of Verulam MSS,* 74–76.

12. *Royal Proclamations,* no. 3483, 420.

13. Sawle Family Accounts, Jan. 25, 1668, CF/1/3501, Cornwall Record Office; *Cal. Treas. Bks. 1667–68,* 7, 14, 61, 267; *Cal. Treas. Bks. 1669–72,* 613, 616; *Cal. Treas. Bks. 1676–79,* 1368.

14. *Cal. Treas. Bks. 1667–68,* 14, 86, 306, 315, 474, 553, 597; *Cal. Treas. Bks. 1669–72,* 18, 192, 202, 212, 292, 307, 434, 553, 1229; *Cal. Treas. Bks. 1679–80,* 866.

15. Rutter vs. Gay, E 134/26, Charles II/Michaelmas 35, Nat. Arch.; Petition of Edward Rutter, 1667, 83 H47, Harleian Charters, B.L.; Petition of Edward Rutter, 1674, 112 C48, Harleian Charters, B.L.; *Cal. Treas. Bks. 1669–72,* 149, 164, 281, 283, 655, 754, 1030–31.

16. Webb, Webb, and Even, vs. Finch and Rutter, E 134/23, Charles II/Michaelmas 17, Nat. Arch.; Trevisa vs. Rutter, E 134/27, Charles II/Easter 24, Nat. Arch.; Trevisa vs. Rutter, E 134/27, Charles II/Trinity 1, Nat. Arch.

17. Chandaman, *English Public Revenue,* 95–96.

18. *Cal. Treas. Bks. 1669–72,* 576; *Cal. Treas. Bks. 1672–75,* 20, 34, 163, 708; *Cal. Treas. Bks. 1676–79,* 18, 149–50, 159, 1242, 1400–02; *Cal. Treas. Bks. 1679–80,* 632–33; *Cal. S.P. Dom. 1676–77,* 574–75.

19. C 110/1/11, 14, 26; C 110/2/; C 110/3/, Robert Nailer's Papers, Nat. Arch.

20. *The Several Acts of Parliament Made for Establishing, Ordering, and Collecting of His Majesties Revenue Arising by Hearth-Money: Abstracted also in an Index, and Margented Accordingly, for the Benefit of Such Persons as are or May Be Concerned Therein* (London, 1668).

21. C 103/16, Papers of Sampson Hele of Gnaton and Hallwell, Nat. Arch.

22. *Royal Proclamations,* no. 3697, 448; Henning, *House of Commons,* 2:655–56; Eveline Cruickshanks, Stuart Handley, and D. W. Hayton, eds., *The History of Parliament: The House of Commons, 1690–1715,* 5 vols. (Cambridge: Cambridge University Press, 2002), 5:311–12.

23. *The Several Acts of . . . Hearth Money* (repr. London, 1678 and 1681).

24. H.M.C., *Lord Montagu of Beaulieu MSS,* 174–75.

25. Chandaman, *English Public Revenue,* 102–3; Henning, *House of Commons,* 3:259–60.

26. *Cal. Treas. Bks. 1681–85,* 548, 571, 677.

27. *Royal Proclamations,* no. 3743, 454.

28. *Calendar of Treasury Papers, 1556–1696* (London: HMSO, 1868), 96–97; Chandaman, *English Public Revenue,* 105.

29. *Cal. Treas. Bks. 1681–85,* 1362–67.

30. See Appendix.

31. Hamilton, *Quarter Sessions,* 205. QS 79/3/65, 81, 109, 174, 206, Devon Record Office.

32. C 103/16, Papers of Sampson Hele of Gnaton and Hallwell, Nat. Arch.; Entry Books of Correspondence with the Treasury, CUST 48/3/160–69, Excise Board and Secretariat, Nat. Arch.; *Cal. Treas. Bks. 1685–89,* 748–49, 1244.

33. *The Declaration of His Highness William Henry, By the Grace of God Prince of Orange, &c. of the Reasons Inducing Him, To Appear in Armes in the Kingdome of England, for Preserving of the Protestant Religion, and for Restoring the Lawes and Liberties of England, Scotland and Ireland* (The Hague, 1688).

34. Tenths were a levy upon ecclesiastical incumbents traditionally equal to 10 percent of annual rental incomes on ecclesiastical property under the incumbent's authority, but often in practice were a fixed sum rather than a percentage of income.

35. *Royal Proclamations*, no. 3942, 475.

36. 1 William & Mary, c. 10, *Statutes of the Realm*, 6:61.

37. *Royal Proclamations*, no. 4012, 481; Anchitell Grey, *Debates of the House of Commons from the year 1667 to the year 1694*, 10 vols. (London, 1763), 9:139.

38. *Cal. Treas. Papers 1556–1696*, 96–97, 195; *Cal. Treas. Bks. 1689–92*, 69–70, 758.

39. John Brewer, *The Sinews of Power: War, Money and the English State, 1688–1783* (London: Unwin Hyman, 1989), 66; Douglas C. North and Barry Weingast, "Constitutions and Commitment: The Evolution of Institutions Governing Public Choice in Seventeenth-Century England," *Journal of Economic History* 49, no. 4 (Dec. 1989): 822; P. K. O'Brien, "Fiscal Exceptionalism: Great Britain and Its European Rivals from Civil War to Triumph at Trafalgar and Waterloo," in *The Political Economy of British Historical Experience, 1688–1914*, eds. Donald Winch and P. K. O'Brien (Oxford: Oxford University Press, 2002), 252–53, 257. For the compositions of the county commissions, compare J.P. Lists, May 1680–July 1683, C 193/12/4, Nat. Arch., and J.P. Lists, 1678–1699, C 231/8, Crown Office Docquet Books, Nat. Arch., with 31 Charles II, c. 1, *Statutes of the Realm*, 5:901–3, and 1 William and Mary, session 2, c. 1, *Statutes of the Realm*, 6:107–9.

40. Dickson, *Financial Revolution*, 55 n.4, 254 n.3, 300, 493 n.2; North and Weingast, "Constitutions and Commitment," 826–27.

"Fictitious Cash": English Public Finance and Paper Money, 1689–97

Richard Kleer

SUPPORTERS OF THE BANK OF ENGLAND HAD TO FIGHT AN UPHILL battle to get the new institution approved by parliament. Although the basic idea was first proposed in 1691 it was not implemented until 1694. And even in that year there was a long and passionate public debate about whether the plan should be allowed to go forward.

Traditionally, resistance to the new institution has been traced to opposition politicians (supposedly worried the bank would bind financiers to the current administration) or to parliament as a whole (which apparently feared the bank would make the Crown financially, and so politically, independent of the House of Commons). In this same vein, the so-called National Land Bank, established in 1696, has been deemed parliament's rejoinder to the Bank of England. The new institution was to be better representative of parliamentary concerns as its assets were to be based upon land rather than stores of gold and silver coin in the case of the Bank of England.

I argue, by contrast, that much of the resistance to the Bank of England came from within the royal administration itself. The institution turned on a fundamental innovation in financial practice, one that the Crown's financial officials feared might prove unworkable. I show, too, that, despite its name, the National Land Bank was based upon monetary assets every bit as much as was the Bank of England. And I demonstrate that the new bank was forced to take this particular form because the advocates of land banks had encountered much the same kind of resistance from within the administration as had plagued supporters of the Bank of England.

Contemporary critics of the Bank of England maintained that it was born of an attempt by the ruling administration to cement its hold over the nation's political machinery. Jonathan Swift, writing some two decades after the occasion, claimed that a faction within William's administration had sought a loan from the nation's leading financiers in order to bind them to his regime: "It was not to be doubted that Money'd Men would be always firm to the Party of those, who advised the Borrowing upon such good Security, and with such exorbitant Praemiums."[1] Later in the eighteenth century, Henry St John, viscount Bolingbroke, wrote to similar effect. Although the war could have been financed from taxes alone, he charged, the political leaders of the day deliberately rejected this strategy: "It was said that a new government, established against the ancient principles and actual engagements of many, could not be so effectually secured any way, as it would be if the private fortunes of great numbers were made to depend on the preservation of it, and that this could not be done unless they were induced to lend their money to the public, and to accept securities under the present establishment."[2] By implication, opposition politicians resisted the bank because they recognized that self-interested officers of the court were trading the nation's financial birthright for short-term political advantages.

A similar story has been told more recently by Denis Rubini and by John Brewer, according to whom members of parliament, having won considerable new powers in the Glorious Revolution of 1688–89, fought to retain those powers during the early years of the new reign.[3] They did not see themselves as disloyal to the Crown. Rather, they subscribed to the view that MPs should represent "country" rather than "court," meaning they should pursue policies in the long-term interests of the nation and its monarch rather than those of the Crown's current coterie of ministers. The principal weapon of this "country" party was control of the purse; if William were kept on a tight budgetary leash he would be compelled to call parliament annually into session. Were his ministers successful in authorizing William to borrow from one or another bank, the king might escape parliament's grasp. Country MPs disliked the Bank of England in particular because it was "inherently anti-agrarian, too much allied with commercial interests and with the growing bourgeoisie" and stood to profit from escalating the war with France.[4] According to this version of history, the storied National Land Bank, established in 1696, represented an attempt by the country element within the House of Commons to seize back the reins of power. By this time the members had accepted the inevitability of long-term borrowing; the war had become costly enough that it could no longer be funded on a pay-as-you-go basis. So the House of Commons designed a bank more to its liking. As its name suggests, the assets of the National Land Bank would be "based primarily upon the land" rather than upon trade and money.[5] And it would be made "more representative of and more answerable to the parliamentary classes."[6] The hope was that the new bank would displace its competitor, or at least channel any profits back to landed men rather than to the merchants who dominated the Bank of England.

While the success of the Bank of England no doubt helped advance the cause of those ministers who had supported it, a purely political interpretation risks overlooking certain important features of the early resistance to that institution.[7] The bank represented a novel experiment in English public finance. It was created to afford a loan of £1.2 million to the Crown, accounting for more than one-fifth of the financial resources that parliament approved for that fiscal year (1694–95). This loan differed from previous forms of public borrowing in two important respects. Although it was in principle a perpetual loan (no express arrangement was made for repaying the principal), creditors would be able to recover their investment at will simply by selling their shares in the bank (in effect their part of the loan) to someone else. And, for the first time ever in England, the loan was to be paid over to the government in the form of paper currency rather than in gold and /or silver coin as had until then been the custom.[8] Officials within the treasury were keen on the first innovation. Individuals who were not keen to tie up their capital in long-term investments might nevertheless agree to participate in a loan of this kind. The paper-money aspect of the proposal, however, proved a major stumbling block; it was this feature that caused the plan to be held back for three years. And even then the bank was finally approved only because treasury and bank officials reached a compromise agreement that retained the main features of the paper-money scheme while simultaneously insuring the government against financial disaster.

Although the National Land Bank was indeed intended to shift financial and political power back to the House of Commons, in other respects recent commentators have been led astray by mere appearances. It was very much in the interests of the new bank's supporters to include strong connections to land-based assets in the basic design of their proposed institution. But the proposal could only have become a genuine land bank if treasury officials had agreed to accept yet another major innovation in financial practice: a new paper currency that would be made legal tender (i.e. that contemporaries would be forced to accept as the legal equivalent of gold and silver coin). Compared with such a proposal, the Bank of England was a thoroughly conservative project. Given that its supporters had had to fight for years to get even so conservative a scheme approved, there was never any realistic chance at this time for a true land bank to be implemented. The so-called National Land Bank, for reasons that will be explained below, was, in the end, a land bank in nothing but name. It was for all intents and purposes a second Bank of England.

A SHORT INTRODUCTION TO CONTEMPORARY ENGLISH PUBLIC FINANCE

The Nine Years' War (1689–97) put tremendous strains upon England's public finances. Before the war, public spending had been running at about £2 million per year. By 1694–96 annual expenditures had reached an average of about £6 million per year. This meant the government was constantly on the look out for large, new revenue sources. In the early years of the war, existing customs and excise taxes were expanded as much as possible. Nonetheless, parliament soon found itself obliged to approve a large new "land tax," which placed 25 percent of landlords' annual rent rolls at the Crown's disposal. As spending continued to outpace revenue some commentators (such as excise-tax officer Charles Davenant) proposed a "general excise," the equivalent of a modern value-added sales tax. Most contemporaries found this proposal entirely reprehensible, arguing that it would permanently saddle the nation with a vastly enlarged and very invasive tax-collecting bureaucracy. Starting in the 1693–94 session, recourse was had instead to novel financial expedients such as term annuities (granting the state a large lump-sum payment in exchange for the guarantee of a stream of smaller annual payments from the state that would continue for as long as certain explicitly identified people survived), tontines (annuities in which the shares of deceased participants were redistributed among the remaining survivors), and lottery loans (to which investors were attracted both by a healthy rate of interest and by the prospect of large, one-time cash prizes for a few lucky lenders).

In addition to long-term loans, the government of the day also had increasing recourse to short-term borrowing to tide itself over between when it was authorized to begin spending and when it actually received the tax revenues on which that spending was ultimately based. For this purpose the exchequer (the treasury office responsible for receiving taxes and loans) issued "tallies": interest-bearing, transferable claims upon a specified tax, payable in order of issue as the corresponding revenues arrived in the exchequer. Tallies were not an entirely desirable form of public security. This is because revenue did not always arrive at the anticipated pace, forcing some of those who had lent short term to sell their tallies to some third party, often at a sizeable discount. On occasions when revenue was particularly uncertain the government itself was forced to issue tallies at a discount (in effect lenders were credited with a larger sum than they had actually contributed to the exchequer). Tallies were also an expensive form of borrowing. They typically paid 7 to 8 percent interest, higher than the prewar norm for public loans of 5 to 7 percent and above the legal maximum on private loans of 6 percent (although a little below the average of 8.3 percent that was paid during these years on long-term public loans).[9]

England's system of public finance was at the time much more decentralized than it is today. The treasury was administered by a committee of four or five "lords," led by the "first lord" (who alone of the treasury officers had the privilege of meeting on a regular basis with the king) and the chancellor of the exchequer (normally the Crown's principal manager of revenue-related measures in the House of Commons). The treasury did not as yet house a staff of paid professionals whose responsibility it was to design and vet revenue measures. Instead, the treasury lords regularly received proposals from freelance individuals or, on occasion, solicited outside advice from recognized experts. If one of their schemes actually made it through the rigors of a parliamentary session, such financial "projectors" (as contemporaries referred to them) could hope for a sizeable cash reward or, better still, appointment to some lucrative office within the treasury's grant (often one associated with the very revenue scheme they themselves had proposed). Revenue measures had to be arranged in consort with the cabinet (at this time nothing more than an ill-defined and fluctuating body of influential core members of the court party) as in order to gain the required number of supporting votes the Crown might have to agree to sponsor other, nonfinancial measures favored by one or more MPs or make strategic patronage offers of one kind or another. While the majority of revenue schemes came to the House of Commons by these means, members of parliament not affiliated with the court sometimes made revenue proposals of their own. Indeed, in the run-up to the session in which the National Land Bank was created, cabinet officials outside the treasury negotiated directly with independent members of parliament upon a joint political and financial program. Officials outside the treasury could also get revenue measures onto the legislative agenda through direct access to the king or members of his cabinet. It was difficult, although not impossible, to secure approval for revenue schemes that originated from outside the treasury. But in an age when party discipline did not yet exist and ministers were therefore unable to count upon stable majorities, even schemes that came from the treasury itself had to be designed to appeal to a broad spectrum of parliamentary opinion. Indeed, to be successful financial projectors had to pay close attention to the winds of political fashion and tailor their proposals accordingly.

The Bank of England

The proposal that was eventually to become the Bank of England was first brought to the treasury lords late in 1691 by William Paterson, a Scotsman and West Indies merchant with considerable experience of banking practices on the European continent but a political outsider in London. Paterson recommended that the government borrow a large part of its financial needs for that session, but on an entirely novel basis. The documentation is sketchy, but the key details appear to have been along the following lines.[10] The Crown would borrow £1 million in perpetuity (although with an option after some years to repay the loan). This would ease parliament's task in the coming session as it would need to find enough revenue only to pay the interest on the loan. Because few people were keen to have their capital tied up indefinitely in a single investment, contributors would be permitted to sell their share of the loan to someone else whenever they pleased. The interest rate would be significantly lower than that usually paid by the treasury on government debt, perhaps 5 or 6 percent. Collectively, the lenders would have to provide only £200,000 in the preferred currency of the day, gold or silver coin. This specie would not be paid over to the exchequer but would be retained by the consortium for its own purposes. Instead, the loan would be paid to the exchequer in paper "assignments" or "bills of property"—what later came to be called "bank notes." The treasury would use these paper notes to pay its suppliers and creditors. Anyone holding such notes would be free to call upon the consortium and demand the equivalent value in specie; the consortium would be bound by law to honor any and all such requests. This was the sole purpose to which the £200,000 of specie contributions would be applied. But in Paterson's estimation few people were likely to come calling for specie. For the notes were to carry a healthy rate of interest, roughly three-quarters of the interest rate on the original loan. The remaining one-quarter of the treasury's interest payments would go to consortium members themselves, in compensation for their specie investment and time and trouble.

Paterson's proposal offered advantages on all sides. Members of the consortium would receive an attractive rate of interest. For a loan of £1 million at 6 percent the exchequer would pay his consortium £60,000 per annum. Consortium members would get to keep only a quarter of this for themselves (the rest would go to the persons holding the new paper notes). But as their actual investment would only amount to £200,000 (the specie reserve required to circulate the paper notes), even that one quarter would net them an effective rate of return of 7.5 percent per annum (or better if it turned out that £200,000 was more than enough to honor the occasional demands for specie from their note holders). Because shares in the proposed "fund of perpetual interest" were to be transferable, consortium members could convert their investment back to ready cash whenever necessary. The government would get a loan at an interest rate well below what it was accustomed to paying and could defer principal payments to some more manageable time. The government's suppliers would also benefit. Since tallies could only be converted to specie at fluctuating, market-determined discounts, suppliers would very likely prefer the proposed paper notes—with their guarantee of being convertible to cash, at full face value, upon demand. In effect, the consortium would be holding exchequer tallies, paying out a slightly lower rate of interest than that available on tallies, but furnishing suppliers with a more liquid, secure form of IOU in return.

Not all the treasury lords were keen on the idea. In the one surviving report of the House of Commons' debates on Paterson's project —a discussion on January 19, 1692—one treasury lord (Sir John Lowther) and the mint master (Thomas Neale) spoke for the proposal while the chancellor of the exchequer, Richard Hampden, went on record against it.[11] Paterson himself later complained that the treasury had been the principal stumbling block in getting the project implemented. He claimed that they were unfamiliar with European banking practices, of "the principals of trade and revenue," and exhibited a hidebound attachment to "the old Norman way of borrowing money."[12]

There is no official record of the reasons offered by the treasury lords against Paterson's proposal. But we can glean a few hints from comments made by William Lowndes (assistant to, and four years later himself, the treasury secretary) upon a similar paper-currency project submitted to the treasury in October 1691. One of Lowndes's concerns was that in future all taxes would be paid in "this fictitious cash," as the general public would rather hold specie than paper. Loans in specie might also grow scarce as lenders expecting to be offered repayment in paper rather than coin would be reluctant to contribute their loans in specie. If the exchequer ran short of specie, the discount on tallies was sure to rise sharply—tally holders traditionally expecting payment of principal and interest in specie.[13] But for Lowndes the primary stumbling block seems to have been a fear that the general public would altogether reject the proposed new paper currency. He pointed out that tallies were as secure an investment as one could imagine (being government securities), were generally repaid within a year, and offered interest of 7.5 or 8.0 percent. By comparison, the proposed paper currency would pay only 5 percent (similar to Paterson's proposal for 6 percent) and, being private securities, carried a greater degree of risk than tallies. What member of the general public, Lowndes therefore wondered, would prefer such a currency to tallies?[14] Similar reasoning would be offered again by certain unnamed "officers of the revenue who had been in the management of the tally trade" when Paterson presented his proposal again in 1693–94. If the resale value of tallies had sometimes fallen 20 to 40 percent below their face value, the discount on Paterson's proposed new paper currency, which was not nearly so good a form of money, was sure to be more than 50 percent. The king would lose half the benefit of the loan right off the top and syndicate members would go bankrupt not long after.[15]

Whatever their reasoning, the treasury lords informed Paterson they were only prepared to proceed if he lined up a "voluntary society of monied men" who would be responsible for contributing the whole of the loan in specie should the bills fail to take.[16] This demand threatened to wreck Paterson's entire scheme. On the terms he had proposed, investors could earn the going rate of interest on their specie investment only if that specie were used to circulate a paper currency in which the loan was actually to be paid. With the risk that they might have to contribute the whole of the loan in their own specie, investors would have found the interest rate of 6 percent proposed by Paterson completely unacceptable. In a compromise move, Paterson assembled a syndicate of "upwards of twenty persons of estates and reputation" who, should the new paper currency fail to take with the general public, were at least prepared to lend to the treasury (presumably still at the promised 6 percent rate of interest) the £200,000 of specie that they had intended to use as a reserve for circulating that paper currency. When the treasury lords stuck to their guns, the syndicate countered with requests for a higher rate of interest, to have both the notes and the specie reserve counted toward the principal of the loan, and to have the bills made legal tender—that is, to abandon the requirement for the syndicate to convert their notes into specie upon demand by the holder.[17] All these requests were incorporated into a new version of the proposal that Paterson put to a House of Commons committee early in 1692. The committee indicated a strong interest in one component of the scheme (the idea of a "perpetual fund of interest," the rights to which could be transferred from one investor to another) but categorically refused the legal-tender concept.[18] Paterson offered to proceed without legal-tender status (indeed, he later professed to find the very idea repugnant). But the syndicate as a whole proved less sanguine and the project eventually foundered on this rock. When Paterson made much the same proposal again in 1692–93 the treasury still insisted upon a syndicate committed to paying the full amount of the loan in specie should this prove necessary.[19]

In the end, the two sides met somewhere in the middle. At the start of the 1693–94 session an unnamed minister of state (whether inside or outside the treasury is not clear) urged Paterson to attempt the project once more. Paterson tendered the treasury a new version, this time for a loan of £1.2 million at 8 percent interest.[20] Again the treasury lords were prepared to proceed only if a consortium of moneylenders agreed to pay in the full amount of the loan, "or at least . . . some considerable part thereof," in specie should the consortium's paper notes fail to be accepted by the general public. Paterson assembled a new syndicate that was, like its predecessor, prepared to turn over the 20 percent specie reserve to the exchequer if the loan project went bad but that balked at the idea of having to pay in the whole of the intended loan in specie. The resulting impasse was resolved only when Michael Godfrey (a prominent City merchant) and some East India interlopers (merchants trading on their own account into Asia in violation of the legal monopoly over all English trade to that region that had been granted to the East India Company) decided to throw their support behind Paterson's project. Others followed their example and the plan began to gain wide support in court circles and among the broader London public. This opened the door to a new compromise solution. The treasury's concern all along had been that the general public might not accept the new paper currency. Now prominent merchants and politicians were indicating they thought the idea a sensible one, improving the chances for a favorable reception if it were actually implemented. The treasury therefore relented a bit. No longer would Paterson have to assemble in advance a syndicate of investors committed if necessary to paying the full amount of the loan in specie. Instead, the treasury would seek parliament's approval for taking out a loan on the terms proposed. With that approval in hand, an invitation would then be issued to members of the general public to subscribe to the loan in the requisite amounts. As long as subscriptions (i.e., guarantees to pay in specie) were collected for at least 50 percent (not the full 100 percent previously demanded) of the targeted amount of £1.2 million, the treasury would agree to accept payment of the loan in paper notes. There was some risk to the prospective investors, however. For if subscriptions fell short of the 50 percent target, anyone who had already subscribed would be required to pay in the full amount of their subscription in specie. For their part, Paterson and company agreed to a specie reserve of 25 percent, somewhat higher than the 20 percent reserve they had previously been proposing.[21] Paterson's group compensated themselves for this additional expense in part by lowering the rate of interest they would pay out to anyone holding their bills.[22]

The same kind of conservatism evident within the treasury also exhibited itself in the Commons. Neale's new proposal first came before the House in a resolution from the committee of ways and means reported on February 1, 1694. The House would seek a loan of £1 million at an annual cost of £96,000 (an 8 percent interest rate as the £200,000 specie reserve was also to count as part of the "loan"). A pamphlet published by Neale around this same time commented on Paterson's scheme and then offered a cheaper alternative. The Crown would issue £2.3 million in "bills" to be paid out to the king's creditors. The bills would pay an interest rate of 6 percent per annum, would be transferable, and would be accepted in tax payments. There was to be no specie reserve; the paper notes would be purely fiduciary. The proposal was probably designed to make Paterson's scheme sound almost conservative by comparison, since the latter was for less than half the amount, paid a higher interest rate, and featured paper notes convertible into specie upon demand. This was perhaps part of the committee's reasoning in opting to recommend Paterson's scheme to the House. But a debate on the committee's resolution immediately broke out. It must have been heated, for time ran out and discussion had to be postponed to a later day. After further debate on February 4, the committee was directed by the House to bring forward a new resolution. Two days later it recommended another of Neale's projects, this one for a lottery loan of £1 million at the substantially higher cost of £140,000 per annum. In his diplomatic report to the Court of Brandenburg, Frederick Bonnet speculated that the initial measure had been rejected because the Commons was uncertain a loan could be raised upon the terms proposed. No one would want to lend given that the Commons insisted upon a right of making the principal redeemable after a certain number of years and that any capital subscribed could not subsequently be withdrawn. These do not seem very plausible reasons, especially as one of the principal features of the scheme was the right to transfer shares in the bank. Much more significant is the fact, also reported by Bonnet, that fourteen of the richest members of the House, with country politician Paul Foley (who would be elected speaker of the House the next year) at their head, had offered to contribute most of the loan in specie ("argent comptant"), though on condition of being paid an interest rate of 10 percent. This suggests that the Commons feared the scheme would fail because of its paper-currency component. Certainly that was the very reasoning that Foley had offered when Neale had recommended a version of Paterson's scheme to the Commons on December 15, 1692: "you can have no fruit of that unless you will force tallies or paper to go for ready money."[23] And fear of paper money was likely one of the principal factors in the Commons' decision to prefer Neale's lottery scheme despite its significantly greater expense.[24] Tickets in the lottery would be purchased (i.e., loans to the Crown would be contributed) in standard money, not some new, untried paper currency. In any event, the administration had to wait until April 1694 before it could find an expedient for resurrecting Paterson's proposal and at long last get it accepted.

It should be noted that Paterson's original proposal was itself very tame compared to other paper-money projects being promoted in the early years of the war. In 1690, Hugh Chamberlen (a renowned midwife and for a while physician to Charles II) twice requested a House of Commons committee hearing on a plan that must have seemed utterly fantastic to his contemporaries.[25] He promised to furnish £100 million without need of any new taxes. Existing local rates for poor relief and highway maintenance could be cut in half to £1 million and the other £1 million earmarked for the next one hundred years as security for a new issue of £100 million worth of a "new species of [paper] money." No specie reserve would be required. Instead, revenues from the local rates would be used to retire £1 million of the notes annually, ensuring they would always be in demand and so would retain their value. It seems Chamberlen was also counting upon legal-tender status for the notes. Of the total sum, £50 million would be spent upon highways and the poor; another £10 million for the war, £20 million for the expenses of the "fund" (Chamberlen was careful to emphasize that there would be "above *three hundred new employments fit for noblemen and gentlemen*") and the rest upon other worthy projects. It is unclear whether the Commons ever gave Chamberlen an actual hearing upon this specific proposal.

Plenty of other paper-money projects, more restrained than Chamberlen's but more innovative than Paterson's, were afloat early in the new reign. In 1690, Sir William Killigrew, a playwright and courtier to Charles II, proposed a temporary legal-tender paper issue of £2 million.[26] Since the general public and revenue officials alike would be required by law to receive them, no one would hesitate to accept such notes at their face value. A modest new parliamentary tax would suffice to pay interest at the rate of 6 percent per annum and to redeem each year a portion of the notes outstanding. The entire issue could be retired within a decade or so, ensuring a merely temporary burden on the public coffers. During the session in which Paterson first brought his plan before the House of Commons, two other perpetual-loan projects were circulating—both stipulating payment in legal-tender paper currencies. One suggested a target of £4 million with a new tax sufficient to pay interest at 5 percent per annum.[27] The other, no longer extant but described in Lowndes's 1691 report to the treasury lords, aimed for £2 million at an overall interest rate of 5.5 percent.

The National Land Bank

The Bank of England as it was finally approved by parliament in 1694 conformed in all essential respects to Paterson's original proposal. Resistance from the treasury slowed the project but did not alter its basic form. The same thing cannot be said of the so-called National Land Bank established by parliament in 1696. This institution was but a pale imitation of the original concept of a land bank and, in the end, did not even deserve its own title. But this change of form is owing to exactly the same kinds of pressures that we have already seen to be at work in the case of the Bank of England: firm resistance from within the treasury to a project that was considered too innovative and risky. The story is a little different from that of the Bank of England in that several projects were competing for parliament's attention. But the various projects collectively evolved along a continuum that clearly demonstrates administrative resistance to radical change.

The professed goal of the several land bank projects of the decade was to help improve the financial situation of England's landowners. The war, in particular the new land tax, had significantly diminished their incomes (at a time when many of them had already mortgaged large parts of their rent rolls to finance the lavish spending demanded of them by courtly fashion). At the same time, the war was enriching merchants and financiers, many of whom were earning handsome rates of interest on their loans to the Crown. Yet the wealth owned by landowners—long streams of annual rents—was, they believed, of more real value to the nation (being based upon tangible output) than the specie from which "monied men" were deriving their new-found wealth. What landed men needed was some way of parlaying their particular assets into the same fantastic returns that were being amassed by merchants and financiers. Land-bank projectors promised to make this fond dream a reality.

The basic strategy for achieving this end was to create a new paper currency backed by land rents rather than by specie. This is very apparent in the first land-bank scheme to come before parliament in the war years, brought forward by Chamberlen and Sir Dalby Thomas (a prominent London merchant) during the session of 1691–92. The scheme built from Chamberlen's earlier proposal for a large one-time issue of paper notes based on the security of a stream of annual revenues. But Chamberlen and Thomas now suggested a new revenue source: land rents rather than highway and poor rates.[28] Landowners would be invited to "subscribe" (i.e., commit themselves to pay) half the annual rents from their estates for the next one hundred years. A new "mint" or "office" would promptly issue "bills" or brass "tickets" for the full one hundred years' worth of the rents thus subscribed. Forty percent of these bills would go to the subscribers for their own use. Another 40 percent would be invested on their behalf in a joint-stock fishery (an investment scheme sure to evoke public support given the increasingly successful inroads being made by the Dutch in this trade). The rest would become the property of the proposed office, allegedly as due compensation for its expenses (though from this sum Chamberlen guaranteed to furnish £1 million per year in war loans at 4 percent per annum). Subscribers would be required to pay their annual rents into the office in its own bills, meaning that the bills would gradually disappear from circulation over the course of a century. Later that session, Chamberlen offered a slightly modified version of this project.[29] Landowners could subscribe as much as two-thirds of the value of their annual rents. And 20 percent of the bills were to be set aside for the war (no interest rate was specified), the share for a joint-stock fishery being reduced to 20 percent.

Had the plan worked as designed, it would clearly have been beneficial to landowners, even those whose estates were already mortgaged. Mortgage loans typically did not exceed twenty times the annual rental income earned on a given property. So with the 40 percent of office bills subscribers were to receive for their own use, they would have been able to pay off their existing mortgages, leaving them free to spend the remaining half of their annual rental incomes. And if the planned fishery company had delivered even a modest 5 percent rate of return they would have won back the other half of the annual incomes arising from their estates.

Although the Chamberlen-Thomas proposal won approval from a Commons committee early in 1692,[30] it was never reported back to the House. We can easily guess the reason why. Its principal weakness was that no one other than the subscribers themselves had a clear incentive to treat the office's notes as money. The notes were to pay no interest to their holders and would not be convertible into specie upon demand. Chamberlen maintained that they would always be in demand since subscribers were required to pay their rents in that currency and the office guaranteed to retire from circulation all the bills thus paid in. But this was a very slender reed, and Chamberlen and Thomas were forced to fall back upon a much more effective solution: making the new currency legal tender. But to such a concept the treasury lords would have been firmly opposed. They had resisted even a specie-backed currency such as Paterson was proposing around the same time on the grounds that the public might refuse to accept it. Legal-tender paper was even more subject to this objection since it offered only the threat of a stick, and no carrot whatsoever for its acceptance as money. Had the bills once fallen to a discount in the open market, it would be too late to prosecute those individuals who had refused to accept them as legal tender; the government's financial situation would already have been irretrievably damaged. Legal-tender status could only help in the short term if a considerable part of the general public had already become accustomed to a new paper currency and was prepared to accept it voluntarily—in which case legal-tender status would have been unnecessary. The idea also had bad associations given that the recently deposed James II had just forced a kind of legal tender currency upon Ireland. Specifically, he had decreed that coins made of brass and copper were to circulate for 2*s.* 6*d.* even though the metal contained in them was worth nowhere near that much.[32] Since these coins lost most of their value after William forced James out of Ireland (to the considerable loss of those unfortunate enough to be holding them), they had become something of a byword for ill-advised monetary projects.

The basic idea of a land bank was nevertheless very attractive to landowning MPs, and it is not surprising to see it returning in several subsequent sessions. The first occasion was in December 1693, when

Paterson's paper-money project had suddenly come into vogue. Chamberlen begged a new hearing on the plan he and Thomas had presented two years earlier.[32] This time around, Chamberlen offered to let parliament nominate eight commissioners (who would serve alongside others appointed from among the land's key judicial officials) to oversee the work of the office—at salaries of £1,000 apiece per annum.[33] A Commons committee reported in February 1694 that the plan "is practicable and will tend to the benefit of the nation."[34] But of course that session the prize went to Paterson and company. Chamberlen complained of unfair treatment; his "fund" had been rejected for reasons that were just as applicable to the new bank but that parliament had somehow agreed to overlook in its case.[35] The Chamberlen camp also published two vitriolic attacks upon *A Brief Account of the Intended Bank of England*, in which pamphlet Paterson had commented rather unflatteringly upon their project.[36]

In the session after the Bank of England was finally approved, another project for a land bank, far more credible than Chamberlen's, was brought before the House of Commons. Like the Bank of England, it centered around the offer of a new war loan that would be paid into the exchequer in paper money. This new project was the brainchild of one John Briscoe, about whom little is known other than that he had promoted several nonbank projects in the early 1690s and had corresponded with Chamberlen in 1693 about the good doctor's banking project.[37] In two editions of a long and rambling *Discourse* and in an accompanying abstract, Briscoe proposed inviting landowners to "settle" their estates with public commissioners (some appointed by the Crown and others by parliament).[38] Having ascertained good title, the commissioners would issue out "bills of credit," in denominations of £5 to £100, amounting in total to the anticipated sale value of the settled estates (by convention twenty times their annual rental income). The bills would be made legal tender and loaned *in toto* to the Crown for the war at an interest rate of 3 percent per annum.[39] The commissioners would take one-sixth of the interest for their salaries and costs and pass on the rest to participating landowners. It seems Briscoe was aiming for a loan of £5 million: the entire cost of the war that year.[40]

The plan had considerable attractions but one glaring weakness. The administration would dearly have liked to find funding at such a low rate of interest. With a loan that was both large and perpetual, parliament's hunt for revenue sources that session would have been greatly simplified. Participating landowners would have appreciated the modest return of 2.5 percent on their "investment" and would have valued far more Briscoe's recommendation that they be exempted from the onerous land tax expected to be renewed that session. However, as there was no incentive whatever for the general public to receive the bills (bearers were not to be paid any interest and no specie reserve would be available to circulate the bills), legal-tender status would be essential. Briscoe maintained, to no avail, that resort to a legal-tender clause would cheat no one, since the bills would still be backed by the real value of the rental properties subscribed to the scheme, ensuring that note holders would be recompensed should anything go wrong.

Given the treasury's noted resistance to receiving loans even in paper currencies convertible upon demand into specie, it should not be too surprising that Briscoe's project went nowhere. William Brockman (an MP then deemed a Whig and a country supporter) drafted a suitable bill and presented it to the House of Commons in March 1695.[41] It went to a committee late in the session but was never reported out. Chamberlen used the occasion to bring his own land-bank project once more to the attention of parliament, arguing that landowners would fare better under his system than Briscoe's and attacking the Bank of England at great length.[42] But there is no evidence that he ever received a hearing that session.

In the wake of these signal failures, the summer of 1695 brought a proposal for a new and far more conservative kind of "land bank." The project was managed by John Asgill and Nicholas Barbon and became known to contemporaries as the Lincoln's-Inn Bank (after the location of one of its offices in London). Little is known about Asgill before this time. He was a young man, recently called to the bar, a former business associate of Briscoe, and a trustee of the London Orphans' Fund in 1695 when Paterson reorganized its creditors into a nascent bank. Nicholas Barbon was considerably older, an MP in a borough [Bramber] small enough that its support could be bought by the highest bidder, and a heavily indebted London builder and property developer. Their plan was to gather £100,000 in specie from interested investors and lend out some part of it upon mortgages at 3.5 percent per annum. They would print transferable "bills or notes of credit" for the amounts loaned (each bill indicating the particular estate from which it derived) and issue the notes out to anyone bringing the equivalent amount in specie to the bank. To entice specie holders the bills carried an interest rate of 2 percent per annum (payable quarterly to the bearer). Some fraction of this new specie would in turn be loaned out upon further mortgages, resulting in still more bills being issued, and so on. Anyone could bring their bills to the bank and have them redeemed in specie upon demand (hence the need for a specie reserve).

Granted, this was still a land bank in the sense that its currency would have the backing of land-based assets, but far from being paid interest for subscribing their rental incomes or being able to free themselves from debt, landowners would be mortgaging their estates (albeit at very attractive rates of interest) to monied men. Asgill and Barbon clearly aimed to mimic the Bank of England by promising to pay interest on their notes and to convert them into specie upon demand. The principal beneficiaries of the plan would therefore have been the original specie subscribers, followed by those who were prepared to deposit specie at the bank short-term in exchange for paper notes. In the final analysis, it was a land bank only in the sense that its lending would be confined, or so its projectors promised, exclusively to landowners.

Since legal-tender status was not required, Asgill and Barbon did not need to wait upon a parliamentary statute but immediately set about implementing their scheme. They issued a broadside describing the project and in late May opened two offices—one at Lincoln's-Inn to receive subscriptions to the specie reserve and another in the Strand to exchange specie for bills.[43] A series of ads in the London *Post-Boy* invited subscriptions and reported totals received to date. By July 13 the initial specie target had been reached and a subscribers' meeting was appointed to elect twenty-one trustees. In August a two-page *Account* advertised the concept to potential borrowers.[44] A formal constitution appeared a few days later, listing several dignitaries among the trustees: Lord Jermyn, baron of Bury; Sir Charles Hedges, an admiralty court judge; Sir Leonard Robinson, chamberlain of London; Mordecai Abbott, customs cashier; and two MPs, Philip Foley (member for Bewdley and brother of Paul) and Edward Harley.[45] That month the bank also began publishing a *Monthly Account* in which it was announced that the specie reserve had been raised first to £250,000 and then to £350,000. The first bills were issued in October. In November, however, as additional specie was apparently slow to come in, the subscription books had to be reopened and a new slate of trustees elected. A list of subscribers published that month included Sir Joseph Herne, former governor of the East India Company and a leading partner in a syndicate that had serviced much of the government's overseas financial needs before being displaced by the upstart Bank of England the previous fall.[46] By early 1696 the bank had loaned £45,000 upon land and allegedly had mortgage loans for another £100,000 under consideration.[47]

It is highly unlikely however that Asgill and Barbon ever envisioned making mortgages their principal line of business, for, as table 1 shows, a land bank constructed upon the lines they were proposing would have afforded rates of return far inferior to those being earned by investors in the Bank of England. Moreover, at the time mortgages were a notoriously expensive way of lending money; land titles had to be inspected and the rental value of properties ascertained. And gentry were often relatively high-risk borrowers: heavily indebted but willing to use social and political status to put off their creditors to another day.

Table 1. *Comparative rates of return for three English banks, 1695*

	Interest rate (%) charged on loan(s)	Interest rate (%) paid on bills in circulation	Gross rate (%) of return assuming 25% specie reserve
Bank of England	8.0	3.0	20.0
Lincoln's Inn Bank	3.5	2.0	6.0
National Land Bank	3.0	0.0	5.2

Unless the two projectors were working as selfless benefactors, they must have had some larger end in view. And indeed they did. They were out to win the sizeable new government loan contract anticipated from the coming parliamentary session. During summer 1695 the court worked closely with the speaker of the House of Commons, Paul Foley, and his nephew and fellow Herefordshire MP, Robert Harley, in drawing up a plan for raising the requisite public funds, or "supply" as contemporaries called it.[48] Already in June Foley had submitted a design for raising £7 million.[49] Very likely it included plans for a major new long-term loan. This would explain why Edward Harley (Robert's younger brother) and Philip Foley put themselves forward in July as trustees for the Lincoln's-Inn land bank and why Edward wrote his father immediately after being elected: "I trust God will pleas to give his blessing to it so as that it may prove of service to ye whole nation."[50] By implementing their project before the session began Asgill and Barbon were trying to ensure their paper bills would already be in circulation and widely accepted by the general public as money. This would greatly diminish the same kind of doubt, arising from treasury and the House of Commons, that had proved such a stumbling block to Paterson's proposed paper-currency war loan. In titling their new institution a land bank and promising to lend at low rates of interest to landowners, the projectors were trying to curry favor with England's beleaguered and disgruntled gentry and their parliamentary representatives.

Briscoe understood the implied threat to his own dream of supplying a large, new paper-currency war loan. In order to match his competitors' bold new strategy, he quickly reworked the fundamentals of his scheme. In early June 1695 Briscoe announced that he was ready to put "into practice, so far as it is capable of being done without an Act of Parliament," what he was now calling the "National Land Bank."[51] He was at first vague on the details.[52] Landowners who subscribed their estates would receive bank bills for three quarters of the sale value (calculated as twenty times the annual rental). They were to pay interest at roughly 3 percent per annum, but would be entitled to a proportionate share of any profits. Further details would be released only at the first subscribers' meeting—to be called once subscriptions had reached £100,000 in annual rental value. Subscribers were free to withdraw at that point if they didn't like what they heard. Of course, without legal-tender status and apparently intending to pay no interest to those holding the bank's notes, Briscoe would need a specie reserve to have any hope of making the bills circulate as money. Asgill and Barbon were quick to point out that Briscoe had not explained where he would get the cash.[53] For several weeks Briscoe avoided the issue and then in July announced that although he had a plan he was not releasing it for fear others would steal his ideas.[54] Periodically he issued broadsides showing subscriptions coming in from almost every county and steadily approaching the £100,000 target.[55] In early August he finally revealed his plans for raising a specie reserve.[56] Anyone subscribing specie would receive 3 percent interest on their contribution (compared to the 3 percent interest that land subscribers would have to *pay*) and a proportionate share of the profits. Briscoe later claimed that within a month he had received pledges for £150,000 of specie.[57] The target for land subscriptions having been reached, meetings began on September 10. At one of their first meetings, the trustees of the new National Land Bank resolved to apply for a "parliamentary establishment" (i.e., the same kind of corporate status that the Bank of England had needed to issue its paper notes).[58] The slate of 36 directors elected in October was not so distinguished as that for the Lincoln's-Inn Bank, but it did include seven MPs (among them Briscoe's earlier collaborator Brockman). Over the next three months they published a list of subscribers, approved a constitution and a design for the bills, acquired office space, hired employees, and set salaries.[59] As with the Lincoln's-Inn Bank, specie subscriptions were slow to be paid in. But by January 1696 the directors had begun to consider specific mortgage loans.

Briscoe's new project, like the new Asgill-Barbon scheme, had little call to be styled a land bank. While landowners would have been able to borrow upon slightly more favorable terms here than at the Lincoln's-Inn Bank, the paper currency would ultimately be backed by the specie reserve rather than land assets, and the benefits would have gone principally to the money subscribers. And it is unlikely that lending would have been confined to mortgages since on this basis the project could not have afforded rates of return the least bit attractive to potential investors. Gross profits would have amounted annually to 2.25 percent of the bills in circulation (3 percent interest on loans to the land subscribers less the 3 percent interest paid to money subscribers on the 25 percent specie reserve). Gross profits were to be divided between land and money subscribers in proportion to the value of their subscriptions (though money subscriptions were to be weighted at 1.33 times the value of land subscriptions). Assuming Briscoe had achieved his target ratio of 1 to 4 between money and land subscriptions, money subscribers would have received 1.33/5.33 of gross profits (which would have amounted annually to roughly 0.56 percent of the value of the bills in circulation). Since money subscribers would have had to contribute only one quarter of the bills in circulation expressed as a percentage of their actual investment their share of gross profits would have generated an annual rate of return of four times this figure, or 2.25 percent of the value of the bills in circulation. Adding this to the 3 percent they were to be paid directly on their specie investment, money subscribers would have received an overall rate of return of 5.25 percent per annum.

Like the 6.0 percent rate of return on mortgage lending implied by the design of the Lincoln's-Inn Bank, this was far below the estimated 20 percent rate of return being afforded to the Bank of England's subscribers. The project would only have been of interest to potential investors if the National Land Bank were authorized by parliament to lend to the Crown at an interest rate comparable to the 8.0 percent being charged by the Bank of England on its loan, or if the bank could make loans that did not call for three-quarters of the profit to go to land subscribers.

Chamberlen tried unsuccessfully to join in this game. By mid-August he was publishing plans for a modified "Office of Land Credit."[60] It would issue bills of credit on security of rent subscriptions, still for one hundred times the estate's annual rental value. But now its bills were to be redeemable for silver or gold coin upon demand. To furnish the necessary specie reserve, landowners would have had to ante up in hard cash ten times the annual value of the rents subscribed (payable in installments over four years). Of the bills issued on the security of their estates, landowners would receive 60 percent for their own use (likewise paid out in installments over the first four years). A further 20 percent, plus their specie contributions, would be invested on their behalf in a suitable joint-stock company (Chamberlen did not explain how the specie payments could both be invested in a joint-stock company and serve as a reserve for circulating bills). A "constitution" was being drafted and bills would begin to be issued as soon as an annual rent charge of £50,000 had been subscribed (all subscriptions to be void if that target were not met). Starting in late September, Chamberlen ran a series of eight advertisements in *A Collection for Improvement of Husbandry and Trade* (a London commercial weekly) inviting landowners to subscribe their estates. In the issue for November 29 it was announced that the £50,000 target had been reached and an inaugural meeting would soon be called. But landowners must have had difficulty raising the necessary quantities of cash, for from late December another eighteen *Collection* advertisements appeared inviting specie subscriptions directly from "monied-men." Chamberlen first offered to repay them in four annual instalments at an interest rate of 15 percent. This must not have sufficed, for the offer was later improved to include a share of the profits from the joint-stock corporation.[61] In the end, the first subscribers' meeting was not called until June 1696 and a constitution appeared only in July.[62] So the Office of Land Credit did not figure in attempts during the session of 1695–96 to derive some part of the year's supply from a parliamentary land bank. The extreme nature of Chamberlen's earlier proposals no doubt played a role in this.

As many had no doubt been expecting, early in the new parliamentary session Briscoe approached the treasury with a new scheme for a paper-currency war loan.[63] He would ask subscribers to the new National Land Bank to approve a perpetual loan of £2 million at 5 percent, or a term loan (for any sum the treasury cared to name) for 25 years at 7.75 percent. The loan would be paid into the exchequer exclusively in bank bills, but the bills could be redeemed for specie upon demand. While legal-tender status was not part of the design, Briscoe did ask that the exchequer accept bank bills for taxes and loans—a favor already being extended to the Bank of England. Briscoe did not specify what rate of interest, if any, he planned to pay on bank bills. Assuming the bills bore no interest and profits on this loan were to be divided with land subscribers after the pattern of his mortgage loans, specie investors would only have earned a rate of return of 7.25 percent. Were the National Land Bank to pay the same 3 percent on its bills as had the Bank of England, the rate would have fallen to 4.25 percent. So it seems very likely that Briscoe had quietly proposed redistributing more of the gains toward money subscribers.

Although it is very likely that around the same time Asgill and Barbon also offered terms for a new war loan, no record survives of such a proposal. But in early February 1696, Briscoe and the Asgill-Barbon group joined forces to form a "Land-Bank United" and put a new proposal.[64] They would loan £2 million in perpetuity at 7 percent. They would collect money subscriptions for the full amount of the loan, receiving a grant of incorporation if at least half this amount had been subscribed before an appointed deadline. They would also accept land subscriptions for £140,000 (in annual rental value) as an additional security. For their pains, land subscribers were to receive a quarter of the profits and be entitled to borrow up to three-quarters of the sale value of their estates at 3.5 percent. For the next seven years the bank would lend an additional £500,000 per year at 3.5 percent to nonsubscribing landowners.

It is difficult to know what to make of this proposal. The editor of the *Calendar of Treasury Books* believed the plan was to pay in the whole £2 million loan in specie and to issue out bills for the mortgage loans.[65] This is certainly consistent with the actual wording of the loan proposal, which called for "25 per cent [of the money subscriptions] to bee payd down & ye remaining 75 per cent by 3 quarterly payments of 25*l.* [percent] each."[66] But J. Keith Horsefield rightly resisted this interpretation since "both Briscoe and Asgill recognised the need for a [specie] reserve." He calculated that the bank could have maintained a (barely-adequate) reserve by lending £1.3 million in cash and the rest in bills.[67] However, even this seems implausible since specie owners could have invested their assets elsewhere at a better rate of return.[68]

Two other possibilities come to mind. One is that the bank did indeed hope to contribute a large part of the loan in specie because under the circumstances this might have proved very rewarding despite the relatively low rate of interest. In January 1696 parliament had passed an act entitling specie holders to receive full face value for their clipped silver coin if it were used to pay taxes or lend to the exchequer before May 5, 1696. Had the proposed bank paid over its loan in heavily clipped coin, specie subscribers could have evaded a potential 50 percent loss of the nominal value of their contributions. A major problem for this interpretation is that subscriptions were to be paid in gradually over the next year, but the subsidy for clipped coin was to hold only until May. Had subscribers to the proposed new land bank been able to obtain the premium only upon their first specie installment, it would not have been sufficiently profitable to contribute the loan entirely in specie. A more likely explanation is that the National Land Bank intended to supply the loan in bills alone and expected investors to have to contribute only a quarter of their subscriptions in actual hard cash. Subsequent calls would have been issued only in the event that a 25 percent specie reserve proved inadequate. This is exactly how the Bank of England had proceeded—whose founding document had likewise called for the full amount of the subscriptions to be paid in within a year—and is consistent with the original design of the National and Lincoln's-Inn land banks.[69] Certainly Briscoe later assumed that the land bank actually approved by parliament was going to pay the exchequer in bills.[70]

In any event, the alliance did not last long. This is probably because the new loan offer shared the principal weakness of the 1695 version of Briscoe's National Land Bank: a low rate of return for specie investors. This was an unavoidable side effect of promising a considerable share of the profits to land subscribers without requiring any tangible contribution of them. It seems to have been a sticking point with the House of Commons, leading the committee eventually to jettison the whole idea of land subscriptions.[71] The Briscoe camp tried to revive the idea, suggesting that actual specie contributions could be extracted from land subscribers over the years to come.[72] But these compromise solutions never took; the United Land Bank partnership quietly fell apart and Briscoe struck out on his own again.

In the first few days of March 1696 Briscoe published a third edition of the *Discourse*. In so doing he was in effect recommending to parliament once more the possibilities of a legal-tender approach—on which basis alone the concept of land subscriptions would have proved feasible. On March 6 the House of Commons resolved to borrow the rest of the supply for that session from "a national Land-Bank, to be settled by new subscriptions."[73] Despite the similarity in name, it was not Briscoe's project that MPs had in mind. Later that month he submitted a new loan offer in which bank bills were once again to be payable in specie upon demand.[74] The proposal was much like the one he had submitted to the treasury earlier that session, albeit (predictably) offering a larger share of the profits to monied men. This too proved unsuccessful, so in April, as a most amusing pamphlet relates, Briscoe carried his supporters in the House of Commons over to the camp of the Bank of England.[75] The new alliance failed; the supply act finalized late that month gave the loan contract to the Lincoln's-Inn group.[76] Asgill and Barbon, but not Briscoe, appeared on the list of commissioners for taking subscriptions to the new "National Land Bank."[77]

The new institution had nothing more than the vestiges of a land bank about it. According to the 1696 act, commissioners were directed to accept "such voluntary subscriptions as shall be made of land" (§10). But land subscribers were not explicitly assigned a role in its operations or any share of the profits. The bank's commission declared the aim of incorporation had been to enable the subscribers "to lend moneys on securities of land att low interest" (§29), but this was a relatively minor aspect of its overall operations. The directors were merely required to lend £500,000 upon mortgages at 3.5 percent, a much lesser sum than the war loan of £2.564 million that the bank was expected to advance to the exchequer. In the big picture, the offer to lend upon mortgages was just a device for distributing a small share of the bank's anticipated profits to a lucky few landowners. Granted, the bank was authorized to issue paper bills in whatever amounts it issued loans upon land (although security for these bills had to derive from the individual estates and not from the bank in general (§31)).[78] But it has already been shown that this kind of business could not have come anywhere close to matching the profits available from other lines of investment, meaning that little or none of the new bank's resources would have flowed into this channel.

In all essential respects the new institution was instead a money bank—a slightly-modified copy of the Bank of England. Commissioners would accept subscriptions "for and toward the raising and paying"[79] of £2.564 million into the exchequer. The loan would be perpetual with interest at 7 percent per annum. The subscribers were to be incorporated if half the loan were pledged before August (§16). One clause (§17) decreed subscriptions null and void if commissioners didn't receive a down-payment for a quarter of the amount subscribed.[80] This suggests the exchequer was to receive paper bills that would be payable on demand, for the circulation of which the bank would maintain a 25 percent specie reserve. In sum, the new bank, just like its predecessor, conformed to the treasury's very conservative ideas about employing paper money for public purposes. The only real risk in this design was that commissioners should fail to collect subscriptions in the required amount.

Unfortunately for the treasury this risk proved far from small; it became the occasion for financial disaster later that same year. In May the government called in a large part of the nation's silver coin to be recoined. The resulting scarcity of specie prompted a series of bank runs, inducing many to lock up whatever stores of gold or silver coin they possessed. In this uncertain environment subscriptions to the new bank reached a grand total of £2,100 beyond the £5,000 contributed by the king himself—far short of the £1.1 million or so required for incorporation. In these circumstances the treasury struggled to scrape funding together for the army in Flanders. So little money arrived, and even that after such a delay, that William was almost forced to abandon the war. A formal peace was negotiated the next year.

The creation of a "National Land Bank" that was in the end little more than a money bank suggests that the specific form of the new institution had less to do with political than with technical considerations. Land-bank projectors such as Chamberlen and Briscoe were attracted to the idea of a legal-tender paper currency because it alone could afford the financial legroom they needed to promise tax relief to England's landowners. But if the treasury lords had objected to a loan built around a paper currency backed by a fractional specie reserve they would have been even less inclined to support banking projects that rested upon the legal-tender concept. This may explain why Briscoe's first land-bank proposal was brought to the House of Commons by Brockman, an MP without any evident connections to the treasury. We will probably never know whether resistance stemmed principally from the treasury or from the members of the House of Commons in general. The important point, however, is that the general idea of a land bank only began to make serious inroads on the public-policy agenda when recourse was had to the more conservative banking model pioneered by the Bank of England—a design based on a paper currency backed by a fractional specie reserve. Unfortunately for land-bank projectors and their supporters, in bowing to the conservatism of public-policy makers they were simultaneously forcing themselves to surrender the essence of the land-bank concept and any hope they had of rendering substantial assistance to England's landowners. In the end, the National Land Bank promised to afford nothing more than a select number of low-interest mortgages (although the marketing campaign of Asgill and Briscoe played this small subsidy for all it was worth). The design of the new institution was intended above all to maximize the prospects for that season's financial program, rather than to throw profits or administrative control into the laps of England's gentry.

As for the Bank of England, the evidence is clear that it was resisted not so much by parliament as by the administration itself.[81] Paterson's project turned upon a major innovation in public finance: lending to the exchequer in paper currencies rather than specie. The treasury lords were worried this experiment might fail. They initially sought to insure themselves against disaster by demanding that a consortium of lenders be prepared to contribute the full amount of the loan in specie should the paper currency fail to take. They agreed in the end to let the experiment proceed if members of the general public were prepared to guarantee payment of at least half of the loan in specie. Treasury officials must have estimated the risk of failure to be fairly high, for in insisting upon this change they were relinquishing the considerable economies in public finance that would have been available had they accepted Paterson's original scheme. The subsequent failure of the subscriptions for the National Land Bank suggests that they were perfectly right to worry.

Sensible administrative conservatism does not make for nearly so interesting a story as a struggle between parliament and crown for control of the purse. But as the latest survey of England's financial revolution indicates, recent research has shown the term "revolution" to be overworked. "We are often left with duller, but perhaps more faithful, pictures of the nature of change as a hesitant progression."[82]

Notes

1. [Jonathan Swift], *The History of the Four Last Years of the Queen* (Dublin, 1758), in *The Prose Writings of Jonathan Swift*, vol. 7, *The History of the Four Last Years of the Queen*, ed. Herbert Davis (Oxford: Blackwell, 1973), 69–70.

2. Henry St John, viscount Bolingbroke, *Some Reflections on the Present State of the Nation, Principally with Regard to Her Taxes and Her Debts, and on the Causes and Consequences of Them* (London, 1753), in *The Works of Lord Bolingbroke*, ed. Henry Bohn, 4 vols. (London, 1844; repr., London: Frank Cass, 1967), 2:443.

3. Dennis Rubini, "Politics and the Battle for the Banks, 1688–1697," *English Historical Review* 85, no. 337 (Oct. 1970): 694–98. John Brewer, *The Sinews of Power: War, Money and the English State, 1688–1783* (London: Unwin Hyman, 1989, 144–54.

4. Rubini, "Politics," 697.

5. Ibid., 698.

6. Brewer, *Sinews*, 153.

7. For a recent account of the political repercussions of the battle of the banks see Mark Knights's entry on Charles Montagu in Eveline Cruickshanks, Stuart Handley, and D. W. Hayton, eds., *The History of Parliament: The House of Commons, 1690–1715*, 5 vols. (Cambridge: Cambridge University Press, 2002), 4:862–63.

8. Stephen Quinn notes one prior occasion (in 1689) when the exchequer accepted a loan in paper currency, in this case in the notes of a select few London goldsmiths (see Quinn, "Tallies or Reserves? Sir Francis Child's Balance Between Capital Reserves and Extending Credit to the Crown, 1685–1695," *Business and Economic History* 23, no. 1 [1994]: 47). But this was for much smaller amounts and seems to have been an exceptional, one-time arrangement for which the goldsmiths in question had had to secure a special allowance.

9. P. G. M. Dickson, *The Financial Revolution in England. A Study in the Development of Public Credit, 1688–1756* (London: Macmillan, 1967), 47.

10. The following account has been constructed from the following sources: *The Journals of the House of Commons, volume 10: 1688–1693* (London, 1802), 632; *The Journals of the House of Commons, volume 11: 1693–1697* (London, 1803), 75, 79, 81; [William Paterson], A Proposal for Setling a Transferable Ffund of Perpetuall Interest [1693], ff 87–88, MS Adv. 31.1.7, National Library of Scotland [hereafter

N.L.S.]; [William Paterson], *A Brief Account of the Intended Bank of England* ([London], 1694), 4–5; [William Paterson], *Some Account of the Transactions of Mr. William Paterson in Relation to the Bank of England and the Orphans Fund: in a Letter to a Friend* (London, 1695), 1–5; [Thomas Neale], *A Proposal for Raising a Million on a Fund of Interest by Setling One Hundred Thousand Pounds Yearly to Pay 8 per cent. for One Million Two Hundred Thousand Pounds, of Which the King to Have a Million* ([London], 1694), 1; Leopold von Ranke, *A History of England Principally in the Seventeenth Century* (Oxford, 1875), 238; Narcissus Luttrell, *The Parliamentary Diary of Narcissus Luttrell, 1691–1693*, ed. Henry Horwitz (Oxford: Clarendon, 1972), 321–23; D. W. Hayton, "Foley, Paul I," in Cruickshanks et al., *House of Commons*, 3:1057–74.

A Brief Account of the Intended Bank of England is generally acknowledged to be from Paterson's own pen, but not *Some Account of the Transactions of Mr. William Paterson.* This is presumably because the latter work was subscribed by one "J.S." The writing styles of the two pamphlets, however, are identical. And at times the author of the later work slips into the first person when speaking of events that could only have been witnessed by Paterson himself. The ascription to "J.S." was very likely tongue-in-cheek. One of Paterson's critics, Hugh Chamberlen, had humorously suggested that *A Brief Account* was written by "Jerry Squirt." Squirt was the name of a character in a contemporary comedy; in the play Jerry would "carp and quibble, pun and play the fool with every thing that came before him" ([Hugh Chamberlen], *Some Reflections on* the "Brief Account of the Intended Bank of England," *Whose Author's Name is Supposed to be Mr. Jerry Squirt* ([London], 1694), 3). So in signing *Some Account* with the initials "J.S.", Paterson may have been thumbing his nose at Chamberlen.

11. Luttrell, *Parliamentary Diary*, ed. Horwitz, 140–41.

12. [Paterson], *Some Account*, 2.

13. William Lowndes, Remarks upon the Proposals for Establishing a Fund to Raise Two Millions, 1691, f. 77r., MS Adv. 31.1.7, N.L.S.

14. Lowndes, Remarks, f. 75v., MS Adv. 31.1.7, N.L.S.

15. [Paterson], *Some Account*, 3–4.

16. Ibid., 2.

17. Ibid.

18. *Commons Journals*, 10:632.

19. [Paterson], *Some Account*, 3.

20. Described in [Neale], *Proposal.*

21. The 50 percent target is implicit in the clause of the bank's authorizing statute that made incorporation conditional upon collecting subscriptions for at least half of the loan (5 & 6 W. & M., c. 20, §24, *The Statutes of the Realm*, 12 vols. (London, 1810–28), 6:489). Only with incorporation would the bank become entitled to the corporate seal it would need to issue out "sealed bills" to the treasury. As for a 25 percent specie reserve, I take this to be the meaning of the clause stipulating that unless every person should pay the commissioners a full quarter of their subscription it would become null and void (5 & 6 W. & M., c. 20, §22, *Statutes of the Realm*, 6:488).

22. Early in the session of 1693–94 Paterson was proposing to pay 6 percent on bank bills ([Neale], *Proposal*, 1). But when the bank's first "sealed bills" were eventually issued, they bore interest at 2*d.* per £100 per day or about 3 percent per annum. This lower rate may have been acceptable to government suppliers given

that bank organizers achieved a 100 percent subscription, increasing considerably the security of their bills.

23. *The Journals of the House of Commons, Volume 10: 1688–1693* 744–45.

24. It should be noted that payments on the lottery loans would cease after a term of years rather than go on into perpetuity as with any loans from the Bank of England. Thus part of the higher annual cost of the lottery loans stemmed simply from the fact that the Crown was in effect gradually buying out the principal.

25. Hugh Chamberlen, *Dr. Hugh Chamberlen's Proposal to Make England Rich and Happy* (London, 1690); Hugh Chamberlen, *An Humble Proposal to the Honourable the House of Commons* ([London], 1690).

26. Sir William Killigrew, *To the King and Queen's Most Excellent Majesties, the Lords Spiritual and Temporal, and to the Knights, Citizens, and Burgesses Assembled in Parliament: An Humble Proposal Shewing How This Nation May Be Vast Gainers By All Sums of Mony Given to the Crown Without Lessening the Prerogative* ([London, 1690]).

27. Proposal for a Fund of Current Property, 1691, ff 79–80, MS Adv. 31.1.7, N.L.S.

28. Hugh Chamberlen and Dalby Thomas, *A Proposal for Encouraging of Persons, to Subscribe Towards a Common Stock of [———] for the Erecting and Managing of a Trade by a General Fishery to be with all Possible Moral Security of a Great Gain to the Adventurers, and of No Less Honour and Advantage to the Publick, and is a Benefit not to be Attained by Any Other Methods, as is Strongly Presumed from Arguments that Have All the Appearing Force of Demonstration* ([London], 1691); Hugh Chamberlen and Dalby Thomas, *A Supplement to the Proposal for a General Fishery, Explaining the Nature and Benefit of the Fund Proposed for the Same* ([London, 1691]).

29. Reprinted in [Hugh Chamberlen], *The Tunnage Bank Compared with Dr. Chamberlen's Land-Fund of Credit* (London, 1694), 7–8.

30. Hugh Chamberlen, *Dr. Chamberlen's Petition and Proposals for a Land Bank to Increase Trade* ([London], 1693), 1; Hugh Chamberlen, *A Short Abstract of Doctor H. Chamberlen's Proposal to the Honourable House of Commons the Last Sessions. And Also of Mr. John Briscoe's Present Printed Proposal Compared Together, Whereby the Benefits of Each to the Nation, and Every Freeholder Concern'd, May Plainly Appear* ([London], 1694), 1.

31. James Simon, *An Essay Towards an Historical Account of Irish Coins and of the Currency of Foreign Monies in Ireland: with an Appendix Containing Several Statutes, Proclamations, Patents, Acts of State and Letters Relating to the Same* (Dublin, 1749), 57–65.

32. Chamberlen, *Dr. Chamberlen's Petition.*

33. Hugh Chamberlen, *Some Useful Reflections Upon a Pamphlet Called* "A Brief Account of the Intended Bank of England" ([London], 1694), 18. Behind the scenes Chamberlen promised one MP that after a suitable act should pass, he would receive "a valueable consideration," ostensibly as compensation for his "right of subscription"—i.e., his right to subscribe his lands to the bank scheme (Chamberlen to [——], Dec. 7, 1693, reprinted in J. H. Aveling, *The Chamberlens and the Midwifery Forceps: Memorials of the Family and an Essay on the Invention of the Instrument* (London, 1882), 162–63).

34. *Commons Journals,* 11:80.

35. Chamberlen, *Tunnage Bank.*

36. Chamberlen, *Some Useful Reflections*; [Chamberlen], *Some Reflections on the "Brief Account."*

37. Hugh Chamberlen, *Mr. J. Briscoe, a Director in the National Land-Bank, His Defence of Dr. Hugh Chamberlen's Bank or Office of Land-Credit: in a Letter to the Doctor* (London, 1696).

38. John Briscoe, *A Discourse on the Late Funds of the Million-Act, Lottery-Act, and Bank of England* (London, 1694); John Briscoe, *A Discourse on the Late Funds of the Million-Act, Lottery-Act, and Bank of England*, 2d enlarged ed. (London, 1694). John Briscoe, *An Abstract of the Discourse on the Late Funds of the Million-Act, Lottery-Act, and Bank of England* (London, 1694).

39. This assumed a perpetual loan; the interest rate could be adjusted upward as required if parliament preferred a fixed-term loan.

40. William Brockman, Object. & Answrs on Proposall Abt Land Bank Bill, Feb. 1694/5, f. 54, Add. MS 42593, B.L.

41. John Briscoe, *The Freehold Estates of England, or England It Self the Best Fund of Security* (London, 1695), 1; *Commons Journals*, 11:277, 283, 293; England, House of Commons, Breviate of the Bill for the Improvement of the Freehold Estates of England, and the Incouragement of Trade, Depending in ye House of Commons, March 1694/5, ff 44–49, MS 152(5), All Souls' College.

42. Chamberlen, *Short Abstract. Some Observations By Way of Answer to a Pamphlet Called* "England's Glory or the Royal Bank" (London, 1695).

43. [John Asgill and Nicholas Barbon], *A Proposal for a Subscription to Raise One Hundred Thousand Pounds for Circulating the Credit of a Land-Bank* ([London], 1695). [John Asgill and Nicholas Barbon], *An Account of the Land-Bank, Shewing the Design and Manner of the Settlement, the Profits to the Subscribers, the Advantage to the Borrowers, the Conveniency to the Lenders, that it Wil Be the Support of the Nobility and Gentry of England, and a Public Good to the Whole Nation* (London, 1695), 2.

44. [Asgill and Barbon], *Account.*

45. [John Asgill and Nicholas Barbon], *The Settlement of the Land-Bank, Established Anno Dom. 1695* ([London], 1695).

46. [John Asgill and Nicholas Barbon], *A List of the Names of the Subscribers to the Land-Bank* ([London], 1695).

47. John Asgill, *Several Assertions Proved, in Order to Create Another Species of Money than Gold and Silver* ([London], 1696).

48. Henry Horwitz, *Parliament, Policy and Politics in the Reign of William III* (Manchester: Manchester University Press, 1977), 155–56.

49. Henry Guy to Lord Portland, June 5, 1695, f. 2r., Portland MS PwA 506, Nottingham University Library.

50. Edward Harley to Sir Edward Harley, Aug. 1, 1696, f. 17, Add. MS 70018, B.L.

51. John Briscoe, *An Account of the National Land-Bank* (London, [1695]), 1.

52. John Briscoe, *Advertisement. I Have Been Desired by Some Gentlemen, Who are Well-Wishers to the Intended Land-Bank to Publish my Answer to the Following Queries, Propounded by Several who have Read my Proposals* (London, 1695); John Briscoe, *Advice to the Free-Holder*, reprinted in John Briscoe, *To the Lords Spiritual and Temporal and Commons in Parliament Assembled* (London, [1695]), 2–4; John Briscoe, *The Freehold Estates of England, or England It Self the Best Fund of Security* (London, 1695).

53. John Asgill and Nicholas Barbon, *The Freeholder's Answer to Mr. John Briscoe's Proposals for a National Bank: Shewing the Reasons Why They Will Rather Borrow Money of the Land-Bank Already Establish'd, than Subscribe to His Proposals* ([London, 1695]), 1.

54. John Briscoe, *Mr. Briscoe's Reply to a Pamphlet, Intitled,* "The Freeholders Answer to Mr. John Briscoe's "Proposals for a National Land Bank"" ([London, 1695]), 1.

55. John Briscoe, *An Account of the Value of the Estates in the Several Counties Subscribed Towards the Fund for a National Land-Bank, from Thursday the 11th of June, to Saturday the 13th of July, 1695* (London, 1695); John Briscoe, *The Following Proposals for, and Accounts of, a National Land-Bank Having Been Printed at London. Its Proveable Many Gentlemen Who Would Have Subscribed Thereto, by Reason of the Distance of their Dwelling from Thence, Have Heard Nothing, or Had but an Imperfect Account of it; for Informing Whom, True Copies of Several of Mr Brisco's Papers are Herewith Reprinted, in Order to be Dispersed in Several Counties* (Edinburgh, 1695), 8; John Briscoe, *An Account of the Value of the Estates in the Several Counties Subscribed Towards the Fund for a National Land-Bank, from Thursday the 11th of June, to Saturday the 3d of August, 1695* (London, 1695); John Briscoe, *Proposals for Raising Money for the National Land-Bank* (London, 1695), 2.

56. Briscoe, *Proposals for Raising Money.*

57. Minutes of the National Land Bank, 1695–96, f. 3r., MS 61, Goldsmiths' Library.

58. Ibid., f. 13r.

59. *A List of the Names of the Subscribers of Land and Money Towards a Fund for the National Land-Bank* ([London, 1695]).

60. [Hugh Chamberlen], *A Brief Narrative of the Nature & Advantages of the Land-Bank, as Proposed by Dr. Hugh Chamberlen, the First Author of Founding a Bank on an Annual Revenue* (London, 1695); Hugh Chamberlen, *A Proposal by Dr. Hugh Chamberlain in Essex-Street for a Bank of Secure Current Credit to be Founded Upon Land* (London: E. Whitlock, 1695); [Hugh Chamberlen], *The Several Articles or Parts of the Proposal Upon Land-Credit Rationally Explained* (London, 1695).

61. [Hugh Chamberlen], *The Office of Land-Credit: Encouragement to Mony'd Men* ([London], 1696).

62. [Hugh Chamberlen], *The Constitution of the Office of Land-Credit Declared in a Deed by Hugh Chamberlen Senior, M.D. and Others, Joynt Undertakers and Managers Thereof: Inrolled in Chancery, Anno Dom. 1696* (London, 1696).

63. John Briscoe, Proposals Humbly Offer'd to the Right Honble the Lords Comrs of the Treasury, [1696], f. 114r., MS Adv. 31.1.7, N.L.S.

64. John Briscoe, *Reasons Humbly Offered for the Establishment of the National Land-Bank* ([London, 1696]), 2; [John Asgill, Nicholas Barbon, and John Briscoe], *Proposals Made to the Honourable House of Commons, by the Land-Bank United, for Raising Two Millions or More* ([London, 1695]); [John Asgill, Nicholas Barbon, and John Briscoe], A Scheme for a Nationall Land-Bank, [1696], ff 104r.–105v., MS Adv. 31.1.7, N.L.S.

65. William Shaw, ed., *Cal. Treas. Bks. . . . Introduction to Vols. 9–17 . . . 1695–1702*, xlix.

66. [Asgill, Barbon and Briscoe], Scheme, f. 104r., MS Adv. 31.1.7, N.L.S.

67. J. Keith Horsefield, *British Monetary Experiments, 1650–1710* (Cambridge: Harvard University Press, 1960), 204.

68. Under Horsefield's version of the scheme, cash investors would have earned only 7.9 percent overall (assuming they received three-quarters of both 7

percent on the government loan and 3.5 percent on mortgage loans, which latter would have averaged a little under £2 million over the first 7 years of the project). The simple expedient of discounting tallies already paid 8 or 9 percent and every specie holder was doubtless anticipating far better returns once the recoinage began in May and specie of any description became very scarce.

69. *The Commission for Taking Subscriptions for 1200000l. Pursuant to the Act of Parliament* ([London], 1694), 4.

70. See Briscoe's letter of June 25, 1696 to the chancellor of the exchequer, Charles Montagu, reprinted in Shaw, ed., *Cal. Treas. Bks. . . . Introduction to Vols. 11–17. . . 1695–1702,* lxvi.

71. *A Second Discourse About Banks: Between a Brigadier, a Lawyer, a Merchant and a Goldsmith* ([London, 1696]), 1.

72. Thomas Neale, *The National Land-Bank, Together With Money: So Composed, as Not Only to Be Easie Understood and Easily Practiced, But More Capable Also of Supplying the Government With Any Sum of Money in Proportion to What Fund Shall Be Settled: as Likewise, the Free-Holder With Money at a More Moderate Interest, Than If Such Bank Did Consist of Money Alone Without Land* ([London], 1696); *The Only Way of Subscribing Land as to Make It Really Useful, as Well for the Supply of the Money to Be Now Raised for the Publick, as for the Advantage of the Subscribers of It, Is to Let It Be Enacted* ([London, 1696]).

73. *Commons Journals,* 11:495.

74. John Briscoe, *To the Knights, Citizens and Burgesses in Parliament Assembled* ([London, 1696]).

75. *Mr. B——coe's Reply to the Almanack, Being Land and Money United: or, B——coe & the B——k of E——nd Joined* ([London, 1696]).

76. 7 & 8 W. 3, c. 31, §§10–41, *Statutes of the Realm,* 7:132–37.

77. *The Commission for Taking Subscriptions to the National Land-Bank* ([London], 1696), 1.

78. 7 & 8 W. 3, c. 31, §§10–41, *Statutes of the Realm,* 7:132–37.

79. This wording indicates the subscriptions were not themselves to be paid in, but were only to support and guarantee payment of the loan—leaving the exact means of payment unspecified (7 & 8 W. 3, c. 31, §§10–41, *Statutes of the Realm,* 7:132–37).

80. Ibid.

81. Granted, strong criticisms were voiced of the project when it first came before parliament. But contemporaries generally attributed this antipathy to causes other than Country party worries about long-term loans making the Crown financially independent of the Commons. Paterson aptly observed that parliament had previously approved two schemes for long-term borrowing (in 1693 a tontine loan anticipated to raise £1 million and in early 1694 a lottery loan for another £1 million) with relatively little discussion. The "unusual opposition" raised against the Bank of England, he concluded, derived instead from the personal interests of "three sorts of people": "the Jacobites, who apprehend it may contribute to lessen their monarch of France, and some few usurers and brokers of money, and the third sort are commonly such as have not wherewith to trade, unless it be like Haman of old, for whole nations or peoples at once"—a not-very-subtle reference to goldsmith bankers ([Paterson], *Brief Account,* 16–17). In a similar vein, Briscoe speculated that some MPs had opposed his project because they knew "a

Land-Bank would make the Government easy" and "had a mind to distress the Government" (Briscoe, *Mr. John Asgill His Plagiarism Detected; and His* "Several Assertions," *of Which He Pretends to Be the Author, Proved to Be Taken Out of Mr. Briscoe's* "Discourse on the Late Funds" (London, 1696), 25–26). Bishop Burnet later wrote that "enemies of the constitution" had earnestly opposed the Bank of England for "secret reasons": they knew it would considerably strengthen the king's hand in the war against France (Gilbert Burnet, *History of His Own Time: With Notes By the Earls of Dartmouth and Hardwicke, Speaker Onslow, and Dean Swift: to Which Are Added Other Annotations*, 2d enlarged ed., ed. Martin J. Routh (Oxford, 1833), 223–24).

82. Henry Roseveare, *The Financial Revolution, 1660–1760* (London: Longman, 1991), 3.

Greed, Fraud, and Popular Culture: John Breholt's Madagascar Schemes of the Early Eighteenth Century

Arne Bialuschewski

IMMEDIATELY FOLLOWING THE GLORIOUS REVOLUTION, WAR restricted English shipping and made it difficult for London merchants to continue some of their customary trading activities. As a result, large amounts of capital were freed up and its owners went looking for alternative investments. Because of the restrictions on conventional trading practices, it became more acceptable, and perhaps even necessary, to invest in innovative and risky enterprises. Additionally, the ongoing European-wide conflict resulted in a greater probability that capital would be lost either to acts of war or to the vagaries of nature and navigation in that period. One result was a mania for speculative ventures—what Daniel Defoe termed the "Projecting Age."[1] Some projects, such as utility companies for water and lighting, would today be considered perfectly sensible. But others were fantastic schemes that seem in retrospect destined to fail.[2]

One of the most intriguing aspects of the projecting age was a mania for treasure hunting. In 1688, the adventurer William Phips returned to London from a salvaging expedition in the Caribbean, bringing with him bullion and other valuables worth some £210,000 —at the time a princely sum. His success encouraged imitators. In the next several years projectors attracted investors with wild promises of future profits.[3] Although very little is documented about these projects, it seems very doubtful that any treasure hunt of the late seventeenth century yielded returns comparable to Phips's expedition. It is possible that many of the enterprises were entirely fraudulent.

The post-Revolution mania for treasure hunting reemerged in the early eighteenth century in a curious new form. Proposals began to circulate in England and Scotland for confiscating the wealth rumored to have been accumulated by several hundred pirates living in Madagascar.

The Indian Ocean had become a center of pirate activity during the 1690s. Authorities in the English colonies were accustomed to granting commissions for undertaking privateering raids against French shipping in the area. However, upon receiving their commissions many of these ersatz privateers promptly sailed to the Arabian Sea, turned pirate, and preyed upon the richly loaded pilgrim fleets that sailed annually from Surat to Mocha and Jeddah on the Red Sea. Indian leaders threatened to boycott all trade with England unless the home government put an end to a problem that was largely of its own creation. In 1695 William Kidd, a seasoned buccaneer from New York, promised a solution. He persuaded a syndicate of Whig lords to back him in a expedition to the Indian Ocean to hunt down the pirates and bring them and their treasures to London. Unfortunately for English authorities, Kidd himself turned raider, taking two large prizes. Kidd returned to America, where he was arrested, shipped to London, and tried. He was executed in May 1701, and his backers only just managed to escape prosecution.[4] The scandal was enormous.

In the meantime, the Board of Trade discovered an easier and more effective way of putting an end to piracy in the Indian Ocean. An investigation revealed that the pirates were being supplied by merchants from North America. In 1699, the colonial authorities there took measures to cut off all trade with Madagascar. As a result, piracy virtually disappeared from the Indian Ocean. Numerous marauders sought refuge among the indigenous population in Madagascar.[5] The conviction grew within England that the retired pirates were sitting on a veritable gold mine of accumulated treasures. This may have been little more than a myth, but a number of projectors sought to capitalize upon it. Among them was a certain John Breholt, a London shipmaster who specialized in maritime get-rich-quick schemes.

Breholt had a somewhat unsavory past. In 1697 or 1698 he had approached John Egerton, earl of Bridgewater, who was at that time president of the board of trade, to request permission to sail to the Indian Ocean and "treat with ye Pirats upon Condition of becoming good Subjects for the Future."[6] Nothing came of this plan so in 1699 Breholt organized an expedition to dive for sunken treasures off the Cuban coast. This venture turned out to be a complete failure, and disputes with the crew over payment led to charges of piracy against him in Charleston and in the Azores.[7] After about a year of imprisonment in Lisbon, Breholt made his way to London. In 1702 he began working on another treasure hunt in the West Indies, this one financed by—among other worthies with ties to the then-government—Thomas, Lord Fairfax of Cameron, and Richard Savage, Earl Rivers. In the spring of 1704, when preparations were already at an advanced stage and several thousand pounds had been spent, rumors spread that Breholt intended to sail for Madagascar. In a sworn affidavit, a sailor accused Breholt's partner, the former shipwright, Peter Dearlove, of having once participated in an assault on an Indian pilgrim fleet in the Arabian Sea.[8] As a consequence, the venture was shelved and Breholt decided to leave London.

In April 1705, Breholt appeared in Edinburgh. His stories of fabulous pirate riches in Madagascar were received with keen interest by the common people, particularly in the local taverns. Breholt claimed to represent the pirates settled on Madagascar and proposed to negotiate a general amnesty in return for a considerable part of their booty, which he announced to be five million pounds.[9] Unfortunately for Breholt, the Scottish economy was in an agonizing decline and there was clearly not enough venture capital available to fund his proposed voyage.

Throughout his stay in Scotland, Breholt lived at the expense of George Mackenzie, earl of Cromarty, who had recently resigned as Scottish secretary of state. Cromarty was a member of the council general of the Company of Scotland, but he belonged to a minority faction within the company that saw the commercial future of Scotland in the Indian Ocean rather than in Mesoamerica, where a colonial scheme in Darien had failed badly, causing many of the problems the country was facing at that time. For Cromarty, Madagascar was an overseas market where the Scots could set up a highly profitable trading base. He envisioned shipping slaves to Brazil, where gold had recently been found. The large profits this trading connection promised to yield would be an important source of capital formation.[10] It appears that Breholt was Cromarty's designated shipmaster.

Sometime in the spring or summer of 1707, Breholt, still resident in Edinburgh, began pushing again for a treasure project. The basic premise was the same as in 1705: to offer the Madagascar pirates a formal amnesty in exchange for a share of their ill-gotten booty. An expedition of the kind Breholt proposed required significant funds, perhaps as much as £25,000.[11] To raise this much capital, it would have been necessary to find a significant number of investors. A list compiled in the course of a later official investigation into the venture indicates the individuals whom Breholt was able to draw into the scheme.[12] The plan seems to have drawn considerable support from among the London Scots, a group of Scottish merchants who had migrated to the metropolis in the late seventeenth century. Probably the greatest contribution was meant to come from George Douglas, earl of Morton. His family owned large estates in the west of Scotland, which secured him a steady income. The earl had some experience with maritime projects, having in 1703 been the main investor in a vessel that had sailed under the commission of the Company of Scotland to the East Indies.[13] Another London Scot who agreed to participate was Sir David Nairne, who had been secretary depute for Scotland prior to the 1707 Anglo-Scottish Union. Like many other businessmen of his day, he made a living from his connections with office holders and the military. His business dealings must have been quite successful; he was the second largest shareholder in the Bank of Scotland with an investment of £23,000.[14] Further funds were meant to come from Sir James Gray and Richard Toulson. Unfortunately little is known about them.

There was also a second group of investors associated with some influential Whigs. Among the most prominent backers were Thomas Hopkins and Charles Howard, earl of Carlisle, both of whom had held various offices in the government and were deeply involved in the partisan conflicts of their times. Carlisle had once lived principally on his land revenues. Several lucky investments during the glory years of projecting in the 1690s, as well as success at the gaming table, had enabled him to build Castle Howard, one of the most conspicuous buildings of the age. It appears that Carlisle had known Breholt for quite some time and had probably backed the failed expedition to the Caribbean in 1699.[15] Carlisle must have possessed an adventurous spirit if he was willing to overlook these losses and join Breholt in a new and very risky enterprise.

Further support for the Madagascar scheme came from three other Whigs, Sir John Bennett (a reputable attorney and MP for Morpeth), Charles Egerton (brother of the earl of Bridgewater and MP for Brackley) and William Wallis (MP for Steyning).[16] These persons were probably not experienced investors who were likely dragged into the venture by acquaintances and who perhaps saw the scheme as the opportunity of a lifetime. Visions of pirate treasure may have proved too hard to resist.

Fragmentary biographical evidence suggests that most, if not all, of Breholt's investors knew each other personally. For example, Morton and Carlisle had served as commissioners for the Union, in which position they had worked along with Nairne and other members of the Whig oligarchy. In the absence of an anonymous financial market, most capital transactions took place within political and business networks. Even the trade in stocks in the early eighteenth century was marked by a large degree of party endogamy.[17] Personal connections were evidently key to investment behavior.

It was a necessary prerequisite for Breholt's enterprise to obtain a commission from the lords of the admiralty or from Queen Anne. In August 1707 Breholt tried to include Sidney, Lord Godolphin—lord high treasurer, chief architect of the Act of Union and, alongside John Churchill, duke of Marlborough, the queen's leading minister—as a secret partner in the scheme. This would have secured his support for a commission for an expedition to Madagascar.[18] This attempt, however, turned out to be fruitless. Therefore, in the following month the efforts to obtain the necessary political support for the privateering venture intensified. This part of the project was coordinated by Martin Laycock, a solicitor and an old acquaintance of Breholt who had tried to salvage the treasure hunt Breholt had been forced to abort in 1704. Laycock was assisted by Bennett and by Paul Jodrell. In a letter introducing them to the secretary of state, Charles Spencer, earl of Sunderland, Laycock described them as "men of Substance and knowen abillaty to undertake such a Trust."[19] Bennett had previously held various legal offices. Jodrell had served as the clerk of the House of Commons, in which capacity he had prepared the parliamentary investigation of the Kidd affair.[20] Both men were conversant with the legal and political aspects of an expedition of this sort.

To assist in obtaining the necessary backing from the authorities, the projectors set up an elaborate system of lobbying. Sometime in the fall of 1707, for example, they approached some individuals involved with the new East India Company, an enterprise established in 1698 by interlopers to break the monopoly of the old, Tory-dominated East India Company. The new company was a natural ally, since many of its traders had been accused by the old company of being or supporting pirates. Although there is no evidence that the new East India Company ever backed Breholt's Madagascar scheme as a corporate body, one of its directors, Sir Streynsham Master, supported the plan when it was considered before the board of trade.[21]

The administrative apparatus of the early eighteenth century was marked by personal cupidity, private interest, and a political culture that combined administrative skill with the operation of a thriving system of clientage and graft. Officeholders on all levels sought to combine the public good with their own interest. Public office was regarded as a legitimate source of profit, and corruption was widespread. The projectors of the Madagascar scheme therefore understood that if they wanted to acquire political support they would have to pump some funds into the system, and so a considerable number of shares in the enterprise were designated for influential government officials: Godolphin and Marlborough, for example, were offered fifty shares each.[22] Although the value of a single share in a successful mission was estimated at £1,000, this offer did not suffice to bring about the anticipated result. The projectors next tried inflating the value of the booty they intended to bring back from Madagascar. In November 1707 Laycock presented a memorandum to Sunderland which claimed that the pirates had accumulated more than £20 million and were willing to part with a quarter of it for the queen's amnesty. This figure was supported by the testimony of six retired pirates. According to Laycock's rough estimate, the total gain for the exchequer would have amounted to £6 million. Laycock's calculation is based on an estimation of the listed worth of five identified pirate crews, the value of whose hoard of treasure he estimated as £20,240,000. These pirates, he wrote, "would readily give the Fourth Part of what they were worth for their Pardon; so that, by a modest Computation, the Fourth Part of the whole would bring in above Six Millions Sterling to the Government."[23] The reasoning employed here by Laycock—the math is obviously wrong, and he omitted mention of any monies that would be paid to investors in a Madagascar expedition—indicates the unsolid nature of the entire scheme. The sum of £6 million represented more than a third of the national debt at that time.

Given the fact that the government was notoriously short of funds, it may seem a little surprising that the authorities never seriously considered sanctioning the Madagascar scheme. There was no financial risk to them, and if the plan turned out to be successful the public coffers would have profited considerably. The queen seems to have been willing to back ventures of this kind, as is attested by the fact that in the spring of 1707 Fairfax had received a renewed patent to loot wrecks in the West Indies, with a one-eighth share payable to the Crown.[24] The explanation may lie in the fact that the Madagascar scheme served no strategic goals (it would not, unlike Fairfax's venture, help to undermine the financial resources of either the Spanish or the French crowns) and bore considerable political risks. In fact, Breholt's Madagascar scheme resembled the Kidd affair in several respects. The attendant dangers of the latter scheme were still burned into the collective consciousness of London's political elite. The leading government ministers may have feared that a similar failure of the proposed new expedition would endanger their careers, if not the future of the entire government.

While the authorities hesitated to issue the necessary commission for an expedition to Madagascar, Breholt endeavored to increase popular support for his project. After his return to London in September or October 1707 he organized a series of public meetings to promote his Madagascar scheme. On several occasions Breholt spoke at the King's Head Inn on the Strand, a well-known Whig haunt. Large crowds were reported to have listened attentively to his talk.[25] It appears Breholt was a charismatic speaker, for witnesses praised his rhetorical skills. The gatherings were also well prepared public-relations events. On one occasion a shipwrecked sailor who had recently returned from Madagascar—the son of the famous Admiral John Benbow—testified to the willingness of the pirates to come to England.[26] On another occasion a woman who claimed to be the abandoned wife of Henry Avery spoke about her personal tragedy. In 1695 Avery had plundered a rich Indian prize and thereupon vanished with his booty, leaving his wife in desperate conditions. Following this presentation, Breholt got forty-eight "Wives and other Relations of the Pyrates" to sign a petition to Queen Anne pleading for the proclamation of a general amnesty for all pirates.[27]

The media of the day also reflected on the Madagascar schemes. In October 1707 Defoe's *Review* published an essay which in vivid language championed the plan to send vessels to Madagascar and bring the pirates to Britain where they would share their immense treasures with the Crown. Moral objections against the scheme were put aside. In Defoe's view, all respected founders of great empires were, in fact, robbers. He specifically referred to the example of Rome, which, like England, had relied on the illicit use of force to establish its empire.[28] In November 1708 the *Monthly Miscellany* carried an article fusing the emerging Madagascar myth with the legend of the mutineer and pirate Henry Avery. The heroic story was further elaborated in a booklet that appeared in June 1709. In this account the pirates had retired to Madagascar where they were joined by marauders of all nations and eventually acquired Avery as their king.[29] The narrative of Avery's life ended with an appeal to the Crown to offer the pirates a general amnesty. Both publications were clearly designed to appeal to a broad readership. They provide a mixture of the highly marketable themes of escapist adventure, rebellion against unjust authority, and a unique example of advancement.

Unfortunately for Breholt and his backers, the Madagascar scheme was headed for even more troubled waters. In the latter half of 1708 rumors were revived that Breholt had connections with piracy. Though Breholt tried to reassure the investors and emphasized that three or four vessels were almost ready to sail to Madagascar, he did not manage to regain their confidence. In the spring of 1709 the privy council instructed the board of trade to undertake an investigation into the Madagascar scheme. A number of witnesses came forward to provide damaging evidence against Breholt. It was alleged he had twice conspired to acquire a vessel with the intention of joining the Madagascar pirates.[30] When this evidence became public, the Madagascar scheme was virtually dead in the water.

Two years later when the South Sea Company was established, a pamphlet suggested expanding its trading privileges to Madagascar. Shortly after that publication, Breholt petitioned to the company to get a license for an expedition to Madagascar to deal with the pirates. But this privilege was not granted.[31] After that the Madagascar myth quickly faded away. Breholt turned his attention to a new project: building lighthouses on the Welsh coast.[32] Thereafter he disappears from the historical record.

The few examples from the late seventeenth century of men amassing fortunes virtually overnight offered ample scope for the talents of projectors, who specialized in drawing wealthy and not-always-well-informed investors into their nets. Breholt's Madagascar scheme is a telling example. It was fostered by a projector who understood the value of publicity in advancing his cause. In the absence of any reliable knowledge about conditions in Madagascar, Breholt managed to manipulate the popular myth of a treasure island for his own ends. His project exposed some of the weaknesses of the period's financial markets and relied upon information being inadequate or difficult to obtain and upon the manipulation of the resulting lack of knowledge through propaganda. Many of his potential investors were inexperienced and perhaps quite naïve. Visions of fabulous treasure may have made them ignore the great risks associated with business dealings in uncharted waters.

Yet it would be too easy to dismiss this episode as a pure public-relations fiction. Even though the Madagascar scheme was never translated into action, it bore witness to a thriving venture capitalism, to the willingness of some to search for business opportunities at the edges of the then-known world, and to the existence of a considerable amount of risk capital.

Notes

1. Daniel Defoe, *An Essay upon Projects* (London, 1697), 1.

2. Christine MacLeod, "The 1690s Patent Boom: Invention or Stock-Jobbing?" *Economic History Review* 2nd series, 39, no. 4 (Nov. 1986): 557–71; Henry Roseveare, *The Financial Revolution, 1660–1760* (London: Longman, 1991), 42–45.

3. Peter Earle, *The Wreck of the Almiranta: Sir William Phips and the Search for the Hispaniola Treasure* (London: Macmillan, 1979), 217–23.

4. Robert C. Ritchie, *Captain Kidd and the War against the Pirates* (Cambridge, MA: Harvard University Press, 1986), 50–227.

5. Arne Bialuschewski, "Pirates, Slavers, and the Indigenous Population in Madagascar, *c.* 1690–1715," *International Journal of African Historical Studies* 38, no. 2 (2005): 401–25.

6. Memorandum of John Breholt, [n.d.], Ellesmere MS EL 9179, Henry E. Huntington Library, San Marino, California.

7. Examination of Peter Dearlove, July 29, 1702, ff 128–29, HCA 1/53, Nat. Arch.; petition of Dearlove, Dec. 6, 1703, SP 44/230/135, Nat. Arch. After the failure of the expedition had become obvious, Breholt and the larger part of the crew decided to sail to Madagascar. The troubles in Charleston were caused by sailors demanding some kind of wages. When the *Carlisle* arrived in the Azores, it transpired that Breholt was heading for Madagascar, which led to his apprehension by the Portuguese authorities. The vessel fled the harbor under gunfire. See the deposition of Lawrence Waldron, May 17, 1709, CO 323/6/222, Nat. Arch.

8. Deposition of Charles Blagrave, July 21, 1704, HCA 1/16/78, Nat. Arch. In addition to treasure, it seems likely that Breholt was searching for his brother George, first officer of the *Carlisle*, who had disappeared when the vessel was lost in Madagascar in January 1701. Dearlove later made his way back to England.

9. William Drummond to John Drummond, May 8, 1705, no. 5, GD 24/1/464, National Archives of Scotland [hereafter N.A.S.]; earl of Cromarty to earl of Mar, Oct. 23, 1705, no. 235, GD 305/1/169, N.A.S.; Joseph Taylor, *A Journey to Edenborough in Scotland* (Edinburgh, 1893), 125. It may seem ironic that only a few weeks prior to Breholt's arrival in Edinburgh three English sailors had been executed for the alleged seizure of a Scottish vessel in the Indian Ocean. It later turned out that the ship had been taken by pirates when the Scots tried to trade at Madagascar.

10. Cromarty to Mar, Mar. 9, 1706, no. 11, GD 124/15/279, N.A.S.

11. There is no direct evidence for the cost of an expedition of this kind. But we know that in 1704 Lord Fairfax (one of Breholt's partners in a previous venture) raised £25,000 for a voyage to the West Indies to loot "all Wrecks, Jetsam, Flotsam, &c." See Indenture of shareholders, 24 June 1704, ff 32–33, MS Rawlinson C. 451, Bodleian Library, Oxford.

12. CO 323/6/191–92, Nat. Arch.

13. Journal of the Court of Directors, Nov. 20, 1703, D/1/3, Royal Bank of Scotland Archive, Edinburgh; Morton's articles of agreement, Dec. 6, 1703, ff 219–20, MS Adv. 83.7.5, National Library of Scotland; George Crawfurd, *The Peerage of Scotland* (Edinburgh, 1716), 354.

14. Sir David Nairne to John Stirling, Apr. 15, 1707, MS Gen. 206, University of Glasgow Library; Richard Saville, *Bank of Scotland: A History, 1695–1995* (Edinburgh: Edinburgh University Press, 1996), 12–13.

15. Deposition of Charles Howard, Apr. 18, 1691, f. 40, MS Rawlinson A. 366, Bodleian Library, Oxford. The fact that the vessel in which Breholt sailed to the Caribbean in 1699 was called *Carlisle* seems to indicate that Carlisle had provided the financial backing for the venture. It is not clear whether he knew that the ship was lost in Madagascar.

16. Eveline Cruickshanks, Stuart Handley, and D. W. Hayton, eds., *The History of Parliament: The House of Commons, 1690–1715*, 5 vols. (Cambridge: Cambridge University Press, 2002), 3:179, 961; 5:767–68.

17. Bruce G. Carruthers, "*Homo Economicus* and *Homo Politicus:* Non-Economic Rationality in the Early Eighteenth-Century London Stock Market," *Acta Sociologica* 37 (1994): 165–94; Bruce G. Carruthers, *City of Capital: Politics and Markets in the English Financial Revolution* (Princeton: Princeton University Press, 1996), 160–94. The Fairfax treasure project attracted much capital from known Tories.

18. Breholt to Godolphin, Aug. 16, 1707, ff 418–19, Add. MS 28055, B.L.; Cromarty to Mar, Aug. 21, 1707, no. 287, GD 303/1/170, N.A.S. It is perhaps worth noting that in 1704 Godolphin had invested £500 in the Fairfax treasure project, a project which had not been translated into action by the end of 1707.

19. Laycock to Sunderland, 7 Nov. 1707, ff 163–64, Add. MS 61620, B.L.

20. Sir Josiah Burchett to Paul Jodrell, Apr. 18, 1701, ADM 2/400/10, Nat. Arch.

21. Memorandum of the earl of Morton, Charles Egerton, Streynsham Master, Richard Toulson, Paul Jodrell, and William Wallis, [n.d.], CO 323/6/195, Nat. Arch. For the relations between the old and new company as well as their problems with pirates, see John Keay, *The Honourable Company: A History of the English East India Company* (London: HarperCollins, 1991), 182–88.

22. For some charges of corruption, see, for example, James R. Jones, *Marlborough* (Cambridge: Cambridge University Press, 1993), 219–22.

23. Laycock to Thomas Hopkins, 7, Nov. 15, 1707, ff 165–69, Add. MS 61620, B.L. The memorandum had been drafted in 1703 in the context of Breholt's previous Madagascar scheme.

24. Queen Anne's Letter Patent, Jan. 25, 1704, ff 22–23, MS Rawlinson C. 451, Bodleian Library, Oxford; Robert Harley to Godolphin, Jan. 21, 1707, T 1/101/16, Nat. Arch. The organization of the Fairfax treasure project was very similar to Breholt's enterprise.

25. Paul de Castro, "Dictionary of the Principal London Taverns," 1930, MS 3110/2/384–85, Guildhall Library, London.

26. Providing one further small wrinkle in the whole story, Vice-Admiral Benbow had directed the pursuit and capture of William Kidd.

27. Deposition of Elizabeth Woodstock, Barbara Ramsey, and Anne Rupert, June 16, 1709, CO 323/6/224, Nat. Arch. It later emerged that Charles Egerton had offered Penelope Aubin a share in the venture if she organized the petition of the wives. There are various copies of the petition preserved. See, for example, f. 162, Add. MS 61620, B.L.

28. *A Review of the State of the British Nation*, Oct. 18, 1707. In this article Defoe made a passing reference to the financial markets by noting that pirates were no worse than the respectable traders who were to be found at the stock exchange.

29. *The Monthly Miscellany: or, Memoirs for the Curious*, Oct. 1, 1708; Adrian van Broeck, *The Life and Adventures of Capt. John Avery, the Famous English Pirate (rais'd from a Cabbin-Boy, to a King) now in Possession of Madagascar* (London, [1709]), 9–15. The publication was recorded in *The History of the Works of the Learned* 11 (1709), 380.

30. Resolution of the board of trade, June 2, 1709, CO 324/9/200–201, Nat. Arch.; British privy council minutes, Whitehall, June 2, 1709, PC 2/82/165, Nat. Arch.; deposition of Lawrence Waldron and John Clough, June 16, 1709, CO 323/6/223, Nat. Arch.; deposition of Penelope Aubin, June 20, 1709, CO 323/6/225, Nat. Arch. In several details the contents of the depositions are contradictory.

31. *A True Account of the Design, and Advantages of the South-Sea Trade* (London, 1711), 21; minutes of the Court of Directors, Feb. 13, 1712, f. 56, Add. MS 25494, B.L.

32. Breholt to William Trench, Oct. 18, 1711, f. 120, Add. MS 22671, B.L.

Gulliver's Travels, the Contemporary Debate on the Financial Revolution, and the Bourgeois Public Sphere

J. Alan Downie

"Money we know to be the Sinews of War"
—John Cary, *An Essay on the State of England* (1695)[1]

DESPITE THE ARGUMENT OF THOSE WHO PROFESS TO DISCERN A PARticularized political allegory in part 1 of *Gulliver's Travels,*[2] Jonathan Swift's most incisive and extensive commentary on contemporary politics occurs during Gulliver's lengthy question-and-answer sessions with the wise king of Brobdingnag in part 2. After describing the workings of the English legislative and judicial systems, Gulliver moves on to "the prudent Management of our Treasury, [and] the Valour and Atchievements of our Forces by Land and Sea."[3] Given the circumstances obtaining in the twenty-five years from the accession of William and Mary in 1689 to the death of Queen Anne in 1714, Swift was quite right to have Gulliver make the connection, however innocently, between fiscal policy and military success.

Gulliver sets out on the voyage that leads to his sojourn in Brobdingnag on June 20, 1702, just more than three months after the accession of Queen Anne. He is stranded on shore on June 17, 1703; the ship that rescues him "came into the Downs . . . on the 3d Day of *June* 1706, about nine Months after [Gulliver's] Escape" from Brobdingnag.[4] Therefore, although *Gulliver's Travels* was published in 1726, Gulliver's putative conversations with the king of Brobdingnag take place during the early years of the War of the Spanish Succession, the second major conflict in which England had taken part since the

Glorious Revolution of 1688. The first, variously called the Nine Years' War, the War of the League of Augsburg, or King William's War, was England's "first major military involvement in Europe since the ending of the Hundred Years' War nearly 400 years before."[5] Although Gulliver, while in Brobdingnag, would have been unaware of the decisive allied victory at Blenheim in the summer of 1704, let alone those that were to follow later in the war, it is clear that, despite what happens in the imagined world of *Gulliver's Travels,* Swift is making a point about events that had transpired in the 1690s and early 1700s.

While Swift is quite right to link English military success to the financial management of successive ministers, the king of Brobdingnag asks Gulliver some pointed questions about these matters:

> He fell next upon the Management of our Treasury; and said, he thought my Memory had failed me, because I computed our Taxes at about five or six Millions a Year, and when I came to mention the Issues, he found they sometimes amounted to more than double; for, the Notes he had taken were very particular in this Point, because he hoped, as he told me, that the Knowledge of our Conduct might be useful to him, and he could not be deceived in his Calculations. But, if what I told him were true, he was still at a loss how a Kingdom could run out of its Estate like a private Person. He asked me, who were our Creditors? And, where we found Money to pay them? He wondered to hear me talk of such chargeable and extensive Wars; that, certainly we must be a quarrelsome People, or live among very bad Neighbours; and that our Generals must needs be richer than our Kings. He asked what Business we had out of our own Island, unless upon the Score of Trade or Treaty, or to defend our Coasts with our Fleet. Above all, he was amazed to hear me talk of a mercenary standing Army in the midst of Peace, and among a free People. He said if we were governed by our own Consent in the Persons of our Representatives, he could not imagine of whom we were afraid, or of whom we were to fight, and would hear my Opinion, whether a Private Man's House might not be better defended by himself, his Children, and Family, than by half a dozen Rascals picked up at a venture in the Streets, for small Wages, who might get an hundred times more by cutting their Throats.[6]

This passage is of considerable significance to the general thrust of Swift's political satire. Gulliver's ostensibly innocent remarks about competent fiscal management and military success are exploited by Swift to allow him to reiterate a number of the major themes upon which he had harped since first stating them in 1710–11 in his *Examiner* essays.

I

Skilfully encapsulated in the king of Brobdingnag's incredulity at a kingdom's ability to "run out of its Estate like a private Person," Swift's foremost complaint about the "financial revolution" concerned the long-term effects of the fiscal expedients to which successive governments had resorted between 1689 and 1697 in order to finance the war with France. At the time of the Glorious Revolution, England was not geared up to fight a long and expensive land war, and it quickly became apparent that the revenue that could be raised from current taxation was hopelessly inadequate to the task of financing military and naval operations on the scale that was required. Before the Revolution of 1688, government expenditure had been around £2 million per annum; in 1696 and 1697 it reached £8 million per annum. Whereas income and expenditure had more or less balanced in 1688 and 1689, government borrowing in 1697 approached £5 million.[7] This of course was precisely the point raised by the king of Brobdingnag, since the figures supplied by Gulliver had indicated that government expenditure was almost double the revenue raised by taxation.

The government's first expedient to find the large amount of money required had been to introduce a land tax which could, in effect, be represented to members of parliament and their constituents as an old-fashioned subsidy. Depending on the rate set, a land tax could raise between £500,000 and £2 million a year.[8] When a land tax proved inadequate to the task of financing the war, a series of measures were introduced in the early 1690s to allow the treasury to anticipate the revenue of current taxation in order to continue to pay for the English army then fighting in Flanders. While the most famous and enduring of these measures was the foundation of the Bank of England, they were all governed by the same aim: the desire to reduce taxation in the current fiscal year by spreading the burden out over future fiscal years. It is quite clear that had these expedients not been effective the war could not have been successfully prosecuted. As D. W. Jones remarks, "had the Bank of England not been successfully floated in 1694, there would have been no means of finding the funds to keep troops and allies in the field."[9] And it was not only the army that benefited from the £1.2 million loan that resulted from the bank's incorporation. John Ehrman has demonstrated that of the payments made to the treasurer of the navy between August 1 and December 31, 1694, £640,939 8*s.* 9¼*d.*, or 95 percent, was derived directly from the bank loan, so that "without the Bank of England, there is no reason to suppose that the fleet could have stayed in the Mediterranean for another campaign."[10]

What Swift implicitly satirised in *Gulliver's Travels,* therefore, were the very financial expedients that had enabled England to defend the Revolution settlement and the Protestant succession by force of arms. Raising money by land taxes and funds of interest were the means by which successive governments succeeded, by the skin of their teeth, in keeping the army in the field in Flanders and the fleet in the Mediterranean.

What, then, was the basis of Swift's concern? It is succinctly stated in *Gulliver's Travels* in the form of a single sentence reporting a question posed by the king of Brobdingnag: "He asked me, who were our Creditors? And, where we found Money to pay them?"[11] It was not the first time that Swift had argued that the measures taken to finance the war enriched "the Money'd Men" at the expense of the "landed interest," in that "every new Summ that was lent [to the government at interest], took away as much Power from the Landed Men, as it added to theirs."[12] In the fall of 1710 Swift had been recruited by the head of the incoming government, Robert Harley, to edit the ministerial journal of opinion, *The Examiner.* In his very first paper Swift explained how "that *Power,* which, according to the old Maxim, was used to follow *Land,* is now gone over to *Money*; and the Country Gentleman is now in the Condition of a young Heir, out of whose Estate a Scrivener receives half the Rents for Interest, and hath a Mortgage left on the Whole; and is therefore always ready to feed his Vices and Extravagancies while there is any Thing left. So that if the War continue some Years longer, a Landed Man will be little better than a Farmer at a rack Rent, to the Army, and to the publick Funds."[13] Swift maintained that it was necessary to go back as far as the Revolution of 1688 in order to explain how this state of affairs had come about. Articulating a conspiracy thesis, according to which, having succeeded in getting hold of William III's ear, "an under Sett of Men, who had nothing to lose," had turned him against the "true Lovers of their Country and its Constitution, in Church and State," Swift maintained that "in order to fasten wealthy People to the new Government, they proposed those pernicious Expedients of borrowing Money by vast *Premiums*, and at exorbitant Interest." It was this, Swift argued, that "introduced a Number of new dextrous Men into Business and Credit," as a consequence of which "the Wealth of the Nation, that used to be reckoned by the Value of Land, is now computed by the Rise and Fall of Stocks."[14]

While Swift's version of events remains the classic articulation of the alleged "clash of interests" between the "men of estates" and the "moneyed men" whose wealth in stocks and shares had largely been accumulated since the Glorious Revolution, it can scarcely be regarded as a disinterested account. As his identification with the "landed interest" demonstrates, Swift enthusiastically enlisted on the side of those who sought "to prevent the beggary of the nation, to prevent the moneyed and military men becoming lords of us who have the lands."[15] By insinuating that the financial revolution was the consequence of a conscious policy to ensnare the landed man by rendering him subservient to an entirely new "sort of men" who had actually come into being as a result of the financial expedients of the 1690s, Swift pandered to the prejudices of the country gentlemen who were his target readers.

As soon as the relevant legislation had passed through parliament, writers were lamenting the ill-fortune of "the Nobility, Gentry and Free-holders of *England*, who were almost ruin'd with th[e] Funds, and the Bank [of England]."[16] Not only did it seem as if people were making their fortunes by lending money at vast rates of interest, but the associated taxes on real and personal property fell disproportionately on the gentry. In 1691 the anonymous pamphlet *A Proposal for an Equal Land-Tax: Humbly Submitted to Consideration* had put forward the thesis that "some would have the Gentry take the whole Burden" of financing wars that were being waged in defence of the Protestant succession "upon themselves and a few others," while those whose property did not consist in land got off scot-free or, worse, actually made a profit the longer hostilities continued. Thus, *A Proposal for an Equal Land-Tax* not only argued that the common people, both men and women, should contribute to the "great and urgent necessity . . . of raising great Summes of Money" in the form of a poll tax, it also maintained that "a Poll-Tax that runs upon Titles and Dignities, is of all others the most unjust, because it is most unequall." The reasoning behind this argument is that which, time out of mind, has been put forward whenever a poll tax has been proposed in parliament: "It is very unequall and unjust, that a Squire not worth a hundred Pound, should pay as much as one worth five thousand a Yeare."[17]

A Proposal for an Equal Land-Tax offers a very early example of what was to become a major theme of "old Whig" and Tory propaganda. Throughout the rest of William's reign, pamphleteers increasingly played on the fears of the country gentlemen at large, and more especially those "old Whigs" and Tories who made up the majority of backbenchers in the House of Commons.

Attempting to answer the question "What is a country gentleman?", Geoffrey Holmes concluded that "the average Country member of Parliament" was "a politician who was usually, though by no means invariably, a fairly substantial landowner, largely dependent on his rents for his income, and sharing most of the apprehensions and prejudices common to so many representatives of his social class."[18] Foremost among these prejudices was an instinctive distrust of governments and courts, leading to a clear distinction in the mind of country gentlemen between the respective roles of the executive and legislature. Parliament, the great "state-physician," was supposed to scrutinise the policies of the executive, to decide upon methods of raising revenue, to check expenditure, and to audit accounts; it was imperative that the independence of its members was preserved. Corruption would inevitably follow if the Crown succeeded in compromising the independence of MPs by offering them pensions or places at court. In 1693, the famous "Hush-money Paper" alleged that some £16,000 had been spent in three days out of secret service funds "the last sessions when the house was a little out of humour." "Who are in places we may find out, but God knows who have pensions," it observed; "yet every man that made the least observation can remember that some who opened loudly at the beginning of the last sessions, who came up as eager as is possible for reformation, had their mouths soon stopped with Hush-money." "It is time to have annual parliaments instead of triennial," it concluded, "since privy counsellors and lords of the treasury . . . can so perfectly feel the pulse of a parliament during an interval."[19]

John Oldmixon noted that the "Hush-money Paper" was published by "some *Whigs* who out of Disgust join'd with the *Tories*."[20] In the 1690s, a coalition of radical or "old Whigs" and Tories emerged to form an effective "country" opposition to the court.[21] This new country party sought to protect the rights and privileges of country gentlemen by protesting against what was perceived as the flagrant attempt by the court to interfere with the free proceedings of parliament. Place bills were introduced into the Commons as a means of preventing pensioner parliaments, and triennial bills to prevent standing parliaments. The Triennial Act, which required a new parliament to be elected every three years, finally received the royal assent at the end of 1694. Concerns about an encroaching executive were exacerbated by suspicions about the ways and means of raising revenue adopted to prosecute the war. As soon as peace was concluded at Ryswick in 1697, the focus of opposition propagandists changed to highlight apprehensions about the army that had fought the war, as a fierce campaign for its disbandment, sparked off in November by John Trenchard and Walter Moyle's *An Argument Shewing, that a Standing Army is Inconsistent with a Free Government, and Absolutely Destructive to the Constitution of the English Monarchy*, was fought throughout the parliamentary session of 1697–98, during the general election of 1698, and beyond.

In a seminal essay published forty years ago, J. G. A. Pocock observed that: "The standing army was a bogey intended for country gentlemen, part of a hydra-headed monster called Court Influence or Ministerial Corruption, whose other heads were Placemen, Pensioners, National Debt, Excise, and High Taxation."[22] While concern about a standing army predates the Glorious Revolution,[23] from the 1690s onward it was used by propagandists to appeal to the doubts and fears of the country gentlemen who paid the land tax. Robert Molesworth raised the issue obliquely in 1694 in *An Account of the State of Denmark, as it was in the Year 1692*: "A standing army is composed for the most part of Forreigners, who have no value for the Natives, nor any concern for their welfare. The Court seems to have had this in its eye, when it raised and maintained such an Army, but in process of time the Army is become the People; that is to say, the only thing worth the King's Care and Affection, and the People nothing, so that no Designs, tending to a Revolution, are to be feared from them."[24] Although ostensibly to do with the rise of corruption and the decline of another nation's manners, Molesworth's pamphlet was really about the threat to English liberties posed by an encroaching executive rather than an objective account of Denmark. It prepared the way for the "standing army controversy" of 1697–99. After the publication of Trenchard and Moyle's initial *Argument* against a standing army, more than forty other pamphlets were published arguing for and against the retention of the land-force which had fought the Nine Years' War. Trenchard was still fulminating against standing armies in peacetime more than twenty years later in *Cato's Letters*, "begun in November, 1720, with an honest and humane intention, to call for publick justice upon the wicked managers of the late fatal South-Sea scheme."[25] "Oliver Cromwell headed an army which pretended to fight for liberty; and by that army became a bloody tyrant," he observed: "As I once saw a hawk very generously rescue a turtle dove from the persecution of two crows, and then eat him up himself."[26] While on first blush it may appear surprising that a tirade against standing armies should take up successive issues in a newspaper column ostensibly devoted to the financial scandal of the South Sea Bubble, it will, on reflection, not seem strange at all. *Cato's Letters* attacked the institution of the system of public credit that originated in the 1690s. That system had come about because of the need to pay for the army in Flanders. After the end of the war, the court sought to retain the services of the army that had fought the war. In this way, a standing army came to signify the worst aspects of the financial revolution of the 1690s in the minds of "old Whigs" and Tories.

While the standing army controversy was used by "old Whig" propagandists as a means to heighten apprehensions about the erosion of liberty and property, other characteristics of "country" propaganda in the 1690s were more directly linked to the alleged consequences to the landed country gentlemen of the fiscal expedients to which successive governments had been reduced. The main features of this line of attack are perhaps seen at their most effective in Charles Davenant's inspired rhetorical creation of the archetypal modern Whig, Tom Double. Although it was not published until 1701, *The True Picture of a Modern Whig* explained how, when the Whig lords were in government in the 1690s, "it rain'd Gold and Silver, you wallow'd in the People[']s Wealth, and if you could have held it ten years longer, you had bought all those Country Boobies out of their Estates, who were wont to roar at you in St *Stephen*'s Chappel." What was particularly galling to the backbench country gentlemen whom Tom Double sneeringly dismissed as "those Country Boobies"—and was therefore especially effective as propaganda—was his revelation that he was "now worth Fifty thousand Pound, and 14 years ago I had not Shoes to my Feet." In making Double offer to name another fifty modern Whigs who, from "poor beginnings," had got "Fortunes since the Revolution," Davenant did not hesitate to lay the blame for this unfortunate state of affairs at the door of the financial revolution of the 1690s. "I know the bottom of the transaction with *Michael Godfrey*, when the Bank of *England* was set up," Double explained; "I was the Go-between when the New *East-India* Company was erected."[27]

The True Picture of a Modern Whig even anticipated the thrust of Swift's conspiracy thesis, articulated in *The Conduct of the Allies, and of the Late Ministry, in Beginning and Carrying on the Present War* (1711), that, in reality, the war with France had been waged not to defend the Revolution settlement and the Protestant succession so much as to enrich those who made money out of the conflict. Davenant emphasised the alleged importance to Whig moneyed men in 1701 of renewing hostilities with France: "our Party can reap no Advantage but by a long, bloody and expensive War, begun and carry'd on against all Right and Reason."[28] Swift, in retrospect, reached a similar conclusion had peace not been signed at Utrecht in 1713, he insisted, "a very few Years more of War and Funds would have clearly cast the Balance on the Money'd Side."[29] Little wonder, then, that in *Gulliver's Travels* he makes the king of Brobdingnag, in all innocence, reiterate the long-standing grievances of the country gentlemen who paid the land tax: "He wondered to hear me talk of such chargeable and extensive Wars; that, certainly we must be a quarrelsome People, or live among very bad Neighbours; and that our Generals must needs be richer than our Kings."[30]

Although Swift has become the spokesman for the landed interest as far as posterity is concerned, he was by no means the only contemporary to follow Henry St John's lead in complaining about the growth of "a sort of property not known twenty years ago, [which] is now increased to be almost equal to the terra firm of our island."[31] It is clear that Swift exploited the tradition of "country" rhetoric first articulated in the 1690s by, among others, Molesworth, Trenchard, and Davenant. Thus when in a letter dated March 23, 1734 Swift expressed his own anger against "Standing-Armies in Time of Peace; Projects of Excise, and Bribing-Elections . . . not forgetting septennial Parliaments, directly against the old Whig-Principles, which always have been mine,"[32] it is almost as if Pocock's "hydra-headed monster called Court Influence or Ministerial Corruption" has been taken into account. And in another place, Swift actually took the trouble to explain what was behind his "mortal antipathy against Standing Armies in times of Peace:" "Because I always took Standing

Armies to be only servants hired by the master of the family, for keeping his own children in slavery: And because, I conceived that a Prince who could not think himself secure without Mercenary Troops, must needs have a separate interest from that of his subjects."[33] It is for this reason, one assumes, that Swift made the king of Brobdingnag, a paternalistic prince who "is almost adored by his Subjects," speak out against "a mercenary standing Army in the midst of Peace, and among a free People."[34] By invoking the bugbear of a standing army, Swift was once more pandering to the prejudices of the landed country gentlemen.

II

Given that Swift's writings on the financial revolution were patently following a well-established rhetorical tradition, we should be cautious about simply accepting his thesis that the fiscal experiments of the 1690s, particularly "those pernicious Expedients of borrowing Money by vast *Premiums,* and at exorbitant Interest," were introduced merely "in order to fasten wealthy People to the New government."[35] It fails to take into account the seriousness of the financial situation faced by William and his ministers. In the summer of 1693, the first lord of the treasury, Sidney, Lord Godolphin, wrote to the king to explain that: "We have borrowed money in the city upon the credit for the review of the poll, so as to be able, I hope to carry on the subsistence for some time longer, but this being the last of our funds, when that is once at an end, the revenue being all anticipated, I cannot see any prospect how we shall go on afterwards, no more than a parliament is likely to sit and give any money or credit timely enough to prevent the service from standing still."[36] Unlike Swift, if we wish to trace the financial revolution of the 1690s to its origins, we should begin by accepting the context within which the scheme for the incorporation of the Bank of England was actually proposed to the House of Commons. Desperate to find the resources required for the continued prosecution of the war, the government, in the parliamentary session of 1693–94, resorted to the sale of annuities and the flotation of lotteries, including the so-called "million lottery." When it became clear that even if these expedients were successful, there would still be a shortfall of around £1 million, a final attempt was made to raise £1.2 million by a new kind of war loan.[37] Provided that half of the initial loan of £1.2 million was lent to the government by

August 1, 1694, the subscribers were to be incorporated from that date until 1 August 1705 as "the Governor and the Company of the Bank of England."[38]

It is important to grasp that ministers were not at all sanguine about the possibility of raising £1.2 million by the Bank of England. The war was proving to be disastrous for English overseas trade, and the treasury was simply running out of ideas. Shipping was affected not only by naval manning requirements, but by controls on tonnage, by unseasonal sailings, and finally by inadequate protection while at sea.[39] As a consequence, there had been increased investment in the early 1690s in domestic trade and industry, as well as a sharp rise in the number of joint-stock companies. There was even a "patent boom," which was also "a product of financial markets distorted by war on an unprecedented scale."[40] Despite ministers' pessimism about the bank raising £1.2 million, therefore, the circumstances were such that the sum was raised without any difficulty. First, as Swift observed in *The History of the Four Last Years of the Queen*, among the "many and plausible . . . Motives which prevailed on People to fall in with this Project" was "the Bait of large Interest [which] would draw in a great Number of those whose Money by the Dangers and Difficulties of Trade lay dead upon their hands."[41] As merchants were increasingly reluctant to risk investment in overseas trade, they welcomed the alternative opportunity presented by the bank to put their money to work at a premium. Another attractive feature of the loan was that almost all of it was in paper money, rather than specie. This meant that the rate of return was very high indeed. As the anonymous author of *Remarks upon the Bank of England, With Regard More Especially to Our Trade and Government* (1706) observed: "the 8 *per Cent.* Alone, (when the Legal Interest was but *6*, and the clear Produce of Land seldom *4*) was of itself a sufficient Encouragement to this Undertaking; especially considering that this was Exempt from Taxes, to which other Money, and Stock, and Land were liable."[42]

If it would be wrong to ignore the context within which the scheme to incorporate the Bank of England was put forward, it would be equally wrong to insinuate that the establishment of the bank solved the problem of financing the war. Despite its best efforts, the treasury was unable to accomplish any further long-term financing in 1695 and 1696, and contemporary economic analysts such as Gregory King were pessimistic about the prospects of finding money to pay the bills. King was as politically conservative as Swift. Geoffrey Holmes has demonstrated that the context of King's much-cited "Scheme of the Income and Expense of the Several Famillies of England" is actually a "fundamentally pessimistic, Tory-'Country' view of England's incapacity to bear for long the burdens of large-scale warfare," rather than an objective attempt to offer an analysis of the social structure of England at the time of the Revolution.[43] It is therefore scarcely surprising that, in the chapter of his *Natural and Political Observations* entitled "The State of the Nation Anno 1695," King concluded: "after the year 1695, the taxes actually raised will fall short every year, more and more, to that degree, that the war cannot well be sustained beyond the year 1698 upon the foot it now stands."[44] What is striking is that Swift should, in effect, silently suppress the widespread anxieties expressed in the 1690s about the government's ability to finance the war.

The circulation of bank bills and notes had the effect of increasing the amount of money in circulation, leading to inflation, a mini boom, and a slump which, unfortunately, coincided with the decision to force through a recoinage of "clipped" silver money in 1696. May 1696 was perhaps the worst month for the ministers of the entire war. The last date for clipped money to be accepted at face value for payments for tax was May 4; two days later there was a run on the Bank of England.[45] The resulting financial turmoil made it extremely difficult for the supporters of the National Land Bank (which had been pushed through parliament just a month earlier by the leaders of the "country" party, Paul Foley and Robert Harley), to raise the £2.5 million war loan they had promised to William III. Supporters of the National Land Bank began demanding to be allowed to contribute large parts of the loan in clipped silver, which would have meant considerable losses for the government. On May 22, Godolphin stressed to the king the "necessity of Concluding" with the "very hard" terms of the land bank supporters "or we must take a noble resolution of having no money at all to remitt, or to answer bills, & Consequently lett the Army starve."[46] When the land bank's promised war loan eventually failed, the treasury defaulted on its payments. Only when the Bank of England agreed to remit £200,000 to Flanders in August 1696 was total catastrophe averted.

When the incorporation of the bank was about to be reviewed in 1706, much was made of the unprecedented privileges it had been accorded. For example, the anonymous *Remarks upon the Bank of En-*

gland, With Regard More Especially to Our Trade and Government. Occasioned by the Present Discourse Concerning the Intended Prolongation of the Bank observed that: "When our Money'd Men first sollicited an Establishment of the *Bank* by *Act* of *Parliament*, the Argument made use of for this Design was not only a *present Loan*, but a great show of future Service; which we may suppose from the mighty Powers and Privileges the Parliament gave them, beyond those of any Corporation, or Society, I believe, that ever was Erected in England."[47] This pamphlet's strident comments on the growth of the moneyed interest bears a striking resemblance, *avant la letter*, to the stance adopted from 1710 onwards by Swift himself. What rhetorical strategies of this kind fail to address, however, are the harsh realities faced by treasury ministers as they battled to continue to pay the army in Flanders and the fleet in the Mediterranean, especially in the mid-1690s. Henry Roseveare notes that the government remained the principal client of the Bank of England in its early years, and that, far from transforming financial institutions overnight, "it sought to justify its existence by a series of major services to the state," including the "remittance of funds to the British forces fighting in Flanders."[48] Without those services, it would have been impossible for the nation to have limped on to the conclusion of peace at Ryswick in 1697.

Similar financial difficulties were faced by Godolphin after the renewal of hostilities with France in 1702. Drawing on the work of J. G. Sperling, P. G. M. Dickson concludes that "Godolphin managed the national finances with great care and skill."[49] In *Gulliver's Travels*, however, Swift implicitly criticizes the financial management of Godolphin, and this criticism is made explicit in *The History of the Four Last Years of the Queen*. According to Swift, "the late Ministry raised all their Money to 1710 only by continuing Funds which were already granted to their hands." This, he argued, "deceived the People in general."[50] In suggesting that "the People in general" were misled about Godolphin's financial acumen, Swift was dealing in disinformation. Despite his absurd pretensions in the Preface to *The History of the Four Last Years of the Queen* "to write with the utmost impartiality," Swift clearly wrote with the express intention of discrediting the "late Ministry" of Godolphin, John Churchill, duke of Marlborough, and the Whigs: "I likewise shall State the Debts of the Nation; shew by what Mismanagement, and to serve what Purposes they were at first Contracted; by what Negligence or Corruption they have so prodigiously grown; and what Methods have since been taken to provide, not only for their Payment, but to prevent the like Mischief for the time to come."[51] It was for this reason that little enthusiasm was expressed by the ministers while he was writing *The History of the Four Last Years of the Queen* in the first months of 1713; it was recognisably "a [political] pamphlet" rather than a history.[52]

Criticism of Godolphin's handling of the economy was only one aspect of Swift's attack on the "late Ministry." The way in which the Bank of England had been set up stimulated stock-market activity. If subscribers to the £1.2 million loan wanted to realize their capital, they did so by selling bank stock. While a rudimentary stock exchange dealing in shares already existed, its rapid expansion after 1694 did little to allay the anxieties of the men of estates. As Holmes observes: "The rise and fall of share prices, and, above all, of Bank and East India Company stock, was to be recognised thereafter as 'the pulse of the City & whereby the state of her health is discern'd.'"[53] The emergence of a market dealing in stocks and shares offered writers such as Swift an opportunity not only to identify and attack those who benefited from "a sort of property unknown twenty years ago," but also to insinuate that the establishment of the bank had been a deliberate attempt on the part of the "Money'd Men" to impoverish the landed country gentlemen. By drawing a distinction between those who added to the nation's wealth through investing in trade and those who made money out of investing in the funds and buying and selling stocks and shares—a distinction which was all the more rhetorically effective for being a distortion of the truth—contemporary polemicists such as Swift were able to ridicule anyone so credulous "as to imagine the many Millions in Stocks and Annuities, are so much real Wealth in the Nation; whereas every Farthing of it is entirely lost to us, scattered in *Holland*, *Germany*, and *Spain*; and the Landed-Men, who now pay the Interest, must at last pay the Principal."[54]

III

When using political writings as documentary evidence, due weight should be given to an assessment of their polemical strategy—the complex of ploys and pitches adopted by the pamphleteer as he seeks to manipulate his readers' political perceptions.[55] Competent propagandists such as Swift clearly have such "target readers" in mind, and in order to achieve their polemical objective—in other words, the shift in consciousness that they aim to bring about—they make effective use of what they perceive to be their target readers' political opinions. As competent polemical writing is slanted to a preconceived audience, its value as documentary evidence may be compromised unless due compensation is made by historians for the rhetorical devices of the propagandist. Because it is immensely difficult to disentangle objective "truth" from rhetorical fiction, we cannot afford simply to assume that contemporary writers were attempting to persuade their readers through reasoned argument alone. As any analysis of polemical writing at the turn of the eighteenth century quickly reveals, arguments that purport to consist mainly, if not solely, of "facts" usually turn out to be nothing of the kind.

The consequences of a failure to appreciate that polemical writing often panders to the prejudices, rather than appealing to the reason, of its target readers, can be far-reaching. For instance, Jürgen Habermas's hugely influential thesis about the rise of public opinion as a force in the state emphasises the increasing importance of "rational-critical debate" as "the private people, come together to form a public, readied themselves to compel public authority to legitimate itself before public opinion."[56] Habermas's account of what he calls "The Model Case of British Development" identifies three "events occurring in 1694 and 1695" as marking the juncture at which "political conflict" was carried "into the public sphere." It was the second of these, "the end of the institution of censorship"—that is, the expiry of the Printing or Licensing Act in 1695—which, according to Habermas, "made the influx of rational-critical arguments into the press possible and allowed the latter to evolve into an instrument with whose aid political decisions could be brought before the new forum of the public."[57]

What, then, would happen were Habermas's argument to be applied to the political writings of Swift? As we have seen, distortion, misrepresentation, and downright obfuscation are vital elements in Swift's polemic. Paradoxically, the sort of "rational-critical" discourse characteristic of the public sphere as conceived by Habermas does not necessarily seek to persuade through reason. On the contrary, the most forceful polemics—Andrew Marvell's *An Account of the Growth of Popery*, for example, or Swift's *The Conduct of the Allies*, or the letters of Junius, or Edmund Burke's *Reflections on the Revolution in*

France—appeal not to their readers' reason, but to their emotions. An awareness of polemical strategy, therefore, can offer a valuable corrective to those who, following Habermas, have claimed to recognize the emergence of a bourgeois public sphere in Britain at the turn of the eighteenth century.

Increased awareness of issues relating to the rhetorical analysis of the pamphlet literature of the period can also add to our understanding of the contemporary debate on the financial revolution. In his discussion of the pamphlet literature, Dickson quotes from *The History of the Four Last Years of the Queen.* "Swift admitted that he was 'not very well versed either in the Style or Matter' of financial affairs," Dickson remarks, "but the fears upon which he played were clearly real enough."[58] While it is likely that the fears *were* real enough, I am interested not only in the rhetorical reasons that Swift elected to play upon such fears, but the tactics he used when he did so. In articulating a fictitious conspiracy thesis, which involved not only Marlborough, Godolphin, and the Whigs, but also England's allies in the War of the Spanish Succession, particularly the Dutch, Swift, in *The Conduct of the Allies* and other writings, did not merely play upon the fears of his target readers, he gave them shape. If the pamphlet literature is to be used by economic historians as evidence of contemporary attitudes, then they need not only to present the pamphleteers' arguments, but to consider what their rhetorical purpose might have been—why, in sum, they elected to use each, particular argument.

In the case of Swift, it is apparent that, by insinuating that the political objectives of the "new dextrous Men" who rose to positions of power and influence in the 1690s amounted to nothing less than a calculated assault on the social position of the country gentlemen who owned landed estates, he sought to represent the threat as nothing short of an attempt to alter the balance of economic power within the state. From this perspective, it was no accident that the principal method of raising revenue was a tax on land. Swift admired "the Style of the Men at Ease, *who lay the heavy Burthens upon others, which they will not touch with one of their Fingers.*" This, in turn, provided him with a ready answer to his own rhetorical question: "what have we been Fighting for all this while?" "We have been Fighting for the Ruin of the Publick Interest, and the Advancement of a Private. We have been fighting to raise the Wealth and Grandeur of a particular Family; to enrich Usurers and Stock-Jobbers; and to cultivate the pernicious Designs of a Faction, by destroying the Landed-Interest."[59] Here is Swift in a nutshell, full of objections to the growing prominence of financial markets and implicitly to high taxes, a burgeoning bureaucracy, the standing army, and continental entanglements. Yet as John Brewer has shown, these were the very institutions by which between 1688 and 1714 successive governments, albeit with limited success, had converted short-term into long-term borrowing and by which Britain had ultimately transformed itself into a powerful fiscal-military state.[60] We must therefore sedulously resist the temptation to accept Swift's rhetoric at face value.

Notes

1. John Cary, *An Essay on the State of England, in Relation to its Trade, its Poor, and its Taxes, for carrying on the Present War Against France* (Bristol, 1695), 170.

2. The classic articulation of this thesis is to be found in Arthur E. Case, *Four Essays on Gulliver's Travels* (Princeton: Princeton University Press, 1945), 69–96. For a more recent restatement, see Hermann J. Real and Heinz J. Vienken, "The Structure of *Gulliver's Travels*," in *Proceedings of the First Münster Symposium on Jonathan Swift*, eds. Hermann J. Real and Heinz J. Vienken (Munich: Wilhelm Fink, 1985), 203.

3. [Jonathan Swift], *Gulliver's Travels* (London, 1726), in *The Prose Writings of Jonathan Swift*, volume 11, *Gulliver's Travels*, ed. Herbert Davis (Oxford: Blackwell, 1959), 127–32.

4. Ibid., 148.

5. D. W. Jones, *War and Economy in the Age of William III and Marlborough* (Oxford: Blackwell, 1988), 15.

6. Swift, *Gulliver's Travels*, 130–31.

7. My figures are taken from the tables in Jones, *War and Economy*, 70–71.

8. J. V. Beckett, "Land Tax or Excise: the levying of taxation in seventeenth- and eighteenth-century England," *English Historical Review* 100, no. 395 (Apr. 1985): 295.

9. D. W. Jones, "London merchants and the crisis of the 1690s," in *Crisis and Order in English Towns 1500–1700*, ed. Paul Slack (London: Routledge & Kegan Paul, 1972), 314.

10. John Ehrman, *The Navy in the War of William III, 1689–1697: Its State and Direction* (Cambridge: Cambridge University Press, 1953), 540–43.

11. [Swift], *Gulliver's Travels*, 131.

12. [Jonathan Swift], *The History of the Four Last Years of the Queen* (Dublin, 1758), in *The Prose Writings of Jonathan Swift*, vol. 7, *The History of the Four Last Years of the Queen*, ed. Herbert Davis (Oxford: Blackwell, 1973), 70.

13. [Jonathan Swift], *The Examiner* 13 (London, Nov. 2, 1710), in *The Prose Writings of Jonathan Swift*, vol. 3, *The Examiner and Other Pieces Written in 1710–11*, ed. Herbert Davis (Oxford: Blackwell, 1941), 5–6.

14. Ibid., 5–6.

15. Sir John Pakington's phrase, quoted in Geoffrey Holmes, *British Politics in the Age of Anne* (rev. ed., London: Hambledon Press, 1987), 149.

16. J[ohn] B[riscoe], *A Discourse on the Late Funds of the Million-Act, Lottery-Act, and Bank of England. Shewing, That they are Injurious to the Nobility and Gentry, and Ruinous to the Trade of the Nation* (London, 1694), 52.

17. *A Proposal for an Equal Land-Tax: Humbly Submitted to Consideration* (London, 1691), 15–16.

18. Holmes, *British Politics in the Age of Anne,* 129.

19. [Charlwood Lawton], *A Short State of our Condition, with Relation to the present Parliament* (1693), in *Cobbett's Parliamentary History of England,* 36 vols. (London, 1806–20), 5: appendix, civ.

20. John Oldmixon, *The History of England during the Reigns of King William and Queen Mary, Queen Anne, King George I* (London, 1735), 89.

21. For the emergence of the "country" opposition in the 1690s, see in particular J. A. Downie, "The Commission of Public Accounts and the formation of the Country Party," *English Historical Review* 91, no. 358 (Jan. 1976): 33–51; D. W. Hayton, "The 'Country' Interest and the party system, 1689–*c.* 1720," in *Party and Management in Parliament, 1660–1784,* ed. Clyve Jones (Leicester: Leicester University Press, 1984).

22. J. G. A. Pocock, "Machiavelli, Harrington, and English Political Ideologies in the Eighteenth Century," *William and Mary Quarterly* 22, no. 4 (Oct. 1965): 571.

23. On this point, see the standard account, Lois G. Schwoerer, *No Standing Armies! The Anti-Army Ideology in the Seventeenth Century* (Baltimore: Johns Hopkins University Press, 1975).

24. [Robert Molesworth], *An Account of the State of Denmark, as it was in the Year 1692* (London, 1694), 268–69.

25. These words are quoted from the preface to the collected edition of *Cato's Letters.* See John Trenchard and Thomas Gordon, *Cato's Letters,* ed. Robert Hamowy, 2 vols. (Indianapolis: Liberty Fund, 1995), 1:11.

26. *Cato's Letters,* 2:678.

27. [Charles Davenant], *The True Picture of a Modern Whig* (London, 1701), 5–6, 14, 15. Godfrey was the first governor of the Bank of England. The first East India Company was formed in 1599 to trade with the spice islands. In 1698, the English Company trading to the East Indies was authorized by act of parliament. This New East India Company, backed by Whig interests, was launched in order to compete with the Old East India Company. Davenant is implying that Tom Double is implicated in the shady dealings of the moneyed men. See Holmes, *British Politics in the Age of Anne,* 153–56.

28. [Davenant], *True Picture of a Modern Whig,* 11.

29. [Swift], *The History of the Four Last Years of the Queen,* 70.

30. [Swift], *Gulliver's Travels,* 131.

31. H. T. Dickinson, ed., "The Letters of Henry St John to the Earl of Orrery, 1709–1711," *Camden Miscellany* 26 (Camden Soc., 4th series, 14, 1975): 146.

32. Jonathan Swift to Francis Gant, Mar. 23, 1734, in David Woolley, ed., *The Correspondence of Jonathan Swift, D.D.,* vol. 3, *Letters 1714–1726* (Frankfurt: Peter Lang, 2001), 731.

33. Jonathan Swift to Alexander Pope, Jan. 10, 1721, in David Woolley, ed., *The Correspondence of Jonathan Swift, D.D.*, vol. 2, *Letters, 1726–1734* (Frankfurt: Peter Lang, 2001), 360.

34. [Swift], *Gulliver's Travels*, 130–31.

35. [Swift], *Examiner*, 6.

36. *Cal. S.P. Dom. 1693*, 24.

37. See the essay by Richard Kleer in the present collection.

38. P. G. M. Dickson, *The Financial Revolution in England. A Study in the Development of Public Credit, 1688–1756* (London: Macmillan, 1967), 54.

39. Jones, *War and Economy*, 15–16, 156–61.

40. Christine MacLeod, "The 1690s Patent Boom: Invention or Stock-Jobbing?" *Economic History Review* 2nd series, 39, no. 4 (Nov. 1986): 549–71 (557–58). See also Julian Hoppitt, "Attitudes to Credit in Britain, 1680–1790," *Historical Journal* 33, no. 2 (1990): 305–22.

41. [Swift], *The History of the Four Last Years of the Queen*, 68.

42. *Remarks upon the Bank of England, With Regard More Especially to Our Trade and Government. Occasion'd by the Present Discourse Concerning the Intended Prolongation of the Bank* (London, 1706), 13.

43. Geoffrey Holmes, "Gregory King and the Social Structure of Pre-Industrial England," *Transactions of the Royal Historical Society*, 5th series, 27 (1977): 51.

44. Ibid., 51.

45. On the crisis of the years 1696–97, see, in particular, Jones, *War and Economy*, 20–25.

46. Portland MS PwA 476, Nottingham University Library.

47. *Remarks upon the Bank of England*, sig. A2.

48. Henry Roseveare, *The Financial Revolution, 1660–1760* (London: Longman, 1991), 37.

49. Dickson, *Financial Revolution*, 59.

50. [Swift], *The History of the Four Last Years of the Queen*, 71.

51. Ibid., xxxiv, 1.

52. On this point, see Erasmus Lewis to Jonathan Swift, Aug. 4, 1737, in Harold Williams [and David Woolley], ed., *The Correspondence of Jonathan Swift*, 5 vols. (Oxford: Oxford University Press, 1965; repr. corr. 1972), 5:66.

53. Holmes, *British Politics in the Age of Anne*, 154.

54. [Jonathan Swift], *The Conduct of the Allies, and of the Late Ministry, in Beginning and Carrying on the Present War* (London, 1711), in *The Prose Works of Jonathan Swift*, vol. 6, *Political Tracts, 1711–13*, ed. Herbert Davis (Oxford: Blackwell, 1951), 59.

55. On this point, see J. A. Downie, "Public opinion and the political pamphlet," in *The Cambridge History of English Literature, 1660–1780*, ed. John Richetti (Cambridge: Cambridge University Press, 2005), 549–71.

56. Jürgen Habermas, *The Structural Transformation of the Public Sphere: An Enquiry into a Category of Bourgeois Society*, trans. Thomas Burger (Cambridge: Polity Press, 1989), 57, 85.

57. Ibid., 57–58. The other "events" listed by Habermas are the founding of the Bank of England and the introduction of cabinet government. I draw attention to issues raised by Habermas's failure properly to contextualize the "events" he men-

tions in "Public and Private: The Myth of the Bourgeois Public Sphere," in *A Concise Companion to the Restoration and Eighteenth Century*, ed. Cynthia Wall (Oxford: Blackwell, 2005), 58–79. As Habermas's unreconstructed Marxist account of English history requires a "bourgeois revolution" to have taken place in the seventeenth century, he predates the advent of industrial capitalism by over a century. Although he refers to the writings of Swift, Bolingbroke, Pope, Gay, and Arbuthnot, as well as Addison and Steele, Habermas cites the establishment of the bank as evidence of "a new conflict of interests between the restrictive interests of commercial and financial capital on one side and the expansive interests of manufacturing and industrial capital on the other," rather than between the new, "moneyed" men who invested in the funds and made profits out of the buying and selling of stocks and shares, and the country gentlemen whose property consisted largely of landed estates.

58. Habermas, *Structural Transformation of the Public Sphere*, 27.

59. [Swift], *Conduct of the Allies*, 59.

60. John Brewer, *The Sinews of Power: War, Money and the English State, 1688–1783* (London: Unwin Hyman, 1989).

Misunderstanding What Swift Misunderstood, or, the Economy of a Province

Chris Fauske

APPROACHES WHICH FOCUS ON JONATHAN SWIFT TO EXPLAIN MORE than Swift ignore an almost overwhelming mass of evidence that the dean of St. Patrick's, Dublin often did not understand the complexity of what was going on beyond the immediate neighborhood either of his liberties or of his own mind. This willful ignorance is what made Swift the writer he was: he produced brilliant diatribes laced with witty invective and bolstered by sharp polemical accusations. And he was free to do so because he almost always constructed a straw man upon whom to unleash his wrath.[1]

Consider, since it represents a flourishing of Swift the Irish writer, and is the only one of his tracts that genuinely worried the political powers-that-were, the 1720 *A Proposal for the Universal Use of Irish Manufacture.*[2] *A Proposal* offers no original economic analysis but instead relies upon a routine mercantilist, almost autarkist, conventional wisdom that even in its day was no longer accepted by the vast majority of decision makers in Dublin, Westminster, or Whitehall.

What does distinguish *A Proposal* from both the vast majority of other Irish tracts upon the poverty of the kingdom, and from all Swift's writings up to that point, is that it directly addresses a key Irish constitutional question of the early Hanoverian period. In short, and not unlike a lot of Swift's pamphlets, *A Proposal* claims to be about one thing and is, in fact, about something else. In that distinction can be found the reasons for Swift's choice almost always to simplify his argument to the point of uselessness for the modern reader hoping to use Swift's work to elucidate a broader cultural or contextual point.

Nonetheless, reading Swift on Ireland's economic condition in the first decades of the eighteenth century can illuminate not the economic debate itself, but the points at which the economic debate entered the public consciousness and could be coopted by a skilled enough polemicist for a different campaign entirely.

In *A Proposal*, Swift struggles as he does nowhere else with the political options available to "every Nation (except this wch is no Nation)," as he described Ireland in a letter to Charles Ford.[3] Swift acknowledges in that letter that "I believe my self not guilty of too much veneration for the Irish H- of Lds, but . . . the Question is whether People ought to be Slaves or no."[4] Swift is here alluding to a bill passed into law in April 1720 in the British parliament that would become known as the Declaratory Act.[5] The Declaratory Act was the final stage in a protracted argument between the Irish House of Lords and the British House of Lords as to which house was the final court of appeal. The resulting British act of 1720 declared Ireland to be "subordinate unto and dependent upon the imperial crown of Great Britain," as a consequence of which "the king's majesty [and] . . . parliament assembled, had, hath, and of right ought to have full power to make laws and statutes of sufficient force and validity to bind the kingdom and people of Ireland."[6] Discussing the Declaratory Act, Swift goes on in the letter to Ford to compare the Irish parliament's frequent inability to establish its identity in relation to the British parliament to the "Quarrell against Convocations: they meet but seldom, have no Power, and for want of those Advantages, cannot make any Figure when they are suffered to assemble. You fetter a Man for seven years, then let him loose to show his Skill in dancing, and because he does it awkwardly, you say he ought to be fettered for Life."[7] At the tail end of debate over the Declaratory Act, Swift published *A Proposal* itself, his first significant publication since the collapse of the Tory administration in the last days of Queen Anne's reign in 1714. Much had changed in both Irish and British politics since then.[8] Swift's proposal that, in accordance with basic mercantilist precepts, Irish men and women wear Irish cloth could hardly at face value be taken as controversial, let alone as seditious. The pamphlet has an agenda quite different to that implied by the title, but Swift was a pamphleteer of great skill, and, aware of the political nuances of potentially little interest to the mass of the disenfranchised Irish, Swift delivers much of his critique of British policy toward Ireland in the guise of an economic tract.

Swift's *A Proposal* might look like an economic tract and read like an economic treatise, but it is neither. Despite its apparent interest in matters economic, *A Proposal* fails to mention the various economic projects being discussed in London and in Dublin with specific application to Ireland except for a final, passing reference to "a *Thing* they call a *Bank*," a reference which concludes with an acknowledgment of the currency troubles confronting Ireland: "the Merchants continue to carry off our Gold, and our Goldsmiths to melt down our heavy Silver."[9]

The fiscal trouble confronting Ireland throughout the years leading up to 1720 had less to do with the various factions' public and private interests than with a stark political reality, a reality coincidentally confirmed in the Declaratory Act: Ireland was, essentially, a province of Britain. It was not a colony, for it had its own monarch, albeit a comonarch shared with Britain, and it had its own parliament and privy council. Unlike Scotland, it had not been subsumed into the British political system; unlike the colonies in North America, its political and civil structures were not dependent upon royal or parliamentary patents or charters. None of which would have mattered particularly if there had been a legal definition of a province's rights, entitlements, and obligations. There was not then in British nor in Irish law such a definition, and nor, by the way, is there today. Swift was right to describe Ireland as a "Nation . . . w[ch] is no Nation"; he failed to point out that it had no clearly defined status at all.

Ireland had one other attribute that rendered its position within the emerging British political structure awkward for everyone concerned the monarch retained significant holdings of property and lease rights, as well as of certain tax revenues, and these offered the Crown a source of income unregulated by parliament. Especially after 1688, it was the policy of the parliament in Westminster to seek to keep the Crown dependent upon its authority to grant or deny revenue to the monarch. Whether those revenues were sufficient or not, parliamentary managers in Westminster saw in the Irish Crown revenues a potential means for the Crown to lessen its dependency on legislative supply bills, and so, as one modern commentator has put it, there developed at least the possibility of perceiving that "it followed that Ireland must be kept poor lest the hereditary revenues of the crown in Ireland should grow."[10]

While Swift exploited the polemical opportunities presented by Ireland's undefined constitutional status, it was the senior Irish-born cleric of the Church of Ireland who more fully appreciated Ireland's position. William King, archbishop of Dublin, had long had a fine sense of the delicacy of being a "province" in a larger system. In a letter of January 29, 1697, while bishop of Derry, to Gilbert Burnet, bishop of Salisbury, King had observed that: "Ireland is a province and, generally speaking, it has been the fate of provinces to be under governors who had no interest or concern for their welfare . . . hence the wise man tells us, *Eccl* 5,8: 'If thou seest oppression of the poor and violent perverting of judgement and Justice *in a province* marvell not at the matter,' for this is generally the case of all provinces and particularly of Ireland."[11]

In 1720, King returned to work on a document he had first circulated privately in 1716. *Some Observations on the Taxes Pay'd by Ireland to Support the Government* sought to draw a connection between the English perception of Ireland's condition and the resulting legislative oppression of the province. *Some Observations* circulated among King's supporters and friends and represented a crucial step in identifying Ireland as an integral part of an emerging British state, albeit a part with its own interests and its own identity. In short, argued King, "The people of Ireland do find, that the greatest inconveniences which happen to the Kingdom, arise for the most part from the Misrepresentations of the State & Condition of it."[12] Swift would exploit these "misrepresentations" in *A Proposal* and other Irish tracts, addressing not the situation as it was but writing instead as a polemicist exploiting what the public believed the situation to be.

King returned to *Some Observations* at a time of potentially momentous change in Ireland. The Declaratory Act had seemed to remove the last vestige of political independence from Ireland, but various political factions understood that in the economic sphere Ireland retained some potential room for maneuver within an emerging eighteenth-century sense of patriotism focused not on national identity but on "economic improvement and the relations between [the] public and authority."[13] At the same time, debate was just beginning on a specific proposal for a Bank of Ireland, a plan that would soon give rise to other schemes and which would, in conjunction with another proposal then beginning to appear in the sights of parliamentarians—to mint copper coinage in England for use in Ireland—turn out to offer the Irish parliament a surprising degree of autonomy, even if, in the end, that autonomy could be expressed only by rejection, rather than by adoption of possible solutions.

In the midst of debate around the Declaratory Act, but unrelated to it, a proposal for the creation of a Bank of Ireland was sponsored by an impressive list of Irish landholders and merchants, including James Hamilton, the earl of Abercorn (Viscount Strabane in the Irish peerage), Gustavus Hamilton, Viscount Boyne, and Sir Ralph Gore.[14] Among those listed in the original petition as supporting the proposal was St John Brodrick.

While still in England in 1720, the lord lieutenant of Ireland, Charles Fitzroy, duke of Grafton, had inherited the efforts made to support the bank proposal by the out-going lord lieutenant, Charles Paulet, duke of Bolton. Meanwhile, the support that Abercorn and his backers had received inspired the creation of a second bank scheme, this one offering to pay off £50,000 of the Irish national debt within five years.[15] Grafton referred the competing schemes to the Irish lords justices, William Conolly and Alan Brodrick, Viscount Midleton.

In January 1721, Midleton and Conolly urged approval of the Abercorn proposal. Their support was based in part on the "general want of specie and decay of trade in Ireland," but the economic rationale was only part of the equation.[16] The lords justices' support for Abercorn's proposal was specifically couched in terms that defended Irish parliamentary privilege. In particular, they noted that when it came to paying off the national debt, "it will not be for his Majesty's Service, or the Advantage of the Kingdom, that Recourse be had in any other Manner than the usual and known Methods in Parliament" for raising the revenue for that purpose.[17]

This analysis was intended to remind British parliamentary managers that the Irish parliament was the means by which Irish bills of supply were drafted and approved, and these bills of supply not only funded operations of the administration in Dublin and the costs of the British military garrison, but also the various sinecures necessary to maintain the British presence in Ireland. British parliamentarians were reluctant to remove tax raising powers from the Irish parliament as that would require either incorporating Ireland into the Union, something they did not support, or declaring it a colony funded under an entirely different method, one which, given the economic constraints of the period, no one was sure could be afforded. To deny the Irish parliament's role in public finances was to question the relationships of monarch, ministry, and legislature, a point Midleton and Conolly agreed upon and implicitly reminded the British parliament of in their support of Abercorn's bank proposal. (Viscount Midleton, it is worth noting here, was the father of St John Brodrick, and that fact no doubt influenced his support of Abercorn's proposal, but the language in which he couched his support of the proposal is particularly important in light of later developments.)

Midleton's and Conolly's stated support for Abercorn's proposal in terms that defended the Irish parliament's revenue raising privilege allowed for the temporary alliance of two increasingly determined opponents within the Irish Whig party. The Tories in Ireland had rapidly collapsed in the aftermath of Queen Anne's death, but that did not mean the Whig faction that inherited power in the country was monolithic, and a fierce power struggle had been going on for some time between Brodrick and Conolly. In 1717, Brodrick became lord chancellor and was created Viscount Midleton. He had henceforward to rely on his brother, Thomas, and his son, St John, to keep an eye on things in the House of Commons, where Conolly was speaker.[18] Ironically, it was in both Midleton's and Conolly's interest to ensure the Irish parliament retained as much of its prerogative as it could, or else neither man would have had much influence with which to bargain with the executive in Dublin Castle.

In late May 1721, the British treasury reported that an act of the Irish parliament would be necessary to create a Bank of Ireland, rather than the simpler process of granting a royal charter. The Irish act would be needed to prevent the bank from borrowing beyond its capital and to hold the investors liable in the event of the bank's failure. The treasury here, in fact, was acting just as it had done earlier during various bank debates in England, cautiously and with a determination to ensure the bank did not destabilize the economy by issuing promissory notes unsupported by realizable reserves. The bank charter was issued on July 29, 1721, subject to the proviso that an act of parliament define its limits and role within one year.

In his opening speech to the Irish parliament in September 1721, Grafton referred the matter of the bank charter to the consideration of both houses. The facts on the ground would seem to have ensured passage of the necessary legislation. "Of the 488 individuals who were prepared to subscribe to a national bank, 117 can be identified as MPs," writes Charles Ivar McGrath.[19] The House of Commons ordered in late September that a bill be drafted for establishing a bank.[20] An initial attempt to defeat the bill in the House of Commons by a group of landowners opposed to the concept of a Bank of Ireland was rejected, and later that month a committee of the whole house stated that a "bank on a proper foundation would be beneficial to the kingdom."[21]

At this stage, Conolly was still in control of the debate in the House of Commons and his access to patronage would normally have been sufficient to ensure passage of the bill through the lower house, so what happened next surprised almost everyone. When the subject again came to a debate in the lower house on October 14, one of various notable performances was that of Clotworthy Upton, who "gave a long rambling incoherent presentation [against the bill] which few could follow and no one bothered to answer."[22] That no one answered the speech is not quite correct, but the supporters of the bank scheme had been tactically out maneuvered, for what the House of Commons voted on was not the merits of the bank scheme itself but the first paragraph of the legislation. By debating the heads of the bill, opponents were able to attack broader economic principles rather than the details of the particular proposal. The vote was carried by opponents of the bank 103 to 95.

As with earlier debates in Westminster about the Bank of England and the National Land Bank, debate in Dublin had little to do with how the bank would operate and much to do with what the establishment of a bank would do to the relative positions of the landowners and the emerging capital-owning families. The concern of the landowners was that the bank would strengthen the hand of those dealing with capital and reduce the influence of those whose wealth was tied up in land, land that was often heavily mortgaged. In the course of these debates, Midleton must have sensed the increasing popular discontent with the idea of the bank. Commenting on the later vote in the lower house, Midleton informed his brother, Thomas Brodrick, that the "snare [of the bank] is broken."[23]

In November 1721, the House of Lords had the opportunity to make clear its view of the subject, and it resorted to one of its favorite turns of phrase in resolving that the whole idea was "Prejudicial and of Extream ill Consequence to this kingdom."[24] In the course of the debate various curious pronouncements followed each other closely, not the least of which was Midleton's discovery of "an affair . . . of a pernicious nature," which turned out to be the bank itself.[25] A reversal of such momentous nature could hardly be opposed by lesser placemen, and the House of Lords sealed the fate of the scheme, a scheme in support of which an Irish-born rising star of the church, George Berkeley, privately distanced himself from his fellow clerics.

The final vote in the saga came on December 9, 1721, when the House of Commons again voted on the bill to establish the bank, rejecting the scheme by 150 votes to 80. Of the 117 MPs who had initially been willing to subscribe to the bank, sixty-six "voted for the bank at some point," forty-six of them on the three occasions when there was a division. Twenty-five voted against it every chance they got. Others either split their votes, abstained, or were no longer members of the House of Commons at the times of division.[26]

Despite almost two years of planning, the bank bill died in both Irish houses in fewer than three months. The Brodrick family's sudden defiance of Westminster and the court marked the final commitment of the "Cork Squadron," a bloc gathered around the self-interest of the Brodrick family, to a case-by-case political agenda as influenced as much by personal animosity and opportunity as by any coherent ideology.

But self-interest is not always without public benefit, and Midleton had not been wrong when in his initial support for a bank he had focused on the shortage of specie in Ireland. However, it had not just been a debate between landowners and cash holders that had defeated the Bank of Ireland. Between the public announcement of Abercorn's scheme and the House of Commons' 1721 debates on the bank, the collapse of stock in the South Sea Trading Company in England had significantly changed the perception of many of those who would be involved in the debate. The South Sea Bubble was a stark reminder that the new economy was built upon principles very few people understood and brought with it the sort of financial insecurity that landowners who were cash poor (which was the case for the majority of Irish landowners) could ill afford. "Thus, by good argument and bad, but most of all by the inopportuneness of the time, the proposal to establish a corporate bank in Ireland was successfully resisted in 1720–21, and the country was condemned to another half-century of irresponsible banking."[27]

Swift's contribution to the bank debate was minimal, a passing comment in *A Proposal*, a few occasional, mainly unpublished poems, and remarks in private correspondence, none of which suggest any particular interest in, or understanding of, the merits, for or against, of the scheme. Additionally, once the South Sea Trading Company's stock began its collapse, Swift had a major problem on his hands when it came to making economic pronouncements: he was on record as an outspoken supporter of the legislation that had created the South Sea Trading Company. Here he is writing in *The Examiner* in 1711: "THE ACT for carrying on a Trade to the *South-Sea*, proposed by the . . . great Person [Robert Harley, later earl of Oxford], whose Thoughts are perpetually employed, and ever with Success, on the Good of his Country; will, in all Probability, if duly executed, be of mighty Advantage to the Kingdom, and an everlasting Honour to the present Parliament."[28]

Swift could perhaps later have used that phrase "duly executed" to shift the blame for the collapse of the stock price, but when composing *The History of the Four Last Years of the Queen* he was no less clear that Harley's "chief Concern was to restore the Credit of the Nation, by finding some Settlement for unprovided Debts . . . which former Ministries never had the Care or Courage to inspect."[29]Among the myriad schemes that the unstoppable Harley, at least according to Swift, put into force was one which "as a farther Advantage to the Creditors [allowed them] to be erected into a Company for Trading to the South Seas."[30] Swift might have opposed the Bank of Ireland proposal for a variety of reasons, but linking his opposition to the South Sea Bubble was not a ploy he chose to engage upon, which is perhaps one of the few instances of his integrity as an author surviving from one pamphlet to the next.

The effusive praise of the South Sea Trading Company in *The Examiner* could be dismissed as the necessary trope of a propagandist engaged in one of the livelier pamphlet wars of British literature, but that cannot explain Swift's insistence in continuing to enthuse about the company in *The History of the Four Last Years of the Queen*, a text he started in 1712 or 1713 when he had his eye on the post of Historiographer Royal, but which he worked on intermittently for at least a further ten years, long after the Bubble had burst. Swift never revised his initial comments about the brilliance of Harley's scheme. True, in a lengthy 1720 letter to Alexander Pope, Swift argued that the "scheme of politicks, (now about thirty years old) of setting up a monied Interest in opposition to the landed," had undermined the "possessors of the soil [who] are the best judges of what is for the advantage of the kingdom: If others had thought the same way, Funds of Credit and South-sea Projects would neither have been felt nor heard of."[31] Even here, though, Swift's objection is not to the South

Sea Trading Company itself, but to the conditions that had necessitated its creation.

The problem was not the South Sea Trading Company per se but the system of public credit that had come to flourish in the years after William III committed the English state to his continental wars, wars that continued to drain the public coffers until the administration of Robert Harley brought what proved to be only temporary sanity to affairs. This analysis absolved Harley of the blame for the South Sea Bubble. That the South Sea Trading Company's stock later crashed so spectacularly only served to show the perfidy of the Whigs, the dangers of public credit unsecured by access to specie and land—the only two assets really worth anything—and the tragedy that was the defeat of Robert Harley, earl of Oxford, a man who, "to judge from the preamble to his patent of honour one would suppose . . . to have rescued the nation from daylight robbery."[32]

Economics was never the dean's forte, though he kept meticulous account books and was quite capable of pursuing the last farthing of unpaid debt. Even when he thrusts the economic debate to the foreground of a tract, Swift is not making economic arguments: he is appealing to public perceptions of economic debate. *A Proposal for the Universal Use of Irish Manufacture* is Swift's most nuanced political effort and so is far more radical than the majority of the deliberately provocative pamphlets he wrote. Demonstrating a keener critical instinct than Swift credited to them, the British authorities in Ireland took *A Proposal* seriously, issuing a writ against the printer and seeking proof positive of the identity of the anonymous author. This response stands in marked contrast to later Swift diatribes that were met occasionally by half-hearted efforts at censorship but more commonly by profound indifference

Four years after *A Proposal*, Swift once again demonstrated his ability conveniently to ignore inconvenient facts—and to wait until the debate was decided before joining the fray— in this case in the argument over the proposed introduction of a copper halfpence to help alleviate Ireland's lack of small change, a lack Swift had been far from alone in mentioning during the debate over the bank scheme.

As with so much happening at the time, Irish history got in the way of Irish needs. John Locke had earlier noted that that those who wished to test the viability of base metal coinage should mint such money. Doing so, he wrote, would prove the point that "The *quantity* of pure Silver separable from the Alloy, makes the real *value* of

Money. If it does not, Coin Copper with the same Stamp and denomination, and see whether it will be of the same value. I suspect your Stamp will make it of no more worth, than the Copper-Money of *Ireland* is, which is its weight in Copper, and no more. That Money lost so much to *Ireland,* as it passed for above the rate of Copper. But yet I think no body suffered so much by it as [James II], by whose Authority it was made current."[33]

James II, like other besieged monarchs before him, had minted "gun money," base metal coins with a face value far higher than their metal content secured against promises to redeem them once access to gold and silver had been restored. Upon pacifying Ireland, one of William of Orange's first acts was to authorize the minting of a copper regal halfpence very similar in style to the previous coppers of Charles II and James II. These coins had a face value equivalent to their worth in metal, that is a fraction of a shilling. At the same time, the Jacobite base-metal tokens were declared to be worth their weight in metal rather than their face value.[34] This latter measure was not simply a punitive act aimed at supporters of James II; nor was it unprecedented.

Despite being a step to ensure economic security, William's actions nonetheless secured in the Irish popular imagination the idea that "copper" coinage was unlikely to retain any intrinsic value. In 1724, this idea was not helped by the fact that the contract that William Wood signed to mint the coin—a contract secured through largely disreputable means—stipulated that "no more than 30 pence of coin should be made out of one pound of copper (although copper was worth 12 pence per pound)."[35] This represented an allowable discount of more than 150 percent. However, when Sir Isaac Newton, the master of the mint, was asked to oversee an assay of the coins once the debate was in full swing, the actual value of the coins minted compared to the value of copper turned out to be something much closer to 1:1.[36] Wood, in other words, was making his profit almost entirely from the annual fee of £3,000—no small sum, true, but nothing to do with debasing the coin of Ireland.[37]

By then, it was too late. The proposal for copper coinage combined a public sentiment opposed to base metal coinage with a very real sense among the Irish political class that the method of introducing the coinage once again threatened to erode the remaining prerogatives of the Irish parliament. In other words, the fight over copper coin was to traverse very similar ground to the earlier fight over the Bank of Ireland, with a populist response largely uninformed by the facts reinforcing a policy debate that had little, if anything, to do with economic necessity.

Swift's contribution to the debate over Wood's halfpence conveniently ignored the fact that the coin was to be offered at something close to its actual metal value. Rather, by suggesting that shopkeepers and other small merchants refuse to accept the coin at all, Swift was playing on fears based on ignorance and invoking memories of the plight of the merchants and small landholders between 1688 and 1691, when far more complicated issues had been involved than the mere coining of ultimately valueless brass tokens.

Swift was able to take this tack because Wood and the Walpole government which granted the patent had made one crucial mistake; the patent did not make the currency legal tender. Small change though the coins were, the public perception, based upon real and imagined memories of currency in James II's time, meant that the lack of legal tender status raised popular fears that once in circulation the same government in London that had granted the patent could declare the coins valueless at least as far as payment of taxes and fees were concerned. Ironically, the lack of legal tender status meant that pamphleteers such as Swift could urge the shopkeepers of Ireland to reject the coins as payment for goods without legal jeopardy. This threat would not only prove reasonably significant, it would allow more nuanced pamphleteers to develop a constitutional argument against the coinage. Whatever the practical merits of the coins being made legal tender—and those merits may indeed have been very few—the fact that they did not have that status played an important role in the debate.

David Bindon, in his 1724 *Some Considerations on the Attempts Made to Pass Mr. Wood's Brass-Money in Ireland* seized upon the constitutional issues surrounding the patent and upon the lack of legal tender status (in this case in England), demanding to know how the British privy council's order requiring Irish revenue officers to take the coin could lead to anything other than "the most unheard of confusion that was ever introduced into the Business of a Nation" given that the order was "directly contrary to Two [Irish] Acts of Parliament [passed in Charles II's reign and still] in Force in this Kingdom."[38] The two statutes Bindon referred to required Irish revenue officers to accept payment of taxes for civil and military list expenditures in Ireland in the "Currant Money of England."[39] That the order to revenue officers to accept the coins was tantamount to declaring the coins legal tender in all but name is here conveniently ignored. Numerous other pamphleteers on the anti-Wood side pointed out that letters patent from the government in Whitehall could not repeal the legislation of Charles II, thereby effectively rendering the patent itself null and void as a useful way of providing specie to allow the payment of the public debt in Ireland.

Bindon, Swift, and most other opponents of Wood's scheme chose to ignore the fact that available specie in Ireland in 1722 was reckoned at about £400,000.[40] Wood's patent allowed for the minting of £100,800 over ten years. However, in late July 1724, Wood "agreed to limit the amount of his coinage" to £40,000, but it was a move too late and too pandering to help win the pamphlet war that had grown up around the proposal.[41] That Wood's coins would have addressed Ireland's desperate need of small change to replace the tokens and chits that formed the backbone of most day-to-day transactions in much of the kingdom was no longer the point. Midleton and Conolly had agreed on such a need in 1721 when reporting on the bank proposals, and *The Postboy* would remind its readers that before Wood's patent was granted "there was the utmost Necessity for Copper Money . . . ; so that some Gentlemen who employ hundreds of the Poor [in Ireland], were forc'd to tally with their Workmen, and give them Bits of Cards with their Seal on one Side, and their Names on the other."[42]

It was not just small change that Ireland lacked. Joseph Johnston has shown that a Trinity College, Dublin-owned estate in Co. Carlow was let for 4*s.* 5*d.* per acre in 1705.[43] Thomas Prior's 1729 *Observation on Coin in General* noted that because of silver coin and guineas being exported to England, Ireland was "reduced to [the Portuguese gold] moidores, the most inconvenient coin of all."[44] The moidore was valued at about 17*s.* In other words, you could rent for one year about four acres of farmland in Co. Carlow in exchange for the coin most widely circulated in Ireland. It was not just that the moidore had a relatively high face value. The absence of crowns and half crowns from most people's pockets in Ireland meant that small debts could not be settled with coinage and had to be reckoned by chit or some other token of indebtedness until sufficient expenses had been incurred to allow the moidore, or some other high value coin, to be used to settle the aggregated sum.

In 1728, Swift himself made the point in the pamphlet *A Short View of the State of Ireland* that "within three Years past, the running

Cash of the Nation, which was about five Hundred Thousand Pounds, is now less than two; and must daily diminish, unless we have Liberty to coin, as well as that important Kingdom the Isle of *Man*; and the meanest Prince in the *German* Empire."[45] It is true that Swift in 1728 was seeking for Ireland the right to mint silver-based coin, but the need for cash, and for cash in smaller denomination, was essentially stipulated by all sides of the economic debates in Ireland throughout the first three decades of the eighteenth century, a fact that Swift was quite capable of overlooking should the need arise.[46] By the end of the 1730s, copper coin minted in the Tower of London was circulating freely in Ireland.

None of this interested Swift. Copper coin is only debased in a monetary sense if it circulates, or attempts to circulate, at a face value greater than its weight in metal. Wood's coin was never intended to do so. The real issue for most of those opposing the patent was not economic but political. "We shal speake our minds freely in what maner the nation hath been treated," wrote Midleton, once again a lord justice and now opposing Wood's patent on constitutional grounds similar to his initial support for Abercorn's bank scheme.[47] Archbishop King was even more angry, declaring that the Irish had been treated "with the utmost contempt; endeavoured to be imposed on as fools and children."[48]

In February 1725, Marmaduke Coghill, member of parliament for Trinity College and a future chancellor of the Irish exchequer, sent a lengthy letter to Edward Southwell exploring in depth the options available to the monarch should he wish to cancel Wood's patent and discussing the state of specie in Ireland. Among the observations Coghill made was that "we have but too much reason to fear, that by art or contrivance, these half pence may be brought into the Treasury, and then they must passe, for tho no compulsory methods are used, yet necessity must oblige us to take them, if the Treasury pays them to the army."[49] The threat of such a quasi-legal method of introduction resonated all too clearly among the Protestant Irish. That James's administration in Ireland had effectively compelled the acceptance of its gun money by ordering the army to pay for goods and services using only such coins was hardly a happy historical coincidence.

Swift certainly grasped the potential for making his mark in the debate about Wood's halfpence, and in *The Drapier's Letters*, which began appearing only when the political tide in Ireland had quite clearly shifted against Wood's proposal, he demonstrates all the various rhetorical skills that have helped ensure his reputation. But Swift's eye for self-promotion must not be forgotten when considering how best to evaluate the content of those letters. Consider a remarkable publication of late November 1728, *The Intelligencer* 18, which points out that

> It has been the Custom of all wise Nations, not only to confer immediate honours upon their Benefactors, but likewise to distinguish their *Birth-days*, by Anniversary rejoycings . . . It is for this reason, that I recommend *Saint Andrew's-Day* unto you, to be Celebrated in a most Particular manner, being (as I am very well informed) the DRAPIER's Birth-Day . . .
>
> Consider . . . my dear *Country Men*, the hazard, which this Noble Spirited DRAPIER did run for our Sakes. How like the old Heroe *Camillus*, he flew in suddainly to our Rescue, when *Wood's* Half-pence were . . . [proposed] by our Enemies, to fill their Pockets more plentifully, with our *Gold*, and *Silver*. That he has done his best to save us from Poverty and Slavery . . .
>
> Let us not Act then, in a Christian Country, like the Barbarous Heathens, who frequently, when their greatest Deliverances were wrought, either Slighted, or banished, or Poisoned, or Murthered the *Benefactors*, or the *Heroes*, or reduced them to the Necessity, of Dying by their own Hands.[50]

Perhaps the only saving grace of this panegyric is that it was written by Swift's co-editor Thomas Sheridan, rather than by the dean himself. Lest we forget, this broadsheet was published at almost exactly the same time as Swift argued in *A Short View* for an Irish mint to address the want of petty cash.

At least one Irish cleric did understand the economic principles of the debate, and it is worth exploring his reactions to the Irish economic schemes of the 1720s as a way of demonstrating just how profoundly, whether deliberately or not, Swift misunderstood the Irish economy of the first third of the eighteenth century. Crucially, George Berkeley had spent some time in Rhode Island in the early years of the eighteenth century, years when the colony had undertaken an exercise in fiscal experimentation theretofore unprecedented. Colonial authorities "authorized issues of paper money, borrowed it [from those to whom they had granted authority to print], purchased goods and other property, depreciated it with successive issues, used it when depreciated to repay their indebtedness, and realized egregious profits."[51] It was a period of inflationary enthusiasm described by one modern commentator as "something like a monetary perpetual motion machine."[52]

What distinguished Rhode Island from other American colonies was that the colony had neither a royal charter nor a proprietary grant. "As a result," writes Leslie V. Brock, "Rhode Island was free to multiply" its currency without restraint. In 1720, Rhode Island had a quarter as much paper currency in circulation as did Massachusetts, where the paper currency was secured against specie. By 1730 that ratio had reached 38 percent and by 1740 it had reached 113 percent, even though their populations had grown at the same pace over that period.[53]

Rhode Island's economy functioned reasonably successfully because it could replenish its own specie with gold and silver consequent upon its thriving trade in sugar and slaves with the West Indies. Its domestic fiscal enthusiasms had more serious consequences outside its own borders than within. What Rhode Island needed, or, more specifically, what its neighbors needed, was a state currency that if not specie-backed was at least well regulated, the sort of regulation the British treasury had sought when requiring an act of parliament to authorize the Bank of Ireland.

In Ireland, with far less access to trade and, consequently, to gold and silver specie, the disconnect between appearance and reality was dramatic, as Berkeley recognized when he asked in Query 32 of the 1735 edition: "Whether if there was no gold or silver in the kingdom, our trade might not, nevertheless, supply bills of exchange, sufficient to answer the demands of absentees in England or elsewhere?"[54] Over time, the Irish economy recovered from the travails of the 1720s. When he prepared the 1750 edition of *The Querist* (the first edition to which, incidentally, he attached his name) Berkeley posed the questions "Whether current bank-notes may not be deemed money? And whether they are not actually the greater part of the money of the kingdom?" immediately after his earlier query about bills of exchange.[55] That bank notes supplied, by Berkeley's estimate, more than half the currency in circulation in Ireland by 1750 shows how far the economy of the province had changed from the outset of the eighteenth century, even without much in the way of a planned structural overhaul.

Gold was still available in Ireland in the second decade of the 1700s, but silver was increasingly unavailable. Bank notes were not in wide circulation, but there were numerous other negotiable scrips in day-to-day use. The trouble was that these scrips had no legally defined value and no metal backing to secure them against discounting or other loss of value. They were, in fact, no more secure than Rhode Island's inflation-ridden legal tender. Berkeley actually constructed a reasonably coherent and possibly workable scheme for an Irish bank. That he chose to remain silent about that fact speaks loudly to what was usually being debated in Ireland under the guise of economic debate.

Just as opposition to the Bank of Ireland had succeeded despite the general agreement over Ireland's want of specie, so, too, did Wood's halfpence fail despite the general agreement about the severity of the problem it sought to solve. Both schemes failed primarily for constitutional reasons, although there was genuine opposition to the bank scheme from those who feared a decline in the power of landowners.

Four years after the halfpence controversy, Swift returned to the matter of Irish coinage in *A Short View of the State of Ireland*, wherein he made the point repeated almost immediately in *Intelligencer* 15 (Nov. 1728) that "We are denyed the Liberty of Coining Gold, Silver, or even Copper."[56] It turns out that Swift had no objection to copper coinage per se. And herein lies the secret to understanding Swift's writings about the Irish economy: he did not have a long-term plan. *A Proposal for the Universal Use of Irish Manufacture* carried in its argument a very real intellectual questioning of British-Irish constitutional relations, which is why the executive administration in Dublin Castle replied with a very real political response to the tract's publication. Most often, however, while Swift weighed in on economic matters he barely understood, Irish politicians got on with the more practical business of debating how to manage the affairs of the new provincial state of Ireland.

That such provincial status came with no meaningful precedent to look to for guidance offered a polemicist such as Swift the opportunity to engage in some spectacular grandstanding—and fine writing—while a debate of real and lasting consequence went on around him, a debate that would seek to answer the very last of George Berkeley's published queries: "Whose fault is it if poor Ireland still continues poor?"[57] Such a debate necessitated a series of less than grandstanding policy statements and actions, and some unpredictable adjustments of course.[58]

Given the ill-defined nature of what constituted a province, or a "Nation . . . (wch is no Nation)," the parameters of such a province's financial debate are often no less clear to us in retrospect than they were to many observers at the time. Nonetheless, we can and should assert that one "part of the difficulty which has stood in the way of a clear view of the ideological issues at stake . . . has been a tendency to overestimate the importance of Jonathan Swift."[59]

Indeed, the absence of any serious political response to Swift's increasingly dramatic outbursts helps illuminate just how clearly Swift was conducting a campaign of his own design, a campaign which was largely irrelevant to those actually seeking to engage in addressing the shifting economic and political demands of the time. So it is that while Swift's work should be considered in context it should not be considered as providing a context.

Notes

1. I have argued elsewhere that Swift had an honorable and coherent agenda behind his delighted assaults on his selected targets—that Tacitus rather than Juvenal is the better classical analogy to Swift—but that still does not get to the crux of whether Swift is a reliable commentator on the socioeconomic matters about which he was at times so willing to express an opinion. See Christopher J. Fauske, *Jonathan Swift and the Church of Ireland, 1714–1724* (Dublin: Irish Academic Press, 2000).

2. [Jonathan Swift], *A Proposal for the Universal Use of Irish Manufacture, in Cloaths and Furniture of Houses, &c. Utterly Rejecting and Renouncing Every Thing wearable that comes from England* (Dublin, 1720), in *The Prose Writings of Jonathan Swift*, vol. 9, *Irish Tracts, 1720–1723, and Sermons*, ed. Herbert Davis (Oxford: Blackwell, 1948), 13–22.

3. Jonathan Swift to Charles Ford, Apr. 4, 1720, in David Woolley, ed., *The Correspondence of Jonathan Swift, D.D.*, vol. 2, *Letters, 1714–1726* (Frankfurt: Peter Lang, 2001), 327.

4. Jonathan Swift to Charles Ford, Apr. 4, 1720, in Woolley, ed., *Correspondence . . . 1714–1726,* 327.

5. 6 Geo. 1 c.5. An Act for the better Securing the Dependency of Ireland upon the Crown at Westminster.

6. For discussion of the origins of the Declaratory Act see Isolde Victory, "The Making of the 1720 Declaratory Act," in *Parliament, Politics and People: Essays in Eighteenth-Century Irish History*, ed. Gerard O'Brien (Dublin: Irish Academic Press, 1989), 9–29; D. W. Hayton, "The Stanhope/Sunderland Ministry and the Repudiation of Irish Parliamentary Independence," *English Historical Review* 113, no. 452 (June 1998): 610–36.

7. Jonathan Swift to Charles Ford, Apr. 4, 1720, in Woolley, ed., *Correspondence . . . 1714–1726,* 327.

8. I discuss this period of Swift's career in some detail in the opening chapter of Fauske, *Jonathan Swift and the Church of Ireland.*

9. [Swift], *A Proposal,* 21–22.

10. Joseph Johnston, "Archbishop King's Diagnosis," in *Bishop Berkeley's* "Querist" *in Historical Perspective,* ed. Joseph Johnston (Dundalk: Dundalgan, 1970), 28.

11. Qtd. in Johnston, "Archbishop King's Diagnosis," 23.

12. Qtd. in Oliver Ferguson, *Jonathan Swift and Ireland* (Urbana: University of Illinois Press, 1962), 188.

13. Joep Leerssen, *Remembrance and Imagination: Patterns in the Historical and Literary Representation of Ireland in the Nineteenth Century* (Notre Dame: University of Notre Dame Press, 1997), 16.

14. Viscount Strabane, like many members of the Irish peerage, was also ennobled, as the earl of Abercorn, in the English peerage, and his association with Ireland was largely nominal. His holdings there were managed for him and revenue from his estates used to support his absentee lifestyle. The importance in which Irish peerages were held by all but a handful of native-born Irishmen is most starkly revealed by the steadily declining number of temporal peers in the first half of the eighteenth century ennobled only through the Irish list. By 1751, there were only twenty-eight such peers. Some Irish peers had inherited English or Scottish titles through marriage, often marriages inspired by a need for greater financial security. Others had acquired English titles as a reward for services to the British executive or the Crown. A tradition would later develop of giving Irish titles to sundry non-Irish people for services rendered abroad. For more on the Irish peerage see G. E. Cokayne, *The Complete Peerage of England, Scotland, Ireland, Great Britain and the United Kingdom,* rev. by Vicary Gibbs, Geoffrey White, and R. S. Lea, 12 vols. (London: St Catherine, 1910–59).

15. Michael Ryder, "The Bank of Ireland, 1721: Land, Credit and Dependency," *The Historical Journal* 25, no. 3 (Sept. 1982): 562.

16. Robert E. Burns, *Irish Parliamentary Politics in the Eighteenth Century,* 2 vols. (Washington, D.C.: Catholic University of America Press, 1989), 1:122.

17. Lords justices of Ireland to Grafton, Jan. 7, 1721. Qtd. in Ryder, "Bank of Ireland,' 562.

18. Irish peers who were not also ennobled in the British list could sit in the British House of Commons if elected, and it is perhaps instructive of how little attention parliamentary managers in Britain paid to Irish politics on most occasions that Midleton sat in the British House of Commons for the Whig-controlled constituency of Midhurst from 1717 to 1728. Another significant Irish opponent of many of the Irish policies of the British government, Robert, Viscount Molesworth of Swords, sat in the British House of Commons for the even more solidly Whig pocket borough of St Michael Cornwall for many years.

19. Charles Ivar McGrath, "Review Article: Parliament, People and other Possibilities," *Eighteenth-Century Ireland* 17 (2002): 162.

20. *The Journals of the House of Commons of the Kingdom of Ireland,* 20 vols. (3rd edition, Dublin, 1796–1800), 3:257–58.

21. Ryder, "Bank of Ireland," 565. The chronology herein laid out also depends upon Ryder, though with one error in dating corrected.

22. Burns, *Irish Parliamentary Politics,* 1:129.

23. Qtd. in Ryder, "Bank of Ireland," 565.

24. Burns, *Irish Parliamentary Politics,* 1:129.

25. Ibid., 1:130.

26. McGrath, "Parliament, People and other Possibilities," 164.

27. Joseph Johnston, "Berkeley and the Abortive Bank Project of 1720–21," in *Berkeley's "Querist,"* ed. Johnston, 51.

28. [Jonathan Swift], *The Examiner* 44 (London, June 7, 1711), in *The Prose Writings of Jonathan Swift,* vol. 3, *The Examiner and Other Pieces Written in 1710–11,* ed. Herbert Davis (Oxford: Blackwell, 1941), 170.

29. [Jonathan Swift], *The History of the Four Last Years of the Queen* (Dublin, 1758), in *The Prose Writings of Jonathan Swift,* vol. 7, *The History of the Four Last Years of the Queen,* ed. Herbert Davis (Oxford: Blackwell, 1973), 76.

30. [Swift], *History of the Four Last Years of the Queen,* 76.

31. Jonathan Swift, "A Letter *from Dr* Swift *to Mr* Pope 1721," in *The Prose Writings . . .* vol. 9, 32.

32. David Green, *Queen Anne* (New York: Charles Scribner's, 1970), 249.

33. Patrick Kelly, ed., *Locke on Money,* 2 vols. (Oxford: Clarendon, 1994), 1:311.

34. J. Simon, *An Essay Towards an Historical Account of Irish Coins* (Dublin, 1749), 65. But Sir Isaac Newton would report the Irish coins of William III, like those of Charles II and James II, to be "much inferior in value" to the coins minted by William Wood, which he tested (Isaac Newton, "A Copy of the *Report* made by *Sir Isaac Newton, Edw Southwel,* and *John Scroope,* Esqs; of the *Assay* made of Mr *Wood's Copper Money . . . ,*" in *The Prose Writings of Jonathan Swift,* Volume 10, *The Drapier's Letters and Other Works, 1724–1725,* ed. Herbert Davis (Oxford: Blackwell, 1959), 188). Wood, however, only submitted for assay coins minted after March 25, 1723. He had minted three previous sets of coins and there was a general consensus in Ireland that the earlier mintings were far more debased than those he submitted to the mint for testing (Ferguson, *Swift and Ireland,* 104n).

35. Constantine George Caffentzis, *Exciting the Industry of Mankind: George Berkeley's Philosophy of Money* (Dordrecht: Kluwer, 2000), 66.

36. Newton, "Copy," 187–88.

37. Ireland had had earlier experiences with chartered mints not producing coins of appropriate quality. For example, a patent issued to Sir Thomas Vinery (sometime lord mayor of London and member of the guild of goldsmiths) to mint small silver coins in Ireland had been revoked in 1686 after the treasurer and the mint commissioners reported to the privy council on the inferior quality of the coinage (Louis Jordan, "Chronological Listing of Documents and Events relating to the Massachusetts Mint," July 7, 2005 <http://www.coins.nd.edu/ColCoin/ColCoinIntros/MAMintDocs.chron.html>).

38. David Bindon, *Some Considerations on the Attempts Made to Pass Mr. Wood's Brass-Money in Ireland. By a Lover of his Country* (Dublin, 1724), 2.

39. Sabine Baltes, *The Pamphlet Controversy about Wood's Halfpence (1722–25) and the Tradition of Irish Constitutional Nationalism* (Frankfurt: Peter Lang, 2002), 159.

40. Albert Goodwin, "Wood's Halfpence," *English Historical Review* 51, no. 204 (Oct. 1936): 654.

41. Ferguson, *Swift and Ireland,* 86.

42. *The Postboy* [Dublin] July 31, 1724. Qtd. in *The Prose Writings . . .* vol. 10, 189.

43. Joseph Johnston, "A Sample of Agricultural Rents, 1700–1850," in *Berkeley's* "Querist," ed. Johnston, 103.

44. Thomas Prior, *Observations on Coin in General* (Dublin, 1729), in "Old and Scarce Tracts on Money." *Photographed from the Original Volume Printed for the Political Economy Club, 1856,* ed. J. R. McCulloch (London: P.S. King, 1933), 63.

45. [Jonathan Swift], *A Short View of the State of Ireland* (Dublin, 1728), in *The Prose Writings of Jonathan Swift,* vol. 12, *Irish Tracts, 1728–1733,* ed. Herbert Davis (Oxford: Blackwell, 1971), 11.

46. You will notice, however, that Swift was a sufficiently careful reader of his own work to make the references to the exodus of gold and silver postdate his *Drapier's Letters* rejection of the need for petty cash. His figure of £500,000 as the available money supply in Ireland at that time is on the high end of most contemporary estimates and also, incidentally, further undermines the economic plausibility of his argument in the *Drapier's Letters.*

47. William Coxe, *Memoirs of the Life and Administration of Sir Robert Walpole, Earl of Orford,* 2 vols. (London, 1798), 2:425.

48. William King to John Gorges, Jan. 28, 1724. Qtd. in. Ferguson, *Swift and Ireland,* 85.

49. Marmaduke Coghill to Edward Southwell, sr, Feb. 2, 1725, in D. W. Hayton, ed., *Letters of Marmaduke Coghill, 1722–1738* (Dublin: Irish Manuscripts Commission, 2005), 15.

50. James Woolley, ed., *Jonathan Swift and Thomas Sheridan:* "The Intelligencer" (Oxford: Clarendon, 1992), 197–99. Not only did Swift approve publication of this panegyric, he most likely thought it far from unbecoming. "Swift's deepest admiration and respect," notes F. P. Lock, "were reserved for the hero of a particular type: the man of unbending principle and integrity who (usually) comes into conflict with his society precisely because his standards are too high for it . . . men whose victory was won through nominal defeat" (Lock, *The Politics of* "Gulliver's Travels" [Oxford: Oxford University Press, 1980], 15). Integrity, of course, is far easier to sustain if one is able to remain outside the involvement of actually seeking practicable solutions.

51. Bray Hammond, *Banks and Politics in America from the Revolution to the Civil War* (Princeton: Princeton University Press, 1957), 25.

52. Caffentzis, *Industry of Mankind,* 104.

53. Leslie V. Brock, "The Colonial Currency, Prices, and Exchange Rates," in *Essays in History* 34 (1992), Charlottesville: Corcoran Department of History, University of Virginia <http://etext.virginia.edu/journals/EH/EH34/brock34.htm>, 7.

54. George Berkeley, *The Querist,* in *Berkeley's* "Querist," ed. Johnston, 127.

55. Ibid., 127.

56. [Swift], *Intelligencer,* 178.

57. Berkeley, *Querist,* 175.

58. Then again, perhaps some significant part of the debate over the economy of a political entity governed by some combination of Westminster-appointed officials and locally elected politicians might well be attributed to honest misunderstanding. Evidence for that assertion might also be found in later debates conducted between various North American colonies and the British government. Despite their name, these "colonies" were not colonies in the sense that we now understand the word, having varying degrees of political autonomy. As with Ireland, however, there was regular disagreement about the limits of that local authority. In the debate over the 1773 Currency Act, the New Jersey governor,

William Franklin, chastised the colonial legislature with the warning that continued opposition to the British parliament's financial plans would lead to the judgment that it had acted "in the opinion of every sensible Man . . . a Part extremely rash and imprudent, and big with Mischief." The legislature was unimpressed, concluding one of its replies with the thought that "the reason your excellency and we give such different accounts of the riches of the province, is easy to account for: you see nothing but affluence, we see the distress of the people." (Qtd. in Joseph Albert Ernst, *Money and Politics in America, 1755–1775: A Study in the Currency Act of 1764 and the Political Economy of Revolution* [Chapel Hill: University of North Carolina Press for the Institute of Early American History and Culture, 1973), 289]. It may be that both parties to the debate were to some extent being as honest as they could be.

59. Ryder, "Bank of Ireland," 558.

The Irish Experience of "Financial Revolution" 1660–1760

Charles Ivar McGrath

In historical memory the English financial revolution is so closely related in time and space to the Glorious Revolution of 1688 that the two events often appear inseparable. Yet for some time now, particularly in the work of Henry Roseveare, P. K. O'Brien, and P. A. Hunt, there has been justification for arguing that the financial revolution was less of a revolution and more of an evolution—an evolution in various fiscal practices and understandings that commenced in the 1640s, 1650s, and 1660s, especially in the areas of indirect taxation (levies on consumption rather than on personal wealth) and the professionalisation of the revenue administration.[1] From such a perspective, 1688 becomes a marker for the point in time when the various separate components came together that, when combined, constituted a cumulative revolution in financial practice, with the Glorious Revolution serving as a catalyst.

For Ireland, a similar pattern can be identified. Ireland's early modern financial evolution commenced around the same time as England's, with the assessments and excises of the 1640s and 1650s and the customs and excise acts of 1662. But different circumstances thereafter resulted in slower development in the 1670s and 1680s, until the process gathered pace again in the 1690s with the advent of regular parliamentary sessions centered around the process of short-term additional supply and an emerging confidence within the Protestant community in Ireland in the apparatus of the state as represented by the Irish executive and legislature. Admittedly, unlike in England, the Protestant Irish were a minority of the population, but as the community from which the ruling elite was drawn, and as the main focus of both economic and political power, they were no less significant for that fact.[2]

Yet financially Ireland remained a couple of decades behind England. England's awakening to the possibilities of the various financial innovations of the seventeenth century and the realization of the full potential of a public credit system and a managed national debt occurred in 1688–89 and led to revolutionary developments in the 1690s and thereafter.[3] Ireland's version of those occurrences happened in 1715–16, following the Hanoverian succession of 1714 and the Jacobite rebellion in Scotland in 1715. The reaction within Ireland to these developments saw the latent confidence in the post-Glorious Revolution settlement burst forth into financial innovations exemplified by the advent of a parliament-sanctioned national debt and the emergence of new facilities for managing public credit.

Early financial and administrative developments

The 1640s and 1650s was an exceptional period throughout the British Isles. The financial innovations introduced by the Westminster parliament to fund its wars against Charles I and the reconquests of Scotland and Ireland, in particular the assessment and the excise duties, marked a significant break with the past.[4] In Ireland, the result of such innovations was a remarkable increase in the amount of public income raised in the country. In the early seventeenth century, the annual income for the Irish government from Irish revenue sources fluctuated between £15,000 and £27,000, and was always in need of subventions from England which varied in amount from anywhere between £8,000 and £67,000.[5] By the 1650s, however, the average annual income from Irish sources had increased to about £264,900. Even so, expenditure was at that time such that, on average, a further £213,758 had to be remitted from England each year to cover the Irish government's costs.[6]

The collapse of the Protectorate in 1659 precipitated a reappraisal of the levels of expenditure and taxation throughout the British Isles. A series of interim measures—including a poll tax—enacted by Ireland's convention parliament in 1660 helped to produce in Ireland a net income of £116,887 for the year ending March 1661. As in the 1650s, this was supplemented from England, on this occasion by the sum of £39,000.[7] The final net total was insufficient to meet the costs of government in Ireland for the restored monarchy. It remained for the Irish parliament to come up with a more substantial financial provision for the government's expenditure that would put an end to the need for recourse to the English treasury.

The Irish parliament of 1661–66 voted a financial settlement for the restored monarchy that led over time to a significant increase in net annual yields from £112,158 in March 1662 to a Restoration high of £256,994 in December 1684.[8] Prior to the financial settlement of the 1660s, the hereditary revenue (that is, revenue that had always belonged to the Crown, or which had been granted to it and which it was entitled to collect in perpetuity without the need for further parliamentary sanction) comprised an array of customs duties, Crown and composition rents, alcohol licenses, prizage, and a number of smaller "casual" branches.[9] The 1660s parliamentary settlement expanded these hereditary revenues to included quit rents, import and inland excise, hearth tax, and consolidated, expanded, and increased customs and alcohol licences.[10] The two most import branches of the new hereditary revenues were the excise duties and the customs duties, both of which were indirect taxes.

Although customs duties had existed in Ireland since an English presence had first been established in the country, the 1662 customs act served to consolidate, expand, and increase a wide range of import and export duties, the authority for the collection of which, for the first time ever, rested solely with parliament.[11] The act settled on the Crown in perpetuity the existing duty of 12*d.* in 20*s.*, or 5 percent, which was to be paid for all goods imported or exported by Irish subjects and an additional duty of 12*d.* in 20*s.*, or a further 5 percent, on all exports of Irish goods or manufactures. A series of further additional duties on imports was also included, while all goods imported or exported by subjects of other countries paid double the normal customs. The duties on wines and oils depended on the country of origin, and again on whether they were imported by Irish or foreign subjects. The only items exempt from import duties were bullion and wool. A further duty of 5*s.* per ton was imposed on all goods in every ship or vessel belonging to any subjects of France that came into any Irish port, either to load or unload goods, or to land passengers. The act also included a substantial and permanent book detailing the rates of duties to be imposed upon an extensive list of goods.[12]

Excise taxes had first been introduced into Ireland in 1643, following their imposition in England by both the parliamentarian and royalist sides during the civil war, but it was only with the passage of the Irish excise act of 1662 that a permanent and perpetual import and inland excise was established in Ireland.[13] The tax had two parts. The first part was the import excise, which imposed a standard duty of 12*d.* in 20*s.*, or 5 percent, on all imported goods, with a higher rate of 10 percent for drugs and a lower rate of 2½ percent for raw hemp, flax, tow, tar, rosin, pitch, wax, cable-yarn, and cordage. Jewels, bullion, corn, victuals, arms and ammunition, and several other items were free from duty. The second part was the inland excise which imposed a duty of 2*s.* 6*d.*, or 12½ percent, on every thirty-two gallons of beer or ale over 6*s.* in price, and 6*d.*, or 2½ percent, on every thirty-two gallons of beer or ale under that price. All strong liquors paid 4*d.* per gallon.[14]

The new hereditary revenues voted in the 1660s quickly provided a greater annual yield for government, the result of which was threefold. First, the English treasury ceased paying subventions to Ireland after 1667. Second, by the 1670s annual government income regularly exceeded expenditure, thereby creating a surplus that was siphoned off to English foreign policy expenditure (in 1678, £97,000 was paid from Ireland for naval services and the garrison at Tangiers). And third, the government's ability to cover all expenditure meant that there was no longer any pressing need to summon parliament. This latter circumstance accounted for the fact that parliament was not convened between 1667 and 1688.[15]

The 1662 customs and excise acts also facilitated the establishment of a professional revenue collection bureaucracy. Although the first revenue commissioners were appointed in Ireland during the Interregnum, it was not until the Restoration that a truly new form of revenue management was established with the permanent legislative foundation provided in the two acts of 1662.[16] The acts instituted a revenue commission that was eventually to manage the entire Irish revenue collection system. The system consisted of a countrywide network of salaried underofficers appointed by, and answerable to, the commissioners themselves.[17] The importance of the commission was not immediately apparent in Restoration Ireland because revenue farming remained the norm until 1682. But after the move to direct management that began in 1683, this new institution started to take hold in the changing world of government administration.[18]

The Impact of the Glorious Revolution

The Glorious Revolution of 1688 led to the outbreak of a country-wide war in 1689 in Ireland between the forces of James II and those of William of Orange. One of the most immediate effects of this war was the collapse of the revenue system. In 1688, the recorded net public income was £251,826. One year later, it had dropped to £4,038. By the end of the war in 1691 the net income had recovered to £119,333. Although the annual net yield continued to improve during the 1690s, the recovery was hampered by England's continuing war with France. The returns achieved in the 1680s were not equalled until 1698.

At the same time, the ultimate price of the Williamite victory in Ireland in 1691 was a permanent increase in the cost of government.[19] The single most significant source of increased expenditure in Ireland was on the enlarged army during and after the 1689–91 war. Prior to the Glorious Revolution, the size of the army in Ireland had varied depending on the circumstances: in 1641 it had stood at 3,240; in the 1650s at 30,000; and in 1661 at 7,500, a figure that continued into the 1680s. After 1691, the army fluctuated between 12,000 and 15,000 men until 1699, when the English parliament legislated for a permanent settlement of an army 12,000-strong to be maintained and paid for in Ireland.[20] The effect of the enlarged army on government expenditure was evident in the annual accounts. Whereas in the 1680s the highest annual cost of government had been £243,663, by June 1698 it had leapt to the unprecedented level of £390,627 per annum. Although this figure was reduced to just under £340,000 by the end of the year, the annual cost thereafter tended to fluctuate between £325,000 and £350,000 in the early 1700s.[21]

Given that the hereditary revenues at their best produced about £250,000 a year, the net annual yield was no longer sufficient for the government's needs. The problem was exacerbated by the fact that the annual arrears on government payments grew at a rapid rate, rising from £100,000 in 1692 to £312,314 in 1696.[22] New sources of income had to be found, and parliament was the most logical vehicle for providing it.

The hereditary customs and excise revenues granted in the early 1660s made it relatively straightforward for the Irish parliament to answer the government's growing need for money after the Glorious

Revolution. This was handled by voting an increased levy upon an existing customs or excise duty for a regulated period of time, in order to provide an estimated amount of money. This device of voting short-term parliamentary additional duties had first been used in England in the 1660s.[233] Once it was adopted in Ireland in the 1690s, it meant that as long as government expenditure exceeded the hereditary income parliament would have to be convened on a regular basis.[24]

The first post-Glorious Revolution Irish parliament, which for the first time was a wholly Protestant assembly, met in October-November 1692. Although a short-lived affair dominated by a constitutional crisis known as the "sole right" issue, the session set in train a series of events that centered upon the changing financial circumstances in Ireland. The crisis arose over the House of Commons' claim to have the sole right to initiate supply legislation, a claim that occurred as a reaction to the presentation of two supply bills that had been drawn up by the government before parliament met. Owing to the government's desperate need for cash, the Commons formally waived its sole right claim in order to pass one of the supply bills, for a one-year additional inland excise duty on beer, ale and other liquors, but then rejected the other, for a tax on grain and house rents for one year, on the basis that it had not originated in the lower house in accordance with its sole right claim. Less than a week later the parliament was prorogued on foot of a protest from the viceroy over the sole right claim.[25]

Almost lost within the political fallout were two significant precedents established in 1692. First, both the government and parliament accepted the idea of short-term parliamentary additional duties in the passage of the one-year additional inland excise act. The act imposed additional duties on domestic beer, ale, and strong liquors for one year from November 1692. It was estimated that the increased duties would raise £20,000.[26] And second, in the lead up to the sole right claim the Commons had called for the government's accounts and nominated a committee of MPs for their examination. This select committee was the first of the standing committees that developed in the later 1690s and early eighteenth century into a committee of public accounts, which in turn became the fulcrum upon which every Irish parliamentary session balanced and the nexus of the whole process of parliamentary supply. A more permanent and larger version of the English parliament's elected commission of public accounts of the 1690s, it also predated the British committee of public accounts by more than 160 years.[27] Both of these developments were central to the significant evolution in Irish financial practice in the early eighteenth century.

Between 1693 and 1695 a compromise was negotiated over the sole right claim. The central focus of the compromise was parliamentary supply. It was agreed that at least one government supply bill, which was to be a copy of the 1692 additional inland excise act, was to be passed by parliament. At the same time, the Commons were to be allowed to assess the further financial needs of government, to decide the means of raising the required revenue, and to prepare the necessary further supply legislation.[28]

In August 1695 a parliament was convened on the basis of the compromise agreement. The Commons passed the government's one-year supply bill and, having commenced scrutiny of the government's accounts in the embryonic committee of public accounts, prepared legislation for raising the remainder of the supply requested by the government.[29] The supply bills drafted by the Commons and passed by parliament in 1695 comprised two additional duty acts and a poll tax. Of the additional duty acts, one extended the additional duties on beer, ale, and other liquors imposed in the government's one-year excise act for a further two years and two months from October 1696, while the other imposed additional customs and import excise duties on tobacco, linen, muslin, calicoes, drapery, and wine for four years from December 1695.[30] The estimated income from all of the additional duties imposed in 1695 was £83,000. A further £80,000–£100,000 was to be raised by the poll tax.[31]

In the remaining two sessions of parliament in Ireland during William's reign, in 1697 and 1698–99, the supply processes established in 1695 were built upon. In 1697, the Commons spent the first part of the session examining the government's accounts and deciding upon the means of raising the required income.[32] The results of these deliberations were a new poll tax and an additional duties act. The latter piece of legislation further rationalised the developing policy on short-term indirect taxation by amalgamating the three additional duty acts of 1695 into one piece of legislation which extended the duties on beer, ale and other liquors, for four years from December 1698, and those on tobacco, linen, muslin, calicoes, and wine for three years from December 1699. These amalgamations did not involve any change in the tax rates, with the exception of that on tobacco, which was raised from 60 percent to 100 percent of the hereditary duty from November 1697 onward.[33] The anticipated additional income from all of these taxes combined was between £150,000 and £200,000.[34]

By the time parliament reconvened in 1698, a growing crisis in Anglo-Irish relations centered upon the woolen industries in England and Ireland ensured a difficult session. An attempt was made by the Irish parliament to placate English public opinion by passing a government-sponsored supply bill imposing prohibitive duties for three years on Irish woolen manufacture exports, which were considered too competitive for English products. It proved too little too late, and the English parliament imposed a complete and permanent prohibition on such exports in April 1699. Two other supply acts were passed in 1698 and 1699 by the Irish parliament: a further additional duty on tobacco for four and a half years from December 1698, estimated to raise an additional £19,000; and a land tax designed to raise £120,000.[35] At the conclusion of what had been a troubled session, the English and Irish governments decided there was sufficient income to provide a subsistence rate of pay to the army for the coming three years, and parliament was dissolved.[36] If anything, the Irish House of Commons had been too generous: the government actually avoided further recourse to parliament until after the final additional duties expired in June 1703.

In the period 1703 to 1714, the precedents established between 1695 and 1698–99 regarding supply were consolidated through regular practice in two parliaments, the first of which sat for six sessions, and the second for only one. All of these sessions—in the detailed fine-tuning of the process for preparing the supply legislation in the committees of supply, ways and means, and public accounts, in the creation of a regularized pattern for the imposition of short-term additional duties, and in the refining of the legislative supply process in general—represented a continuing evolution in financial practice in Ireland, and one that was an essential precondition for the development of a national debt after 1715.

In 1703–4, in accordance with the compromise of 1695, the first supply act originated with the government and reimposed the basic schedule of additional inland excise duties on beer, ale, and strong liquors that had expired in December 1702, for one year from September 1703.[37] Thereafter, with the Commons' committee of public accounts moving center-stage of the whole supply process, parliament passed a second supply act that extended those inland excise duties for another year and reimposed the additional duties on linen and muslin that had expired in December 1702, and those on tobacco that had expired in June 1703. These duties, along with an increased duty on imported calicoes, were imposed for two years, to November 1705. There was also a new tax of 4*s.* in the pound for two years on specific pensions and grants made out of the Irish revenue, which had been prompted by the investigations into pensions on the Irish Establishment.[38] The estimated income from the two acts was £30,000 and £90,000 respectively.[39]

In 1705 the main elements of the two additional duty acts passed in 1703–4 were combined together in one parliamentary additional duty act for extending all of the duties to September 1707. The only new duty was on "silks and stuffs made or manufactured in Persia, China, or the East Indies," while the tax on pensions was allowed to lapse. The estimated income from the act was £150,000. In 1707, only one additional duty act was required and this extended all of the existing duties to June 1709, providing an estimated income of £135,000. The voting of these duties for only a year and three-quarters created a problem in 1709, in that the act was liable to lapse before parliament had time to renew it. The problem was solved by the first supply act of the session, which secured the payment of all duties from June 1709 until the date of the enactment of the main supply act in 1709, which in turn followed previous policy by extending all of the duties, though only for one year with an estimated income of £75,000. In 1710 it was necessary once again to pass a temporary act for securing the additional duties during the life of the session. There was no mention in the securing act of the duties on linen and calicoes. The reduced schedule of duties was also repeated in the main supply act, while the duration was for one and a half years, to December 1711, with an estimated income of £123,000. The duties on linen and calicoes did not expire however, as they were instead imposed for seven years and appropriated for specific purposes in an act for improvement of the linen manufacture. In 1711 the schedule of additional duties taxed in 1710 was continued once again, although the duration was increased to two years, to December 1713, with an estimated income of £150,000.[40]

The second Irish parliament of Anne's reign, summoned in late 1713, was dominated by a political showdown between the Irish Tory and Whig parties. The only supply act passed in the session was a government bill presented in accordance with the 1695 compromise, which extended the main additional duties on beer, ale and strong liquors, tobacco, muslin, and silks and stuffs, for three months to March 1714. This bill had been drafted by the government in imitation of the Commons' temporary supply acts passed at the beginning of the 1709 and 1710 sessions. However, before the party conflict could be resolved and further taxes voted, the parliament was dissolved automatically on the death of the queen at the beginning of August 1714.[41]

National debt and public credit

By the time of the succession of the elector of Hanover, George I, to the thrones of Great Britain and Ireland in August 1714, the supply process in Ireland had evolved to a point where the basic principles for the post-Revolution financial relationship between parliament and government had been well and truly confirmed. These principles included the presentation by the government of only one short supply bill at the beginning of a newly elected parliament; the drafting of all other necessary supply legislation in the House of Commons; the control of the ways and means of raising supply by the Commons; and the use of short-term indirect taxation for the provision of the majority of the government's increasing income requirements.

It was also the case that by 1714–15 twenty years of regular parliamentary supply had sustained an unprecedented higher level of income for the government, and had thereby created a sense of stability within Irish financial practice. In the coming years that stability would ensure the growth of confidence within Protestant Ireland in the financial security of parliamentary additional duties.

These three developments—parliamentary control of supply, increased income, and public confidence—were essential preconditions for the next stage in the evolution of Irish financial practice in the early eighteenth century, namely the advent of a national debt and the concomitant availability of public credit facilities. A key aspect of the English financial revolution was the creation and maintenance of a national debt. Similarly, the introduction of parliament-sanctioned government borrowing in Ireland in 1716 was a highly significant occurrence.[42] The first loan of that parliament-sanctioned national debt was raised on the basis of an unlimited vote of credit by the Commons, and the promise in the third additional duty act of the 1715–16 session that provision for repayment of an unspecified principal sum would be made in the next session. In the interim, interest of 8 percent per annum was to be paid out of the general income from the additional duties voted in 1715–16, without appropriation of a specific fund. The government borrowed £50,000, the immediate financial necessity for which was the renewed Jacobite threat following the Hanoverian succession.[43]

Already in 1715 Ireland's military contribution to securing the new regime had involved sending four regiments to England and eight to Scotland, an action which had left the army in Ireland under strength and the Protestant community worried about its own security.[44] Thus the 1716 loan was used to raise thirteen new regiments.[45] The significance of these events was not lost on contemporaries. The Irish chief secretary believed that "never [a] parliament did greater things, especially the vote of credit the like to which was never known here before."[46] The commission of lords justices appointed to govern the country at that time concurred: "Their vote of credit is a resolution without precedent here . . . [and] will very much contribute to [his majesty's] service, which could not possibly have been carried on any other way at this time, in a country where we have no Bank nor East India Company to supply the emergencies of the government."[47]

These remarks highlighted the different stage of development of financial structures and practices in Ireland. The innovations developed in England in the 1690s had not been replicated at that time in Ireland for numerous reasons, including the lack of an overriding need, the absence of the requisite economic climate, the lack of public creditors, and the absence of a robust capital market.[48] By 1716, however, the situation had changed. A boom in the Irish economy following the conclusion of the War of the Austrian Succession provided the requisite climate; twenty years of regular parliamentary supply and government solvency provided the confidence for potential public creditors; and an immediate need existed in terms of the threat from the Jacobite rising in Scotland.[49]

There proved little difficulty in raising the £50,000. In fact, it appears that more money was made available from within the Irish Protestant community than was needed and that, as far as can be ascertained, the loan was made in ready specie.[50] A scheme for raising £100,000 had been put to the government at that time on the basis of issuing interest-bearing treasury bills to the loan subscribers in a variety of denominations in order to encourage their circulation alongside ready specie. But there is no evidence that this scheme was used for raising the £50,000.[51] The people who actually subscribed to the loan demonstrated the extent to which a significant number within the Protestant community felt confident enough to invest their capital in government. The largest subscription (£5,000), came from William Conolly, speaker of the House of Commons. At the same time, seventeen more MPs, four past or future MPs, six peers, four women, three bishops, three judges, three clergymen, two aldermen, and twenty unidentified private people were included on the list of sixty-three individual subscribers.[52]

The additional duties act upon which the first loan was secured in 1716 had not made any provision for repayment of the principal loan. And it had only provided in general terms for interest payments for a two-year period to 1717. Thus, from the outset, the national debt was tied in with the established pattern for short-term taxation and biennial parliamentary sessions.[53] In 1717, parliament started to address the question of servicing the debt as it became apparent that the government's income was not sufficient to clear the principal sum. In the second supply act of 1717 provision was made for the public creditors to continue to receive interest payments out of the government's income in general, including the hereditary revenue, until such time as they were repaid their principal amount.[54] In the following years, as it became more apparent that the government was struggling to pay even the interest on the debt, the same provisions for servicing the debt were included in the main two-year duration supply act passed in each session to up 1727–28.[55]

Increasing expenditure, increasing income

The creation of the national debt in 1716 was, in a broader context, part of the endeavors made in Ireland to facilitate the Irish government's increasing annual expenditure during the period 1715 to 1760. This increase was owing to factors such as the maintenance of the standing army, particular security crises, and the growth in public works projects. Annual expenditure had crept beyond £400,000 by 1718 and continued to rise steadily thereafter to more than £600,000 by the late 1750s and early 1760s.[56]

During 1715 to 1760 the government's year-by-year or annual income continued to increase, primarily through the introduction of new rates on existing parliamentary additional duties and the addition of new commodities to the schedule of goods liable for additional duties. In 1715–16, additional inland excise duties on beer, ale, and liquors and import excise duties on tobacco, muslin, silk, wine, and liquors were imposed along with a direct tax on government salaries, profits of employments, fees, and pensions paid to individuals not resident in Ireland. All of these taxes, along with the further additions detailed below, were continued every session thereafter (the direct tax lapsed between 1753 and 1767). In 1717, further import excise duties on liquors and inland excise duties on beer, ale, and liquors were imposed. In 1719, new import excise duties were imposed on molasses, treacle, tea, coffee, chocolate, and cocoa nuts. In 1725–26, 1727–28, and 1729–30 yet more additional import excise duties were imposed on certain liquors, while in the latter year further import excise duties were also placed on silk goods. In 1731–32, the most recent increased duty on imported liquors was allowed to lapse, though new import excise duties were placed on wine, hops, china, earthen, japanned, or lacquered ware, and on vinegar (these duties lapsed between 1753 and 1759). In 1737–38, new import excise duties were imposed on romals, cotton goods, cotton/linen goods, and cambrics. In 1743–44, additional export customs duties were imposed on hides. In 1745–46, the import excise on cambrics and lawns and the import excise on wine, velvet, and silk goods were increased, while in 1751–52 and 1757–8 the import excise on cambrics and lawns was increased even further. In 1759–60 additional import excise duties were imposed on paper.[57]

All of these parliamentary additional duties remained the mainstay of the government's year-by-year income in the period 1715 to 1760. But in times of particular need or crisis, such as with the creation of the national debt in 1716, other financial innovations were, however briefly, flirted with in Ireland. Further loans were to prove a viable option in 1729 and thereafter. But in the 1720s, two other possible alternatives were investigated, before being discarded for primarily political reasons. These were the failed proposal for the establishment of a national bank in Ireland in 1720–21, and the issuing of a patent for coining copper halfpence and farthings for Ireland to the English ironmonger, William Wood, in 1722.

The failed project for a national bank, 1720–21

It was not long after the creation of a national debt in Ireland that the subject arose of a national bank, such as had been established in England in 1694. These two financial innovations were closely connected. There had been proposals in the late seventeenth century for establishing a national bank in Ireland, though none had met with either encouragement or success.[58] It was not until 1720 that the issue was raised in earnest again. The origins of the idea for a national bank are obscure. However, it is certain that the plan had already been formed when John Irwin published in early 1720 a public notice calling for subscriptions for the establishment of a bank and a paper credit in Ireland as a means of addressing a variety of economic and financial problems. According to Irwin, these problems included the fact that the "value of our exports has been very short of answering our extraordinary imports, and the vast sums that are yearly remitted to Great Britain to pay the rents, salaries and pensions due to persons who reside there," both of which drained the gold and silver from Ireland to England. Also, the "expectation of extravagant gain has prevailed on many persons, to send over all the money they had credit for, to purchase Mississippi and South Sea stocks, though at a most extravagant price," which likewise had drained Ireland of the cash "that should keep up the circulation of trade." Irwin's (and presumably his fellow projectors') plan was "to establish a paper credit upon a good foundation, [so] that bank bills shall pass through the whole kingdom as current and free as gold and silver." The plan was that £500,000 "be raised by subscription to be a fund for securing the payment of all such notes" as the "bank" or "company" should issue. Subscriptions were to commence on May 19, 1720.[59]

The assumption that the plan published by Irwin was already the well-developed scheme of a group of projectors was evidenced by the fact that the intended May 1720 subscription was rapidly filled. In quick time directors of the intended bank were elected, a petition in the name of one of the directors, James Hamilton, earl of Abercorn, was sent to George I desiring that he grant letters patent for a royal charter to establish the bank, and letters were dispatched to Irishmen in London to lobby on behalf of the petition.[60] The lobbyists initially felt it would be difficult to get the petition accepted, given the many similar financial projects abounding in London at the time, unless it could be demonstrated that it was intended as a "lasting and real advantage" to Ireland.[61] Presumably seeing the opportunity for financial gain, a counterproposal emerged from another group of Irishmen,[62] and a minor bidding war ensued as Abercorn's group promised assured interest rates of 5 percent and the new group offered to discharge £50,000 of the national debt within five years. This latter offer caused the two lords justices, William Conolly and Alan Brodrick, viscount Midleton, to report in favor of the Abercorn bank scheme. Both men took particular pains to express their concern that the second bank proposal's offer to clear £50,000 of the national debt would contravene "the usual and known methods" of parliament, which was wholly and solely responsible for providing "any money which shall be necessary to be applied to the use of the kingdom."[63] While the Abercorn scheme might in time have become an alternative source of money for the government, the projectors had not been so blatant as to offer to pay off the whole principal sum of the national debt all at once. Whether such an action would have obviated the need for the government to continue to have regular recourse to parliament for financial supplies was a moot point. But it was certainly the case that the offer of £50,000 was considered to be going against accepted practice in relation to public finances and, therefore, was unacceptable to the lords justices and, presumably, to most of the political nation.

The considerations on the bank proposals occurred at the same time as a long-running contest over the legislative and appellate role of the English parliament in relation to Ireland finally came to a conclusion. The last in a series of contests between the two Houses of Lords over which body was the final court of appeal in Irish legal cases culminated in the passage in the Westminster parliament in April 1720 of "An Act for the better Securing the Dependency of the Kingdom of Ireland on the Crown of Great Britain" (or the "Declaratory Act" as it became known).[64]

For the bank project, the most significant impact of the Declaratory Act was in how the discontent in Ireland prompted the English government to consider whether it might be possible to govern without recourse to the Irish parliament. Such considerations were entered into in September 1720, with a proposal for reducing the size and cost of the army in order to bring the annual cost of the Establishment within the produce of the hereditary revenue. It was posited that if such a reduction could be achieved, then the setting up of a national bank in Ireland, or a fire insurance company, might enable the Irish government to function without the need for recourse to parliament for additional duties every two years (the projectors of the insurance company had offered the government £100,000 for a charter, though this was apparently not an unusual practice and the corporation would hope to recoup such money from their future operations). However, the crux of the proposal was for a reduction in expenditure rather than for the use of loans from a bank or company as a means of avoiding recourse to parliament.[65]

The September scheme of the English government never developed beyond the proposal stage because it was considered too much of a political risk.[66] In the interim, the consideration of the bank proposal had continued on into 1721, by which time the second proposal had been withdrawn in order to avoid jeopardising the overall prospects for a bank.[67] As part of the ongoing consideration in England of the petition for a royal charter, on May 28, 1721 the English treasury commissioners reported to the English privy council in favor of setting up a bank in Ireland, stating that "We are sufficiently convinced of the extreme bad circumstances to which that kingdom is at present reduced for want of money or proper credit to circulate there as well to answer the public revenues as also to pay rents, discharge private debts and contracts and to carry on trade and for other their necessary occasions which bad circumstances are amply represented by others and seem to call aloud for an immediate relief."[68]

They recommended that a charter for the bank be granted, but also that "an act of the Irish parliament would be necessary in order to make effective certain important provisions which the treasury believed should be included in the charter." Although the petitioners were unhappy about this latter recommendation, the English ministry were only prepared to issue the charter on such an understanding. The charter was thus issued on July 29, 1721, and referred for consideration to the Irish parliament in September.[69]

The intention was that the Irish parliament would draft a bill for establishing the new bank upon "a solid and good foundation, [and] under proper regulations and restrictions."[70] The drafting of the bill commenced in late September 1721, but by mid-October had run into trouble. On October 14, the first clause of the draft bill was debated and thrown out in a committee of the whole house by 103–95. Following the report from that committee to the house, it was resolved, by a division of 98–91, that further consideration of the draft bill be put off for two months.[71] When the house returned to consideration of the bill two months later, on December 9, it was rejected, while the proposal for a bank in general, and the charter in particular, suffered the final ignominy of a third defeat, by 150–80, on the question put to the house that "after long and mature deliberation, [the Commons] cannot find any safe foundation for establishing a public bank, so as to render it beneficial to Ireland."[72]

There are many possible explanations for the rejection of the bank project. The initial proposals were made in early 1720 in completely different circumstances to those prevalent in late 1721. The first proposal occurred during the height of the mass speculation (including substantial amounts of Irish capital) in the South Sea Company, at a time when public confidence in such schemes knew no bounds. The collapse of the company in late 1720, however, had an extremely detrimental effect upon the Irish economy and public confidence in general. The Irish economy had already been in decline before mid-1720. Trade restrictions due to quarantines to prevent the plague spreading from the continent increased the hardship, as did the impact of bad weather, which caused famine conditions in the winter of 1720–21. These economic pressures, combined with the innate conservatism of the landed country gentlemen in parliament and ongoing conflicts within Irish politics made the task of the critics of the bank a great deal easier and turned the bank project into something of a sacrificial lamb.[73] Although later commentators have seen the rejection of the bank project as an expression of Irish Protestant patriotism in the face of yet "another English scheme to exploit Ireland,"[74] the evidence suggests otherwise. As Michael Ryder, the author of the most comprehensive study of the episode, has demonstrated, it can more readily be explained as the result of a perception that a national bank would be "corrosive of the political society and values of the country gentry" in its own right.[75]

The Wood's halfpence affair, 1722–25

The failure of the bank project meant that the shortage of ready specie remained a problem in Ireland. In the early 1720s most estimates of the total currency in the country were around £400,000. The most significant shortages were in the area of small silver coin, though problems existed for gold and copper as well. The coinage in circulation in Ireland was made up from English silver coins and guineas, and continental gold coin as follows: louis d'ors, pistoles, double pistoles, doubloons, and moidores. There was little or no continental silver, and the English silver that existed was constantly taken out of the country by bankers and merchants because of the favorable exchange they received in England for silver over gold. The crux of the exchange problem lay in the fact that in Ireland the value of all coins had over time been raised above their intrinsic value, with gold and silver ceasing to bear an equal proportion to each other. There was also great opposition in Ireland to any suggestion of reducing the value of coins in order to bring them back in line with England.[76]

The difficulties arising over the shortage of coinage were seen to be compounded by the absence of a permanent mint in Ireland. Since the Restoration, the norm had been for patents to be granted on occasion to favored individuals or groups in Ireland to mint coin within the country. In July 1722, a new patent was granted for coining copper halfpence and farthings. However, it differed from previous patents in that it had originated as a grant to George I's mistress, the duchess of Kendall, who had sold it for £10,000 to an English ironmonger, William Wood, who was to make the coin in England and export it to Ireland. The original patent was for £100,800 worth of copper coin to be minted over fourteen years, although this amount was eventually reduced to £40,000. However, the best estimates at the time and in later decades of the need for new copper coin in Ireland never exceeded more than £10,000.[77]

The news of the patent prompted immediate opposition within the Irish government and among the wider community. The reasons for opposition were varied and numerous. It was argued that Wood would export the profit arising from the coinage out of Ireland; that the real need was for silver and gold coinage; that the intrinsic value of the metal in the coinage was less than the face value of the coins; that it would not be legal tender; that the existing problem of counterfeiting would be further encouraged; that the patent did not allow for sufficient control of the new currency; that the large amount of copper would drive gold and silver out of Ireland; that it would ruin trade and the economy; that the intention was to illegally force the coinage upon the people; that the English privy council was not empowered to order the Irish revenue commissioners or their collectors to accept the copper coin; that the Irish customs and excise acts of

1662 required all revenue to be collected in "lawful money of England," which Wood's coins would not be; that the patent had been obtained through bribery and misinformation; that any such patent should be granted to an Irish person; that Irish economic concerns would always be second to English; and that, in general terms, it was proof once again that Ireland was to be treated as a subordinate, rather than sister, kingdom.[78]

Leading government officials had made it clear to the English administration since mid-1722 that they were opposed to the patent. The biennial convening of the Irish parliament in September 1723 was the first opportunity for the whole Protestant political community to express their discontent in one forum.[79] Both houses of parliament entered into lengthy investigations that resulted in addresses to the king detailing many of the grievances that had emerged against the patent.[80] The English government chose to try to tough it out, though continuing country-wide opposition during 1724 and an ongoing and extensive pamphlet debate would not allow the problem to go away.[81]

By the end of 1724, the chief governor of Ireland, John, Lord Carteret, who had been sent over from England with instructions to solve the problem, had decided that the patent would need to be withdrawn and that Wood would need to be compensated in some other manner.[82] The threat that the discontent over the patent might result in disruption to the supply process in the 1725–26 parliament ensured that leaving the issue unresolved was not an option. With support from two other Englishmen (the recently appointed archbishop of Armagh, Hugh Boulter and the new lord chancellor, Richard West) Carteret eventually won an agreement in August 1725 for the surrender of the patent in return for a pension for Wood on the Irish Establishment for eight years at £3,000 per annum. The formal announcement of the withdrawal of the patent was thus able to be made when the Irish parliament convened in September, bringing the affair to a conclusion.[83]

Servicing the National Debt

Although the problem of the shortage of coin in Ireland remained, the resolution of the Wood's halfpence affair ensured that the continuing parliamentary provision for the servicing of the national debt was not endangered. However, although parliament continued every two years to vote additional duties and to make a general legislative provision for servicing the principal debt of £50,000 and the interest thereon, a combination of parliamentary parsimony and the absence of a specific fund for servicing that debt meant that the government was unable to meet all of its financial commitments. Instead, a significant annual arrear in payments built up on the Establishment. For example, in 1729 this amount stood at £317,170, the vast majority of which was owed to the army.[84]

Renewed fears of war caused the administration in 1725–26 to hope for a new vote of credit in parliament to address this problem.[85] Instead of sanctioning a new loan, however, the Commons requested that £10,000 from the supplies already granted be set aside for payment of 7 percent interest upon those warrants that had already been issued for army pay but which had not been paid and were thus in arrears. The plan was that "bankers and other monied men" would advance cash upon the security of the warrants, for which they would receive interest payments. The warrants would then in turn "have a currency among the people."[86] The scheme proved successful, and the warrants "were immediately cleared by money advanced by several persons." During the next two years, £8,395 was paid in interest on the principal of £59,967. In 1727–28 another £10,000 from the duties voted in parliament was applied toward continuing the interest payments for a further two years.[87]

The first step toward a more comprehensive provision for the government's financial difficulties occurred in 1729. At the end of that year, the Commons legislated for a new loan of £150,000 for transforming part of the pay arrears into a funded national debt. In so doing, the Commons accepted the need to impose new duties and to appropriate them in order to pay the interest. Any surplus from these taxes, after payment of the interest, was to become a sinking fund for discharge of the principal debt. The original loan of £50,000 made in 1716 was also included in these previsions for repayment from the appropriated fund, which thereby brought the total funded national debt, before interest payments, to £200,000.[88]

As in 1716, there was no shortage of people willing to subscribe to the 1729 loan. Given that the new loan was aimed at clearing part of the pay arrears, priority was to be given by the treasury to subscriptions in the form of warrants for army pay, which were to be treated as "ready money" and were to include those warrants upon which interest had been paid since 1726.[89] Thus, by means of an amended version of the interim measure utilized in 1726 and 1727, any individuals who advanced cash to the army for its pay arrears could subscribe the warrants they held for those payments as part of the loan to the government and receive interest thereon. By March 1730, £52,000 had been subscribed in the form of debentures and warrants for army pay arrears. The majority of the eighty-four subscribers were army officers. Also by that time, £90,000 had been subscribed in ready specie by eighty-six individuals.[90] The need to export £40,000 in coin for the pay arrears of the Irish troops stationed in Gibraltar had necessitated the acceptance of ready specie before all of the warrants had been subscribed.[91] The list of subscribers to the loan demonstrates, as in 1716, their confidence in the central apparatus of the state and their understanding of a public credit system.[92]

The 1729 loan act lowered the interest rate for the national debt to 6 percent. The first reduction of the interest rate on the debt had occurred in 1723, when it was reduced in the relevant supply act to 7 percent, which was in keeping with an act of 1722, which had reduced the legal interest for all financial transactions in Ireland from 8 percent to 7 percent. Public creditors who did not wish to receive reduced interest were to be repaid the full amount of their principal on demand and new creditors found for the same amount.[93]

In 1731–32, a new loan of £100,000 was voted, once again for the purpose of transforming part of the pay arrears into a funded debt. The concept of a sinking fund was put on a more practical standing with the enactment of a clause for any surplus from the appropriated duties to be applied toward discharging the principal by means of a lottery. Whenever £5,000 more than was needed for current interest payments had built up in the treasury, the names of creditors would be drawn by lottery to decide which of them were to be repaid their principal. The interest rate for all of the principal sum of the national debt, which with the new loan stood at £300,000, was reduced to 5 percent. As before, existing creditors could receive full repayment of their principal if they did not wish to receive reduced interest.[94] Later in the same session, parliament reduced the maximum interest rate on private financial transactions to 6 percent as "a consequence of the loan bill," and on the understanding that it would "induce people to lend their money to the government at 5 percent, when all other securities, which are certainly more precarious, are reduced to 6 percent."[95] As before, there was little difficulty finding people to subscribe to the new loan.[96]

In December 1733, repayment of the principal debt of £300,000 commenced from the sinking fund. By March 1741, the principal debt had been reduced to £227,000. Throughout all of this time the interest continued to be paid as well.[97] However, at the same time there had been a slow increase in the pay arrears from £182,695 in 1733 to £210,180 in 1741.[98]

The renewed security crisis following the outbreak of war with Spain in 1739 resulted in the voting of loans of £25,000 in 1740 and £125,000 in 1741, while the Jacobite rebellion in Scotland prompted the voting of a loan of £70,000 at the end of 1745.[99] Once again, there proved little difficulty in finding public creditors.[100] The total funded national debt had increased to £352,000 by early 1742, but had fallen to £335,300 by late 1745 (just before the new loan of that year). And by 1745 the arrears on public payments had fallen to £118,879. On all counts, therefore, the state of Irish public finances was fairly healthy.[101]

Repaying the national debt

The main reasons for the alteration in the government's financial affairs in the 1740s was a significant improvement in the economy and some unexpected savings in government spending, which had been facilitated, ironically, by the large number of Irish regiments transferred to the British military Establishment during the 1739–48 war. The peace of 1748 added to the new economic prosperity. The end result was a significant improvement in the income from the public revenue.[102]

The continuing build-up of a substantial surplus in the treasury in the late 1740s led in 1749 to the Commons taking the unprecedented step of passing legislation for the appropriation of £128,500 of the general surplus in the treasury for the purposes of clearing that amount of the funded national debt. The 1749 debt repayment act was the first step along the road to conflict between the executive and legislature over control of expenditure. While the sinking fund legislated for in previous years had always been tied—at least in theory—to a surplus arising from the appropriated additional duties, the 1749 debt repayment act, while continuing to impose appropriated duties for the future servicing of the debt, also appropriated substantial funds in the treasury, the origins of which were less certain.[103] Such action was perceived by the government as impinging upon the Crown's prerogative with regard to the expenditure of money in the treasury, in particular that arising from the hereditary revenues and more generally that arising from parliamentary taxation not explicitly appropriated in legislation.[104]

In the 1749 debt repayment act, the first £70,000 of the debt, which was the only part upon which interest was charged at 5 percent, was to be cleared in full, with the relevant creditors being assured of full repayment by March 1750. The remaining £58,500 was to be used for the repayment of that same amount out of the remaining principal debt on which interest was paid at 4 percent. The creditors to be repaid were to be drawn by way of a lottery, in keeping with previous practice in the legislation for the sinking fund.[105] The continuing buildup of a surplus in the treasury led to the passage in December 1751 of another debt repayment act that appropriated £120,000 from the treasury in order to further reduce the funded national debt.[106] The creditors to be repaid were once again decided by lottery.[107]

The conflict simmering since the passage of the debt repayment act in 1749 came to a boil in late 1753. Although the dispute took place against the background of a power struggle among the leading Irish political managers, the focus of the conflict between the executive and legislature was upon the control of expenditure.[108] In keeping with the previous two sessions in 1749 and 1751, in late 1753 the Commons drafted a bill for appropriating £77,500 from the general surplus in the treasury for repayment of the funded national debt. There was, however, a significant difference to the 1753 bill: it stated that the sum of £77,500 would clear all of the remaining funded debt. Thus, the bill did not include the usual clauses for continuing the appropriated additional duties intended to pay interest on the debt—after December 25, 1753 those duties would lapse.[109]

However, in 1753, for a variety of reasons both political and constitutional, the Commons chose to reject their debt repayment bill after it was returned with an amendment from England (where it had been under consideration by the king and council in accordance with the constitutional relationship between the two countries).[110] The amendment had been inserted in order to assert the right of the Crown to dispose of the surplus in the treasury. Thus, the rejection of the bill by the Commons brought to a head the conflict over who had the right to dispose of that surplus.

The rejection of the bill in theory threatened the repayment of the remainder of the funded national debt. All previous provision for servicing the debt had been tied in with the two-year duration of each relevant supply act. With the defeat of the bill, there was no legal requirement for the government to pay interest or repay principal. However, in March 1754 a king's letter directing that the national debt be reduced was issued, an action which it was felt would help to maintain credit.[111] Indeed, with the belated release of this ready specie from the treasury, the difficulties arising from an economic downturn in the early 1750s and the concomitant decline in credit for normal commercial activity were alleviated to a degree. For the governments in both Ireland and England the king's letter for repayment was also seen as a vindication of the Crown's right to dispose of the treasury surplus.[112] During the later 1750s the debt continued to be repaid, so that by 1759 it had been reduced to £5,200, the lowest figure reached since its inception in 1716.[113]

Conclusion

In retrospect, the 1750s were a unique phase in the history of the Irish-funded national debt, not least because the debt was almost cleared. However, what may be considered to approximate normality was restored by the end of the decade as the government's finances finally started to feel the impact of a serious economic downturn combined with the increased financial pressure of Britain's return to war with France after 1756. In December 1759, the government once again needed a parliament-sanctioned loan, the immediate cause of which was the widespread fear of a Franco-Jacobite invasion. Within two months of the legislation passing in parliament, the Commons felt obliged to pass a vote of credit for £300,000 because of the landing of the French privateer, François Thurot, at Carrickfergus in February 1760.[114] Continuing concerns about defense saw the debt rapidly increase thereafter. In 1761, a new loan of up to £400,000 was legislated for and a further vote of credit for £200,000 agreed to.[115] In the mid-1760s three new loans, all of £100,000, were legislated for. Even with the government choosing not to borrow the full amounts voted, by 1769 the principal sum had reached £655,000. Fourteen years later, in 1783, it had escalated to £1,919,386. The demands of such escalating debts saw new innovations in taxation introduced during the same period.[116]

The 1750s had also served to clarify important aspects of the evolved financial practices in Ireland. The central question in the 1753–54 dispute had been over whether the government or parliament had the right to dispose of the surplus in the treasury. The government argued that the surplus was at the disposal of the Crown because it arose from the hereditary revenue and the nonappropriated parliamentary additional duties, an argument that was based on the view that the hereditary revenues in particular were the property of the Crown. The majority of Irish MPs, however, saw the treasury surplus as a sinking fund for the funded national debt, a view that centered on a belief that all public income, whether it derived from the hereditary revenue, parliamentary taxation, or the loans that made up the national debt that had been secured on the "Public Faith," was part of the "Public Wealth," and therefore at the disposal of the nation as represented by parliament.[117] As such, the dispute was over control of expenditure.

Having laid the foundations in the 1660s, from the 1690s through to the 1710s the focal point of the Irish parliament and the Protestant political nation had been upon gaining control of public income. Having achieved that aim, attention began to shift to control of expenditure, an endeavor made more realistic by the creation and maintenance of a funded national debt. The appropriation of specific taxes for payment of the debt marked the first step in that direction, while the appropriation of surpluses in the treasury in 1749 and 1751 represented a significant acceleration in that process. The 1753–54 dispute served to highlight these changed circumstances, but also demonstrated that there was still a distance to travel in Ireland's journey of financial evolution because the Crown was, in the short-term at least, seen as the victor in the dispute.

The period from the 1660s to the 1750s witnessed the emergence of a newfound confidence and sense of identity within Protestant Ireland. This confidence was expressed in part through the actions of that community's representatives in parliament in implementing innovative financial practices for the benefit of the government, and in part through the wider community's willingness to act as public creditors. For a time, an unprecedented, and unrepeated, period of economic prosperity and increased revenue for the government in the late 1740s made it appear that the Irish community of public creditors would no longer be needed. But, with the decline in the economy in the 1750s followed by the outbreak of the Seven Years' War in

1756, it became only a matter of time before the government would have to call upon that community once again.

NOTES

1. Henry Roseveare, *The Financial Revolution, 1660–1760* (London: Longman, 1991); Henry Roseveare, *The Treasury: The Evolution of a British Institution* (London: Allen Lane, 1969); Henry Roseveare, *The Treasury, 1660–1870: The Foundation of Control* (London: Allen & Unwin, 1973); P. K. O'Brien, "The Political Economy of British Taxation, 1660–1815," *Economic History Review* 41, no. 1 (Feb. 1988): 1–32; P. K. O'Brien and P. A. Hunt, "The Rise of a Fiscal State in England, 1485–1815," *Historical Research* 66, no. 160 (June 1993): 129–76; P. K. O'Brien and P. A. Hunt, "The Emergence and Consolidation of Excises in the English Fiscal System before the Glorious Revolution," *British Tax Review* no. 1 (1997): 35–58.

2. C. I. McGrath, *The Making of the Eighteenth-Century Irish Constitution: Government, Parliament and the Revenue, 1692–1714* (Dublin: Four Courts Press, 2000).

3. John Brewer, *The Sinews of Power: War, Money and the English State, 1688–1783* (London: Unwin Hyman, 1989); P. G. M. Dickson, *The Financial Revolution in England. A Study in the Development of Public Credit, 1688–1756* (London: Macmillan, 1967); Linda Colley, *Britons: Forging the Nation, 1707–1837* (New Haven: Yale University Press, 1992); J. G. A. Pocock, *The Machiavellian Moment: Florentine Political Thought and the Atlantic Republican Tradition* (Princeton: Princeton University Press, 1975), 423–61; J. G. A. Pocock, *Virtue, Commerce, and History: Essays on Political Thought and History, chiefly in the Eighteenth Century* (Cambridge: Cambridge University Press, 1985), 98–102, 108–23; M. J. Braddick, *The Nerves of State: Taxation and the Financing of the English State, 1558–1714* (Manchester: Manchester University Press, 1996); Roseveare, *Financial Revolution*; David Stasavage, *Public Credit and the Birth of the Democratic State: France and Great Britain, 1688–1789* (Cambridge: Cambridge University Press, 2003).

4. Roseveare, *Financial Revolution*, 6–7.

5. John McCavitt, *Sir Arthur Chichester: Lord Deputy of Ireland, 1605–16* (Belfast: Institute of Irish Studies, 1998), 37–41.

6. T. J. Kiernan, *A History of the Financial Administration of Ireland to 1817* (London: P. S. King, 1930), 62, 79.

7. Seán Egan, "Finance and the Government of Ireland, 1660–85," 2 vols. (unpub. diss, University of Dublin, 1983), 2:196–224. For the convention parliament see Aidan Clarke, *Prelude to Restoration in Ireland: The End of the Commonwealth, 1659–1660* (Cambridge: Cambridge University Press, 1999), 144–5, 158, 268, 285–87, 301.

8. Egan, "Finance and Government," 2:196–224; McGrath, *Irish Constitution*, 291.

9. Kiernan, *Financial Administration*, 76–80; Egan, "Finance and Government," 1:25.

10. Kiernan, *Financial Administration*, 80–86; Seán Réamonn, *History of the Revenue Commissioners* (Dublin: Institute of Public Administration, 1981), 3.

11. A. J. Donnelly, "The Administration of Customs and Excise in Ireland," 1–2, typescript lecture delivered to the Civics Institute of Ireland, Nov. 1950, National

Library of Ireland [hereafter N.L.I.]; Réamonn, *Revenue Commissioners,* 3–4, 6–8; Kiernan, *Financial Administration,* 76, 79–80; William Edgar, *A Collection of Several Statutes and Clauses of Acts Made and Passed in This Kingdom, and in Great Britain, Relating to His Majesty's Revenue of Ireland* (Dublin, 1720), 280–82; James Fleming, *A Collection of all the Irish and English Statutes now in Force and Use, Relating to His Majesty's Revenue in Ireland* (Dublin, 1749), 1–2; Victor Treadwell, "The Irish Customs Administration in the Sixteenth Century," *Irish Historical Studies* [hereafter *I.H.S.*] 20, no. 80 (Sept. 1977): 384–417.

12. *The Statutes at Large Passed in the Parliaments Held in Ireland,* 20 vols. (Dublin, 1763–1801 [hereafter *Stat. Ire.*]), 2:419–96.

13. T. C. Barnard, *Cromwellian Ireland: English Government and Reform in Ireland, 1649–1660* (Oxford: Oxford University Press, 1975), 28–30; Braddick, *Nerves of State,* 99; Donnelly, "Customs and Excise," 10–11; O'Brien and Hunt, "Emergence and Consolidation," 43–51.

14. *Stat. Ire.,* 2:365–418.

15. Kiernan, *Financial Administration,* 76–86; Egan, "Finance and Government," 1:25; 2:5–7, 222–24; C. I. McGrath, "The Irish Revenue System: Government and Administration, 1689–1702" (unpub. diss., University of London, 1997), 63, 314; A. E. Murray, *A History of the Commercial and Financial Relations between England and Ireland from the Period of the Restoration* (London: P. S. King, 1903), 160–61.

16. Barnard, *Cromwellian Ireland,* 258–59; J. C. Beckett, *The Making of Modern Ireland, 1603–1923* (London: Faber, 1969), 104–5; Réamonn, *Revenue Commissioners,* 8–9. *Stat. Ire.,* 2:365–493.

17. Réamonn, *Revenue Commissioners,* xi–ii, 10, 14–20; *Stat. Ire.,* 2:378–85, 425, 429, 489–92.

18. Egan, "Finance and Government" McGrath, "Irish Revenue System," 141–218.

19. McGrath, 'Irish Revenue System," 9–27, 63–88, 314–17; McGrath, *Irish Constitution,* 49–72, 291–95.

20. Alan J. Guy, "The Irish Military Establishment, 1660–1776," in *A Military History of Ireland,* eds. Thomas Bartlett and Keith Jeffrey (Cambridge: Cambridge University Press, 1996), 211–16; Henry Horwitz, *Parliament, Policy and Politics in the Reign of William III* (Manchester: Manchester University Press, 1977), 222–70.

21. *Cal. S.P. Dom. 1697,* 462, 528, 593; *Cal. S.P. Dom. 1698,* v–vi, 23, 29, 33–34, 57–58, 427–28, 430–31, 437–40; *Cal. S.P. Dom. 1699–1700,* viii–x, 5, 11, 43–44, 65, 68; *Cal. S.P. Dom. 1703–4,* 172–73; *Cal. Treas. Bks. 1681–85,* 738, 1002–12; *Cal. Treas. Bks. 1685–89,* 1742–47; *Cal. Treas. Bks. 1698,* 139–43; *Cal. Treas. Bks. 1699–1700,* 141–57, 364–67; *Cal. Treas. Bks. 1700–1701,* 338–39, 433–46; *Cal. Treas. Bks. 1703,* 123–25; *Cal. Treas. Bks. 1709,* 114–23; McGrath, *Irish Constitution,* 66–67, 293–95; Patrick McNally, *Parties, Patriots and Undertakers: Parliamentary Politics in Early Hanoverian Ireland* (Dublin: Four Courts Press, 1997), 40–41.

22. McGrath, "Irish Revenue System," 63–88, 233–40, 314–17, 325–27; McGrath, *Irish Constitution,* 49–72, 291–95.

23. J. E. Aydelotte, "The Duke of Ormond and the English Government of Ireland, 1677–85" (unpub. diss., University of Iowa, 1975), 30–34, 78, 108; Egan, "Finance and Government"; C. I. McGrath, "Securing the Protestant Interest: The Origins and Purpose of the Penal Laws of 1695," *I.H.S.* 30, no. 117 (May 1996): 26–28.

24. C. I. McGrath, "Parliamentary Additional Supply: The Development and Use of Regular Short-Term Taxation in the Irish Parliament, 1692–1716," *Parliamentary History* 20, no. 1 (2001): 27–54; C. I. McGrath, "Central Aspects of the Eighteenth-Century Constitutional Framework in Ireland: The Government Supply Bill and Biennial Parliamentary Sessions, 1715–82," *Eighteenth-Century Ireland* 16 (2001): 9–34.

25. *The Journals of the House of Commons of the Kingdom of Ireland,* 11 vols. (1st edition, Dublin, 1753–63 [hereafter *C.J.I.* (1st)]), 2:614–15; J. I. McGuire, "The Irish Parliament of 1692," in *Penal Era and Golden Age. Essays in Irish History, 1690–1800,* eds. Thomas Bartlett and D. W. Hayton (Belfast: Ulster Historical Foundation, 1979), 1–31; McGrath, *Irish Constitution,* 73–90.

26. *Stat. Ire.*, 3:245–46; McGrath, "Irish Revenue System," 45.

27. McGrath, *Irish Constitution,* 73–290; Philip O'Regan, "Accountability and Financial Control as 'Patriotic' Strategies: Accomptants and the Public Accounts Committee in late Seventeenth- and early Eighteenth-Century Ireland," *Accounting Historians Journal* 30, no. 2 (Dec. 2003): 105–31; Kiernan, *Financial Administration,* 121–22.

28. C. I. McGrath, "English Ministers, Irish Politicians and the Making of a Parliamentary Settlement in Ireland, 1692–95," *English Historical Review* 119, no. 482 (June 2004): 584–613.

29. McGrath, *Irish Constitution,* 90–117.

30. *Stat. Ire.*, 2:365–493; 3:312–13, 328; McGrath, *Irish Constitution,* 38–39, 42–43; McGrath, "Parliamentary Additional Supply," 35–36.

31. *Stat. Ire.*, 3:289–95; McGrath, *Irish Constitution,* 38–39, 41.

32. *C.J.I.* (1st), 2:840, 842, 844–45, 847–49, 851, 853, 860.

33. *Stat. Ire.*, 3:353–58, 374–96.

34. McGrath, *Irish Constitution,* 40, 43.

35. *Stat. Ire.*, 3:451–73; McGrath, *Irish Constitution,* 41, 43.

36. H.M.C., *Buccleuch MSS,* 2:599–601, 620–21; *C.J.I.* (1st), 2:1123.

37. *Stat. Ire.*, 4:1–2; *C.J.I.* (1st), 3:30.

38. *Stat. Ire.*, 4:7–10; *C.J.I.* (1st), 3:60–64; D. W. Hayton, "A Debate in the Irish House of Commons in 1703: A Whiff of Tory Grapeshot," *Parliamentary History* 10, no. 1 (1991): 156–59.

39. McGrath, *Irish Constitution,* 44–45.

40. *Stat. Ire.*, 4:69–70, 109–12, 187–90, 251–57, 291–93.

41. *C.J.I.* (1st), 3:963, 1001, 1019.

42. McGrath, "Constitutional Framework," 9–34.

43. *The Journals of the House of Commons of the Kingdom of Ireland,* 20 vols. (3rd edition, Dublin, 1796–1800 [hereafter *C.J.I.* (3rd)]), 3:60, 73–76, 80, 86, 92–93, 98, 112; appendix, xxxviii; *Stat. Ire.*, 4:325–7; Kiernan, *Financial Administration,* 145–46; McGrath, *Irish Constitution,* 286–87.

44. SP 63/373/88, 112, 144, 150, 193, 242–43, SP 63/374/26–7, 42–43, Nat. Arch.; *C.J.I.* (3rd), 3:9–10, 73–75, 92; appendix, lxxvi.

45. Duke of Grafton and earl of Galway to James Stanhope, Jan. 30, 1716, SP 63/374/63–65, Nat. Arch.

46. Charles Delafaye to [Robert Pringle], Jan. 30, 1716, SP 63/374/59–60, Nat. Arch.

47. Duke of Grafton and earl of Galway to James Stanhope, Jan. 30, 1716, SP 63/374/63–65, Nat. Arch.

48. McGrath, "Irish Revenue System," 1–7.

49. L. M. Cullen, *An Economic History of Ireland Since 1660* (2nd edition, London: Batsford, 1987), 43–44; McGrath, *Irish Constitution*, 50, 54–55, 64, 70–72.

50. Charles King to ——,Feb. 15, 1716, SP 63/374/101–2, Nat. Arch.

51. A scheme by Charles King, Feb. 4, 1716, SP 63/374/70–71, Nat. Arch.

52. *C.J.I.* (3rd), 3: appendix, cxiii–cxiv.

53. *Stat. Ire.*, 4:325–27; *C.J.I.* (3rd), 3:92.

54. *Stat. Ire.*, 4:433–38.

55. *Stat. Ire.*, 4:504–8; 5:1–5, 75–81, 137–42, 201–6.

56. *House of Commons' Parliamentary Papers, 1801–1900: Public Income and Expenditure, Session 1868–69*, xxxv, 366 pt. i, 255–321, 434–39; Eoin Magennis, "Coal, Corn and Canals: The Dispersal of Public Moneys, 1695–1772," *Parliamentary History* 20, no. 1 (2001): 71–86; Eoin Magennis, *The Irish Political System 1740–1765: The Golden Age of the Undertakers* (Dublin: Four Courts Press, 2000), 40–61; Guy, "Irish Military Establishment," 211–30.

57. *Parliamentary Papers*, xxxv, 366 pt. i, 434–39. The additional duties in 1714 were valued at about £85,000 per annum, though by 1778 they had risen to about £240,000 per annum. See The Charge of the Establishment of Ireland for one year compared with the present Revenue, 1714, ff 110–12, MS 2022, Trinity College, Dublin; *C.J.I.* (3rd), 10: appendix, xii–xiii, xix; *Stat. Ire.*, vols. 4–7; McGrath, "Constitutional Framework," 11–19. For a list of the biennial parliamentary sessions see D. W. Hayton, "Introduction: The Long Apprenticeship," *Parliamentary History* 20, no. 1 (2001): 23–25.

58. Richard Lawrence, *The Interest of Ireland in its Trade and Wealth Stated. In Two Parts* (Dublin, 1682), 2:3–5, 10; Hugh Chamberlen, *Papers, Relating to a Bank of Credit, upon Land-Security; Proposed to the Parliament of Scotland* (Edinburgh, 1693); Hugh Chamberlen, *A Proposal and Considerations Relating to an Office of Credit upon Land Security: Proposed to their Excellencies the Lords Justices: and to the Lords of the Privy Council; and the Parliament of Ireland* (London, 1697); F. G. Hall, *The Bank of Ireland, 1783–1946* (Dublin: Hodges Figgis & Co., 1949), 15.

59. *To the Nobility, Gentry and Commonalty of this Kingdom of Ireland* [Dublin, 1720]. The only known extant copy of this pamphlet is in the N.L.I. manuscript collection (59–61, MS 2256). See Michael Ryder, "The Bank of Ireland, 1721: Land, Credit and Dependency," *Historical Journal* 25, no. 3 (Sept. 1982): 560.

60. Lord Abercorn, Viscount Boyne, Sir Ralph Gore, Oliver St George, St John Brodrick, Francis Barnard, Thomas Coote, Michael Ward, Henry Sandford, James Macarthy, and John Irwin to Lord Percival, 2 June 1720, 8–9, MS 2256, N.L.I.; Ryder, "Bank of Ireland," 559–61.

61. Lord Percival, Sir Gustavus Hume, Sir James Stanley, Edward Southwell, Joshua Allen, and William Maynard to [Abercorn], June 18, 1720, ff 17–18, MS 2256, N.L.I.; Ryder, "Bank of Ireland," 561.

62. Petition of George, Lord Forbes, and Brabazon Ponsonby, [undated]; Grafton to Abercorn, 6 Aug. 1720, 11, 21–22, MS 2256, N.L.I.

63. *C.J.I.* (3rd), 3: appendix, cci; Ryder, "Bank of Ireland," 560.

64. Edmund Curtis and R. B. McDowell, eds., *Irish Historical Documents, 1172–1922* (London: Methuen & Co., 1943), 186. For discussion of the origins of the

Declaratory Act see Isolde Victory, "The Making of the 1720 Declaratory Act," in *Parliament, Politics and People: Essays in Eighteenth-Century Irish History*, ed. Gerard O'Brien (Dublin: Irish Academic Press, 1989), 9–29; D. W. Hayton, "The Stanhope/Sunderland Ministry and the Repudiation of Irish Parliamentary Independence," *English Historical Review* 113, no. 452 (June 1998): 610–36.

65. Memorial relating to schemes proposed for making such savings upon the military part of the Establishment of Ireland, as may bring the charges of the government there within the produce of the hereditary revenue, Sept. 1720, SP 63/379/61–64, 66–70, Nat. Arch.; D. W. Hayton, *Ruling Ireland, 1685–1742: Politics, Politicians and Parties* (Woodbridge: Boydell and Brewer, 2004), 230–31; Hayton, "Stanhope/Sunderland Ministry," 620.

66. Hayton, "Stanhope/Sunderland Ministry," 630–31; Sabine Baltes, *The Pamphlet Controversy about Wood's Halfpence (1722–25) and the Tradition of Irish Constitutional Nationalism* (Frankfurt: Peter Lang, 2003), 97–98.

67. British privy council minutes, Whitehall, July 12, 26, 1720, May 7, 28, 1721, PC 2/86/222, 228, PC 2/87/197, 211–14, Nat. Arch.; Ryder, "Bank of Ireland," 563.

68. British privy council minutes, Whitehall, May 28, 1721, PC 2/87/212, Nat. Arch.

69. Ryder, "Bank of Ireland," 563–64.

70. *C.J.I.* (3rd), 3:257–58.

71. *C.J.I.* (3rd), 3:267–68; Joseph Griffin, "Parliamentary Politics in Ireland during the reign of George I" (MA thesis, University College Dublin, 1977), 102, 190–93; Ryder, "Bank of Ireland," 565.

72. *C.J.I.* (3rd), 3:289.

73. Roseveare, *Financial Revolution*, 54–58; Ryder, "Bank of Ireland," 557–82; Griffin, "Parliamentary Politics," 100–12; Joseph Johnston, "Berkeley and the abortive bank project of 1720–21," in *Bishop Berkeley's* 'Querist' *in Historical Perspective*, ed. Joseph Johnston (Dundalk: Dundalgan Press, 1970), 44–51; Hall, *Bank of Ireland*, 15–29; James Kelly, "Harvests and Hardship: Famine and Scarcity in Ireland in the Late 1720s," *Studia Hibernica* 26 (1992): 66–69; Cullen, *Economic History*, 44–46.

74. F. G. James, *Ireland in the Empire, 1688–1770* (Cambridge, MA.: Harvard University Press, 1973), 112.

75. Ryder, "Bank of Ireland," 559, 569–82.

76. D. W. Hayton, ed., *The Letters of Marmaduke Coghill, 1722–1738* (Dublin: Irish Manuscripts Commission, 2005), 18–19.

77. Albert Goodwin, "Wood's Halfpence," *English Historical Review* 51, no. 204 (Oct. 1936): 647–55; Baltes, *Pamphlet Controversy*, 105–9.

78. Revenue commissioners to Edward Hopkins, Aug. 7, 1722; same to treasury lords, Sept. 19, 1722, SP 63/380/110, Nat. Arch.; Marmaduke Coghill to Edward Southwell, Jan. 31, 1723, f. 7, Add. MS 21122, B.L.; Patrick McNally, "Wood's Halfpence, Carteret, and the Government of Ireland, 1723–26," *I.H.S.* 30, no. 119 (May 1997): 355–56; Goodwin, "Wood's Halfpence," 647–63; Baltes, *Pamphlet Controversy*, 109–17, 159, 171–73.

79. Duke of Grafton to [Sir Robert Walpole], Aug. 22, Sept. 14, 1723, SP 63/381/3–4, 7–10, 120–24, Nat. Arch.

80. *C.J.I.* (3rd), 3:317–20, 322–25; SP 63/381/145–46, 147, 149, 165–66, 168, 172, 178–79, 180–83, 184–85, Nat. Arch.

81. For county and other addresses in 1724, see SP 63/383/208–9, 227–28, SP 63/384/18, 66, 136–39, 189–91, Nat. Arch. For the pamphlet debate, see Baltes, *Pamphlet Controversy*, 113–265.

82. Carteret to the duke of Newcastle, Dec. 16, 1724, SP 63/384/226–28, Nat. Arch.

83. McNally, "Wood's Halfpence', 362–68.

84. *CJI* (3rd) 3: appendix, ccclxii, ccclxxvii.

85. West to Newcastle, Jan. 27, 1726; Carteret to same, Jan. 28, 1726, SP 63/387/13–14, 17–19, Nat. Arch.; *C.J.I.* (3rd), 3:442–43.

86. Isaac Manley to ——,Feb. 25, 1726; Boulter to Newcastle, March 22, 1726, SP 63/387/73, 114–16, Nat. Arch.

87. Carteret to Newcastle, Dec. 23, 1727, Jan. 11, 1728, SP 63/389/123–24, SP 63/390/1, Nat. Arch.; *C.J.I.* (3rd), 3:490–91, 495.

88. *Stat. Ire.*, 5:337–40.

89. Ibid.

90. *C.J.I.* (3rd), 3: appendix, cccxcvi–cccxcviii.

91. Coghill to Southwell, April 18, 1730, 1–4, Add. MS 21123, B.L.

92. For a detailed assessment of the extent to which a community of people existed in Ireland in the first half of the eighteenth century who were prepared to act as public creditors, see C. I. McGrath, "'The Public Wealth is the Sinew, the Life, of every Public Measure': The Creation and Maintenance of a National Debt in Ireland, 1716–45," in *The Empire of Credit: The Financial Revolution in the British Atlantic World, 1700–1800*, eds. Daniel Carey and Christopher Finlay (Dublin: Irish Academic Press, 2008).

93. *Stat. Ire.*, 5:63–65, 75–81.

94. Ibid., 5:487–92.

95. Walter Cary to Charles Delafaye, Dec. 10, 1731, SP 63/394/141–42, Nat. Arch.; *Stat. Ire.*, 5:508–10.

96. Robert Clayton, bishop of Killala, to Mrs. Charlotte Clayton, Jan. 2, 1732, 158–60, Add. MS 20102, B.L.

97. *C.J.I.* (3rd), 4: appendix, li–liii, lxxiii, cv–cvi, cxxxix–cxl; *Stat. Ire.*, 5:487–92; 6:5–9, 175–80, 393–98, 483–89.

98. *C.J.I.* (3rd), 4: appendix, xxii, xliii, li–lii, lx–lxi, lxxiii, lxxxi, cv–cvi, cxv, cxxxix–cxl, cl.

99. For the 1740 loan, which was raised on the basis of a vote of credit only without any legislation being passed thereafter, see SP 63/403/39–40, 45, 49, 53–57, 61–62, Nat. Arch.; *C.J.I.* (3rd), 4:341–46; appendix, clviii. For the 1741 and 1745 loans, see *Stat. Ire.*, 6:605–12, 702–10.

100. The names of the public creditors from 1745 to 1759 were recorded in a series of ledgers kept by the teller of the exchequer, Nathaniel Clements (MSS 7259–66, Trinity College, Dublin). For Clements, see A. P. W. Malcomson, *Nathaniel Clements: Government and the Governing Elite in Ireland, 1725–75* (Dublin: Four Courts Press, 2005).

101. *C.J.I.* (3rd), 4: appendix, li–liii, lxxiii, cv–cvi, cxxxix–cxl, clvii–clviii, clx, clxx, ccxlviii–ccxlix, cclix.

102. *C.J.I.* (3rd), 4: appendix, clxvi, ccliv–cclvii, cclix, cclxxxii–cclxxxvii; *Stat. Ire.*, 7:6–15, 104–11; Cullen, *Economic History*, 50–99; David Dickson, *New Foundations: Ireland, 1660–1800* (Dublin: Helicon, 1987), 102–3.

103. *Stat. Ire.*, 7:6–15.

104. See Declan O'Donovan, "The Money Bill Dispute of 1753," in *Penal Era and Golden Age*, eds. Bartlett and Hayton, 55–87; Magennis, *Political System*, 62–83.

105. *Stat. Ire.*, 7:6–15. On the basis of figures given in the 1749 act, the total principal of the funded national debt stood at £378,500. However, on the basis of the more exact figures given in the parliamentary journals, the figure was £393,600, of which £85,100 (rather than the stated £70,000) paid 5 percent interest. See *C.J.I.* (3rd), 5: appendix, vi–vii.

106. *Stat. Ire.*, 7:104–11. In the 1751 act, the total for the principal funded debt is given as £237,500. However, as in 1749, a more exact figure of £248,700 can be derived from *C.J.I.* (3rd), 5: appendix, ccl–ccli.

107. See printed lists of loan debentures, 1752, ff 39, 44, MS 7264, Trinity College, Dublin.

108. PC 2/102/363–64, 378–79, 383–85, PC 2/103/515–16, 518–19, 525, 546, SP 63/411/49–55, 214–16, SP 63/412/204, 206–7, SP 63/413/25–26, 103–4, Nat. Arch.; 50–52, 85–86, 100–1, 109–10, 169–71, 173–74, 198–99, 200–1, 215–20, Add. MS 35592, B.L.; O'Donovan, "Money Bill," 55–87.

109. *C.J.I.* (3rd), 5:187–88, 190; duke of Dorset to earl of Holdernesse, Nov. 17, 1753, SP 63/413/73, Nat. Arch. In fact, the principal of the funded national debt stood at £98,000 at the time of the drafting of the bill. See *C.J.I.* (3rd), 5: appendix, cclxx–cclxxi.

110. Lords of the committee of council on Irish bills, Whitehall, Nov. 27, 1753, PC 2/103/515–16, Nat. Arch.

111. Edward Weston to Sir Robert Wilmot, March 26, 1754, T3019/2295, Wilmot papers, Public Record Office of Northern Ireland.

112. O'Donovan, "Money Bill," 69, 74–79.

113. Loan repayments, 1754–59, 49, 55–7, MS 7265, 28, 30, 32, MS 7266, Trinity College, Dublin; *C.J.I.* (3rd), 6: appendix, clxxii–clxxiii.

114. *Stat. Ire.*, 7:619–22; *C.J.I.* (3rd), 7:13; Magennis, *Political System*, 133–43; James, *Ireland in the Empire*, 259–61; O'Donovan, "Money Bill," 69, 74–79.

115. *Stat. Ire.*, 7:809–20; *C.J.I.* (3rd), 7:95, 97–98, 108–10, 117–18, 147–49, 151–52.

116. *Stat. Ire.*, 9:7–17, 272–85, 489–503; 10:6–22, 71–87, 342–56, 647–62; 11:13–29, 311–33, 353–72, 407–22; 12:19–50; R. V. Clarendon, *A Sketch of the Revenue and Finances of Ireland and of the Appropriated Funds, Loans and Debt of the Nation from their commencement* (Dublin, 1791), appendix, xvi.

117. *Reasons for Regulating the Coin, and Reducing the Interest; With a Scheme for Paying Part of the National Debt Without Burthening Ireland* ([Dublin], 1731), 21; *Reflections on the National Debt; With Reasons for the Reducing the Legal Interest; And Against a Public Loan. With Some Advice to the Electors of Members of Parliament* ([Dublin], 1731), 12. *Common Sense: In a Letter to a Friend. To which is prefixed an Explanatory Preface. By the Author of Ireland in Tears* (London, 1755), 48.

Whither the Irish Financial Revolution?: Money, Banks and Politics in Ireland in the 1730s

Eoin Magennis

THIS ESSAY TELLS THE TALE OF IRELAND IN THE 1730S AND HOW THE dull and complex subjects of money and banking occasionally lit up economic and political debate in the period. It is the story of the beginnings of what was to become a transformation in Irish economic fortunes and, at the same time, of continuity in largely wary public attitudes about economic change. It is fair to say that the 1730s are largely unknown even to most Irish historians. This is hardly surprising as it is an unremarkable decade when compared to either "Swift's Ireland" of the earlier period or to that associated with the imperial crisis of the 1770s onward. Also, the tale of economic change is largely ignored outside the pages of economic histories. Briefly stated, the 1730s was a decade of stuttering economic growth and repeated attempts to reform the currency of Ireland. The economic growth began in the middle of the 1730s and may be seen as a striking period of expansion when looked at in the long run. At the time, however, the growth was punctuated by crises and seemed much more conditional. In retrospect, as a consequence of the economic expansion the difficulties with currency appeared settled after the 1730s, while banking and credit appear to have been expanding in a secure manner. Again, at the time this hardly seemed possible: the largest bank in Ireland had closed and the coinage appeared to be as flawed as ever.

As for contemporary writings about economic development, or its absence, in Ireland, there was certainly an outpouring of such material. One pamphleteer in 1735 wrote scathingly about this phenomenon: "Pamphlets upon pamphlets must be wrote to explain the causes and effects of things; the money'd interest against the landed, the landed interest ever jealous of the money'd; the whole world must know all our reasons for every act of prudence or of state."[1] Patrick Kelly has estimated that there were more than 200 broadsheets, pamphlets, and books published on this subject between 1720 and 1750; 108 of these centered on the issues of currency, money, and banking.[2] A graph would show peaks of activity around the national bank scheme (1720–21), Wood's halfpence (1722–25) and the lowering of the value of gold coins (1737). These three episodes perhaps account for three-quarters or more of the 108 pamphlets. Reading through these publications you get a sense of recycled arguments and the impression that political rather than economic points dominate at the peak times. You also get an idea of the key economic arguments which centered on the finer technical points about weights of coins and their quality, or which looked into the role of money and credit in the wider system of trade. There was little, apart from George Berkeley's *The Querist*,[3] that was truly innovative, with most writers apparently influenced by the late seventeenth-century Irish and English economists such as John Locke, William Petty, and Charles Davenant. However, as we shall see, Berkeley's work did not come from nowhere, and, amid suggestions that it was time to tackle the thorny banking problem, it fits into a growing challenge to Locke's views on money.

Money: I

Money, or the absence of it, was a problem that occupied the thoughts of most of the Irish economic writers and a section of its[4] political elite for much of the first half of the eighteenth century. The pamphlets centered on the deficiencies of Ireland's coinage and on recurrent concerns about paper money. In the first place, Ireland had no indigenous coinage as it lacked a national mint, something that placed the country in an unusual position. Lacking a mint made Ireland a wretched kingdom and denied it a right allowed "every petty prince in Germany" as Jonathan Swift put it.[5]

With no coinage of its own, Ireland relied for its specie upon English gold and silver coins alongside a variety of French, Portuguese, and other European coins. The values of the various coins were fixed by government proclamations. According to the best authority on the Irish currency, the proclamation of 1695 depreciated the Irish monetary unit by setting the highest ever values for foreign and English gold coins.[6] The guinea was set at 26*s.* Irish and the pistole at £1 1*s.* The silver coins, including the English crown and shilling and French Lewis, were all undervalued. A further proclamation in 1701 revalued all these coins and reduced their values, which did not redress the problem of the silver coins. Another proclamation in 1712 dealt specifically with the new Portuguese moidore, a product of Brazilian gold. It was valued at £1 10*s.* Irish, which overvalued it according to its bullion value and this favored its circulation in Ireland. This overvaluing of the gold coinage was made even worse when there was no reduction in Ireland following the 1717 British lowering of gold coins.

Thus, by the 1720s Ireland had overvalued gold coins and undervalued silver coins. This led to recurrent outflow of silver specie anytime there was a trade imbalance, an almost constant problem for most of the 1720s and some of the 1730s given Ireland's economic problems and regular harvest failures. The consequence was regular and severe shortages of circulating coins. The supply of copper coins was also problematic as it depended on private patentees and there appears to have been either a glut of coins or else a shortage when the copper coins were taken to the American colonies to get a higher value for them there. The copper coins consisted of a mix of counterfeit or clipped coins and those known as "raps," which had an assumed value below their real one.

The circulation of money remained a difficult problem and one that attracted efforts at reform on several occasions in the 1720s and 1730s. The most infamous attempt at reform was the patent issued in 1722 to increase the amount of copper coins through the production of halfpence and farthings. The events surrounding the expansion of the supply of halfpence and the succeeding debate tell us more about Ireland's dependent relationship with England than about the country's coinage. There is some doubt whether an expansion would have benefited domestic trade and lowered cost transactions in Ireland as it might have driven out the already scarce silver coins. However, the outrage was initially targeted at the fact that the patent was granted first to a mistress of George I and then sold for £10,000 to a Wolverhampton ironmonger, William Wood. The direction of the outrage was subsequently changed by the rumors that Wood was allowed to mint 360 tons of copper into £100,800 in halfpence and farthings. The fear was that this would swamp the Irish economy rather than assist it. This explains the opposition of the revenue commissioners in Ireland and the talk in pamphlets that £200,000 in gold and silver coins would be swept away for this "brass money" (with all the connotations of the Irish experience under James II).[7] The coins were soon named "Wood's Halfpence" and the opposition threatened to make parliament unmanageable and cost one lord lieutenant his office. Not surprisingly, the patent was effectively abandoned by 1725.[8]

The defeat of Wood's halfpence did not, of course, solve the problems with the coinage. As well as periodically lacking small change, Ireland suffered from the undervaluing of silver coins, which meant that private bankers and merchants could make a profit by buying up silver coins in Ireland and exchanging these in England. The most obvious solution was to revalue the silver and / or gold coins but this was fiercely resisted. In 1728, Archbishop Hugh Boulter of Armagh, the key lord justice, recommended that the ratio of gold to silver in Ireland should be brought into line with that in England.[9] This was not a new proposal and had, according to one pamphleteer, been circulating since 1725. At the height of the Wood's halfpence crisis there was little chance it would have been pursued but, with a new king and the political crisis over, such an idea must have seemed possible. Indeed, the same pamphlet alleged that in 1728 there was initially no opposition to the scheme.[10]

Whatever the truth of this claim, the proposal soon ran into trouble in 1729 as Boulter shaped it to bring before the Irish parliament. There was some discussion of the gold reduction scheme at the Irish privy council and witnesses for and against were called to give their evidence. And there the matter was dropped. Boulter had a long list of people he blamed for this setback, including private bankers, patriot politicians, and the speaker of the Irish House of Commons, William Conolly. The scheme, argued Boulter, would deny the private bankers and their political supporters the profit they made on the exchange of money, especially the export of silver coins to England.[11] His supporters focused on the quietness of the private bankers before 1729 and then their mobilization to prevent the proposal being fully debated in the Irish parliament. There was also understandable insistence that the scheme was "first thought of and desired" in Ireland, in order to defend it against any accusations of being a second Wood's halfpence.[12]

One man who was named and blamed by Boulter was the "broken merchant" from Limerick, David Bindon. He was not yet an MP in 1729 although he came from a family of loyal parliamentarians and was certainly an unlikely opponent of government.[13] He was a merchant who had been "broken" by debt in 1725, but by the late 1720s he was studying the law. At the same time he was pursuing his main interest, writing about the economic improvement of Ireland. Over the next thirty years he wrote possibly eight pamphlets and translated a key French economic text by Jean Francois Melon.[14] At the time of the coinage proposal, Bindon appeared in front of the Irish privy council with Dublin merchants to petition against the change.[15] Boulter accused him of being in thrall to the banking interest; however, Bindon's *An Essay on the Gold and Silver Coin Current in Ireland* argued for an adoption of the proportional value of gold to silver found in England to end the trafficking in silver coins. His disagreement with Boulter was that he believed the archbishop had overvalued gold and undervalued silver and would thus cause a further outflow of silver coins.[16]

The majority of the dozen pamphlets written on the subject, as well as the merchants, bankers, and politicians who thought about the issue, were heavily in the debt of John Locke and his writings on currency from the 1695–96 English recoinage. Locke's views, addressed to the working of the domestic economy, suggested that increasing the valuation of silver coins would reduce the amounts paid by debtors, while creditors would benefit from any increase in valuation. Most people at the time applied these ideas in an undigested form, but the debate on money was opened up by those, such as Bindon and Thomas Prior, who asked whether the ideas from England in the 1690s could be applied to Ireland in the late 1720s.[17] One key question posed by Bindon was whether the change in valuations of coins would not mean a shift in exchange rates between Irish and English money and therefore have an impact on exports as well as on domestic dealings.[18] Prior made the case that Locke's theory was wrong in the Irish situation, where, Prior insisted, only one metal (silver) had a standard of value.[19] Bindon went on to argue that different coins (including copper ones) had different uses and thereby found their different values.[20] This challenge to Locke links these writings to Berkeley's *The Querist,* in which he asked "Whether, all things considered, it would not be better for a kingdom that its cash consisted of half a million in small silver rather than five times that sum in gold? Whether the principal use of cash be not its ready passing from hand to hand, to answer common occasions of all sorts of people, and whether common occasions of all sorts of people are not small ones?"[21]

The debate over money also marked a small shift in the political economy of Ireland in another way. The rhetoric of the debate lacked the virulent anti-Englishness of the Wood's halfpence era, possibly because of the dire state of the economy in 1728–29 or possibly because Boulter had indeed sought to engage the Irish elite in his scheme. In 1724–26 there was a great appetite for the kinds of argument that posited that England was out to destroy Ireland's economy, but Boulter's critics did not use this language in 1729–30.

One of those who had employed the fiercest Patriot rhetoric in the mid-1720s was the "Drapier," Jonathan Swift. In the late 1720s, Swift was again exercised by the depth of the Irish economic crisis, when starvation or emigration seemed the two most likely options for many. *A Modest Proposal for Preventing the Children of Poor People in Ireland, from Being a Burden to their Parents or Country,* published in October 1729, lambasted those who offered endless proposals to solve Ireland's problems and castigated both the elite and poor for failing to act.[22] However, on the issue of coinage Swift may have been open to persuasion. James Kelly has speculated that Swift might have avoided entering the lists on the coinage debates of 1729–30 in order to let Boulter's proposals develop.[23]

And so it was that those writers who doubted Locke's monetary theories and eschewed vocal patriotism were most effective in their criticism of the plan to reduce the gold coins. Prior argued that only absentees and "money changers" would profit from the outflow of silver coins that would result, while Bindon believed that if they had acted in their self-interest the bankers would have supported Boulter. By his plan, they would have profited from exporting silver and "the credit of their notes would [have] be[en] proportionately increased."[24] In this debate we can see some signs of the ideas later picked up by Berkeley on money as well as the greater acceptance that Ireland's economic problems would not be solved by blaming England for all its ills.

Banks

Banking was another economic issue that plagued the administration in Ireland. The country lacked a national bank that could issue paper notes accepted by all. In 1720–21, a serious effort to create a national bank with private shareholders on the model of the Bank of England was undertaken. However, the proposal failed to gain sufficient political support in the Irish parliament. Fears of stock-jobbing in the wake of the South Sea Bubble and divisions among the Irish political elite were the main causes of this failure. In addition, the larger questions and suspicions about the state of Ireland's economy and the dependent relationship with Britain came to the fore to complicate matters.[25]

Opposition writings on the bank scheme focused on the belief that corruption would follow in the wake of its establishment, including influence over parliamentary elections and the reduction of parliament "to the condition of [a] cipher."[26] Also, there were doubts expressed about the security of the bank. One writer claimed that land, or "real" security, was preferable to the moveable assets, or "personal" security, which merchants could offer.[27] It should be said that this point was picked up by the national bank's proponents, especially Henry Maxwell. He wrote that private bankers were surely less trustworthy than a public bank which would not "remove all [its] effects into other countries, follow [those] effects [itself] and leave [its] creditors in the lurch."[28] The opponents of the bank, including the latecomer Jonathan Swift, won the argument, at least insofar as the outcome of the scheme. It is also noteworthy that these views, which could best be described as "country" ones, were ones largely borrowed from English debates of the 1690s.

In the vacuum left by the absence of a national institution, private banks expanded during the early eighteenth century to create a small but vibrant sector.[29] The evidence for the early Irish private banks is sketchy but they appear to have been primarily remitters of money between Ireland and London, beginning in the later seventeenth century. This business served, primarily, merchants and, secondly, absentee landowners, all of whom needed money to be sent from Ireland and who were hampered by the regular scarcity of specie in Ireland. Most of these private banks were mercantile in origin and made their money from the commission on dealing in the exchange of money between the two islands. At their peak in the early 1750s, the number of banks stood at eight in Dublin with others in Cork, Galway, Clonmel, Athlone, Waterford, and Belfast.[30] All of this led to a range of private credit services, although nothing on the scale of the paper credit offered in the American colonies or the range of financial innovations available in England or France.[31] Given the economic conditions in Ireland and the proximity of London, there was no necessity to create the version of a "private" financial revolution that other places saw. Dependency and economic problems made Ireland's revolution something of a chimera tied to the creation of a "public" national debt.

The private banking sector was always a volatile one and demands for reform arose after the shocking closure of Burton and Falkiner's bank in June 1733.[32] This bank was Dublin's largest and could be traced back through a complex history to the first regular bank in Dublin in the name of Burton. The Burton family had been bankers to the government on several occasions and made a profitable return from the exchange business, taking care of the pay and allowances of British regiments on the Irish Establishment or Irish regiments sent abroad.[33] The closure rocked the Irish political elite, being described heatedly by one government official as "like the South Sea Affair in 1720."[34] Most of the problems were specific to the bank: debts from other financial concerns associated with Samuel and Benjamin Burton as well as Francis Harrison, all of whom were deceased by June 1733, had been passed to the bank, leaving it with debts of more than £90,000 and with between eight hundred and nine hundred creditors.[35] However, the specific nature of these problems did not prevent a sharp run on the other banks, causing Marmaduke Coghill, one of Ireland's revenue commissioners, to reflect "what slender security people have who lodge their money in bankers hands."[36]

The affair of Burton and Falkiner's bank came before the parliamentary session which opened in Dublin in October 1733. In the event, the ensuing debate in parliament centered on the important but very narrow question of whether the settlements on the estate of the late Francis Harrison and Samuel Burton should be taken care of ahead of the bank's creditors. The debate was sparked by the claims of one MP, Abraham Creighton, who was an heir of Samuel Burton, and his father-in-law, the lord chief justice, Sir John Rogerson. They opposed the bill requiring the compulsory sale of Burton lands in order to pay the bank's creditors. Rogerson pursued a strong case on property grounds (despite a law from George I's time on this very subject), but the British privy council was persuaded by the argument from Dublin that "if this bill miscarries it must put an end to our paper credit here, by an immediate run upon the bankers or gradual forbearing to lodge money there."[37] The bill passed as the scarcity of currency in Ireland made paper credit and the private banks necessary for the exchange business and government payments. The story did not end there, as the trustees appointed by parliament struggled to sort out the tangled affairs of the collapsed bank. There were quarrels over the management of the payment of creditors in 1739–40 which sparked a pamphlet exchange and some newspaper notices but, once more, these reflected personal and narrow concerns rather than taking a wider view of banking.[38]

The narrow terms of the discussion by legislators might have had something to do with the desire not to upset the small private banking sector too much. It may also be partly due to the economic growth that had marked the early 1730s.[39] As prices in agricultural sectors remained stagnant the growth was driven by a boom in linen sales. The boom produced a positive balance in trade and the first, small signs of economic confidence. That said, the closure of Burton and Falkiner's did elicit some comment about the relative merits of private and national banks in the 1730s. The debate opened in 1734 with the publication of an anonymous pamphlet, *A Proposal for the Relief of Ireland, by a Coinage of Monies, of Gold, and Silver and by Establishing a National Bank.* It was published in Dublin, reprinted from a London edition.[40] The author referred to the closure of Burton and Falkiner's, insisting that he meant no "reflection on the gentlemen of Ireland concerned in private banks" despite his argument that they could not answer the public good.[41] In *The Querist,* Berkeley did not mention the failed bank by name but asked: "Whether the wealth and prosperity of our country do not hang by a hair, the probity of one banker, the caution of another, and the lives of all?"[42]

The anonymous 1734 pamphlet walked the thin line between economic patriotism and challenging the colonial status of Ireland. It urged the Irish elite to take control of their own affairs and encouraged Britain to support this effort to create wealth, rather than choose to see it as an expression of independency. The author made the point that "the nation subjected to another must be supported and preserved in its trade and wealth in some degree or the dominion over it is lost."[43] The idea floated in the pamphlet was for a subscription-based bank that would deal with the £300,000 national debt and which could lend money at 5 percent. This, the author said, was based on the Scottish model for a national bank from 1695. The pamphlet expressed a confidence that this proposal could succeed where the 1720–21 project had failed because of the improvements since then in relation to the increases in population, trade, and manufactures.[44]

This anonymous piece was followed in 1735 by a pamphlet written by Daniel Webb, a Cork merchant, also concerned about banking. His views about the private bankers were certainly much more censorious. Indeed, Webb argued that too many of his mercantile colleagues dealt in money and credit and "love the idle traffic of usury."[45] His argument was for cheaper money with lower interest rates and he cited the writings of Arthur Dobbs and the examples of the Danish, Swedish, and Dutch economies in support. If there were concerns about reductions in interest causing runs on private banks then the solution must be for national action.[46]

One problem with banking reform was that there was no agreement on the path to be followed. In 1725 and 1729 Bindon had published two versions of largely the same pamphlet which did not favor a national bank. Instead he took a third way, that modeled on the municipal Lombard banks which lent money to the industrious poor and manufacturers at lower interest rates than the private bankers charged. Berkeley's bank scheme was different again. As he wrote in *The Plan or Sketch of a National Bank* in 1737, "it doth not appear that any scheme of its nature was ever proposed in these kingdoms."[47] The bishop was clearly making the point that his scheme was not like the 1720–21 project, nor like the various ideas floated in pamphlets since then. He was also clear that most of what passed for national bank schemes were "private" rather than "public" ones backed by groups of eager shareholders.

So what were the origins of Berkeley's ideas on banking? It is difficult to tell as his correspondence gives few clues. In his early correspondence with John Percival (the future earl of Egmont), Berkeley appears to have been more of a passive recipient of ideas circulating in the early 1720s.[48] Patrick Kelly convincingly argues that Berkeley's experience in Rhode Island opened him up to the possibilities inherent in paper money and credit. At the same time, he was aware of the "evils" that could arise when legislators sacrificed the public good for private interest or over-rated lands and issued too much credit.[49] Berkeley's own views centered on the question of trust and credit going hand in hand. A run of queries in part one of *The Querist* questioned whether problems associated with money and credit did not have more to do with speculation rather than the money itself: "Whether the evil effects which of late years have attended paper-money and credit in Europe did not spring from subscriptions, shares, dividends and stock-jobbing?"[50]

Berkeley's argument was that bank notes were only useful as they rendered economic services, and, if they did not encourage industry, then their effects could be ruinous, as in the case of the South Sea Bubble or the French Mississippi scheme.[51] As private bankers were more likely to get involved in such speculation, Ireland's best hope lay in a national bank controlled by the public. Indeed, it would also provide a support to the operation of private banks whose books were open to supervision.[52] Berkeley gave plenty of detail in his *Sketch* of what a national bank might look like. First, its funds would be raised by a tax on wines with parliament standing security for deficiencies. This fund would allow for £100,000 in bank notes to be issued to people who had sufficient cash or securities and twenty-one visitors would be appointed (from among "great persons") or selected from among MPs to inspect the books at least four times annually. Berkeley put great store by the role of the Irish parliament and the social elite in the running of this national bank: "A bank where there are no sharers would be free from all the evils of stock-jobbing. A bank, whereof the public makes all the profit, and therefore makes good all deficiencies, must be most secure. Such a bank prudently managed, would be a mine of gold in the hands of the public."[53]

Berkeley's strategy for bringing a national bank about is also a subject on which we can say something. He and Prior clearly believed that the banking issue was important enough to extract from the bigger work. Therefore, "select queries" relating to a national bank were printed just after part three of *The Querist* as a whole was published in March 1737.[54] This was sent as an open letter to *Faulkner's Dublin Journal* and printed as a broadsheet. In November 1737 another open letter was printed on the issue of a national bank. This was not by Berkeley, nor, as his biographer suggests, by Percival.[55] Instead, *The Phoenix or a New Scheme for Establishing Credit* was taken from the 1721 pamphlet by one of the proposers of the 1720 national bank scheme, Colonel John Irwin. In this pamphlet (and in the newspaper article) he had abandoned the earlier subscription-based scheme in favor of a parliamentary bank supported by funds from the revenue and able to issue up to £500,000 in notes.

Therefore, by late 1737 there were many different schemes and ideas circulating on the subject of the establishment of a national bank. In November 1737, Berkeley went to Dublin to take his seat in the House of Lords for the first and only time. However, he never brought his plan before the Lords. Perhaps he feared the condemnation of the House, whose members in 1721 had said that any future proposer of a national bank would be regarded as an enemy of Ireland. Perhaps it became obvious, once he took his seat, that there was no support in parliament for such a scheme. One historian believes Berkeley blamed a combination of private bankers, libertines, and patriot parliamentarians for the national bank not coming about.[56] However, it seems most likely that between March and November 1737 Berkeley was more concerned with the blasters, a club of freethinkers in Dublin, than with banking. He spoke only once in this session and then to denounce the blasters in an inquiry into that club's activities.[57] Whatever the reason, Berkeley was not to see the Irish parliament approve of a national bank scheme in his lifetime.

Money: II

Another reason for the silence over a national bank was that the 1737 parliamentary session was, once again, convulsed by the question of coinage rather than that of paper money. As in 1728–29, Boulter was to the fore. The reforms had begun when the Irish privy council agreed in March 1736 to ask London for a royal proclamation to lower the value of gold coins. The overvalued Portuguese moidores, which Boulter claimed made up half the money in circulation, were cited as the main reason for making a reduction necessary.[58] The proposal approved by the privy council was to reduce the guinea by three pence to make a guinea worth 21*s.* English. Other gold coins were revalued in proportion. At the same time Boulter persuaded British ministers to produce a small amount of copper coins for Ireland to ease the scarcity in small change.

The mid-1730s had indeed seen a growing trade imbalance and complaints about the scarcity of silver and copper coins. This was largely due to the decline in linen exports to England because of high prices, putting a stop to the linen boom that had driven the short-lived economic growth. Against this background a new storm arose over the coinage reforms but it lacked the intensity of the 1728–29 debate, perhaps because there was a widespread acceptance of the need for small change to improve liquidity in the troubled economy.

The episode can be quickly retold. In April 1736 Dublin's merchant elite met and drew up a protest at the reported lowering of the gold. At a second meeting, Swift spoke to the assembled merchants and told them that only absentees, bishops, and officials would stand to gain.[59] The lord mayor and sheriffs of Dublin and then Swift and two MPs presented petitions to the lord lieutenant, Lionel Cranfield Sackville, duke of Dorset, opposing the change. This was to no avail as the lord lieutenant went to London to ask for a royal proclamation. Swift bitterly castigated Dorset whom, he said, "prevailed on us to make a promise to bestow upon England £25,000 a year forever by lowering the gold coin."[60] Attention then turned to the copper coins or "raps" as news of two tons of halfpence being minted in London circulated in Dublin. Again Swift raised the alarm against these "raps," but his attempt in March 1737 to prevent the new halfpence from being used in Dublin failed. Boulter succinctly reported that despite the noise "people of sense are very well-satisfied of the want and goodness of them."[61] The coins were tried, assayed, and accepted as legal tender by the revenue within two months.

The "raps" were soon forgotten in the political and pamphlet debate that opened in 1737 about the planned reduction of the gold coins. There was strong opposition from the two trading centers, Dublin and Cork, and a petition was sent from the latter town to the Irish parliament. In any commentary on this event much of the interest has focused upon Swift's outrage, his threatening talk to Boulter at a mayoral dinner, and his raising a black flag over St. Patrick's Cathedral in mourning for the Irish currency.[62] However, the proclamation was implemented and after a tide of "scurrilous and abusive papers . . . dispersed about town" the storm of protest dissipated.[63] The difference between 1737 and the events concerning Wood's halfpence or 1729–30 was that the opponents of reform were isolated. Swift was regarded by many as an eccentric while the opponents in parliament (Anthony Malone, Sir Richard Cox, and Eaton Stannard) were all relatively new MPs.

There was another difference in that most of the written works at this time were in favor of the reduction, and the pens of Bindon and

Prior remained quiet. One pamphleteer questioned whether "public clamour" over the issue should be taken seriously given that it was "a subject of some nicety in itself," and even the experts disagreed among themselves.[64] Another writer recalled the anger about the "raps" but pointed out that "now it is generally allowed that they were necessary and have been of great service." This same pamphlet accused Swift of inconsistency as he had argued in *The Intelligencer* in 1728 for the lowering of the gold as its high value was a burden on laborers and only benefited bankers.[65] The major work in 1737 was Bryan Robinson's *Short Essay upon Coin,* which cited the usual authorities (Sir Isaac Newton, Petty, and Locke) to support the actions of government.[66] On the other side, there were attacks on the constitutional basis of the reduction as parliament had not given its consent. Also the argument went that only the bankers (as money traders) and absentees would profit, with allegations that £30,000 of Portuguese coins had been exported at a huge profit within three days of the proclamation.[67]

The issue of money could still stir passions and the absence of a national mint was a sign of Ireland's dependent position. However, there seems to have been a growing belief among the Irish elite from the later 1720s that Ireland's economic development would not necessarily be harmed or constrained by being part of Britain's imperial system.[68] Not every initiative coming from British ministers or their representatives in Dublin was seen as inimically dangerous to Ireland. In the case of money, for the likes of Bindon or Berkeley (though not Swift), British schemes were useful if they had the potential to stimulate economic growth. Bindon, in the introduction to his translation of Melon's work, called for the expansion of credit to assist a trading nation such as Ireland. Given the misfortunes which he noted had befallen the private banking sector, he suggested that the circulation of paper money and credit might better be done by a national bank of some sort. Berkeley's philosophy on the usefulness of money or credit in Ireland was outlined in the following queries:

> §Whether the simple getting of money, or passing it from hand to hand without industry, be an object worthy of a wise government?
>
> §Whether it doth not have much import to have a right conception of money? And whether its true and just idea be not that of a ticket, entitling to power, and fitted to record and transfer such power?[69]

Epilogue

Coins, paper money, and banks remained problematic in Ireland. The coinage reform of 1737 appeared to have ended "two decades of enormously disruptive monetary conditions in Ireland," although there was some doubt whether it overvalued the silver Spanish pistoles which made up perhaps 75 percent of the circulating cash.[70] In 1750 the revenue commissioners decided not to accept light (or debased) guineas in taxes, which led to them being removed from circulation and cut to pieces.[71] The pistoles were then devalued in October 1750, but the following year bankers and army paymasters began to refuse to accept them.[72] The privy council ruled out further devaluation on the grounds of confidence in the silver coinage and by July 1751 speaker Henry Boyle, George Stone, archbishop of Armagh, and several of the leading politicians agreed that the Spanish coins should be withdrawn and replaced by better coinage. The privy council, with authority from George II and the Irish lord lieutenant, issued a proclamation to take in the coins at their real value.[73]

Initially all was well with this change because Stone had scouted wider opinion before proceeding with the proclamation. Additionally, the general attitude appeared to be to "thank God they were to have no more of them [the pistoles]."[74] However, problems arose when the Irish government did not manage to replace this source of most of the silver coins in the country. By April 1752, Stone and the leading Irish treasury official, Luke Gardiner, were asking for the defective coins to be replaced with up to £50,000 in good coin. Those officials associated with the Irish government and based in London were asked to lobby the British treasury. Their efforts were to no avail as the British treasury lords asked why a buoyant Irish treasury could not support its own coins. At the same time, an attempt to get the ban on importing English coins lifted was opposed by the Bank of England.[75] Suddenly, the good intentions began to look ill-prepared and the deflation in the money supply began to be blamed for recession in late 1752.[76] This heralded the start of a deeply damaging political crisis in Ireland which encompassed money and the public debt.

As far as banking went, the 1750s appeared to be changed times. In the 1750 edition of Berkeley's *The Querist* most of the references to a national bank were dropped.[77] However, before the decade was out two crises had rocked the private banking world with five banks closing in 1754–55 and another three in 1759–60. An act was passed in 1756 which banned merchants from acting as bankers and assured that the private banks would be dominated by landed interests rather than trade. According to one authority, the 1750s was the decade when Irish banking innovation in the eighteenth century came to an abrupt end: "Banking in Ireland stagnated for forty years after its brilliant debut between 1720 and 1754, and not only did it stagnate but it did so in the midst of very rapid economic development."[78]

This epilogue from the 1750s seems to challenge Berkeley's idea that a flourishing economy needed buoyant credit to support it. However, it may act more as a reminder that the Irish "financial revolution" was indeed a weak one, confined largely to the creation of a national debt. Despite economic growth the dependence of the economy on Britain ensured that innovation in financial circles remained occasional and short-lasting. In terms of thinking about money and banking, the debates of the 1730s reveal a curious mixture of long-held views inherited from Locke and the challenge to these views from Berkeley in particular. The 1750s suggest that in Ireland's economic thinking the ghost of Locke was a more powerful force than the ailing Berkeley, who would die in 1753 without having seen any major changes in Irish banking practices.

Notes

1. Daniel Webb, *An Enquiry into the Reasons of the Decay of Credit, Trade and Manufactures in Ireland* (Dublin, 1735), 15.

2. Patrick Kelly, "The Politics of Political Economy in Mid-eighteenth-century Ireland," in *Political Ideas in Eighteenth-Century Ireland*, ed. S. J. Connolly (Dublin: Four Courts Press, 2000), 106; Henry R. Wagner, *Irish Economics, 1700–1783: A Bibliography with Notes* (New York: A. M. Kelley, 1969); J. W. Hanson, *Contemporary Printed Sources for British and Irish Economic History* (Cambridge: Cambridge University Press, 1963).

3. George Berkeley, *The Querist*, in *Bishop Berkeley's* "Querist" *in Historical Perspective*, ed. Joseph Johnston (Dundalk: Dundalgan, 1970).

4. Kelly, "Politics of Political Economy"; David Bindon, *An Essay on the Gold and Silver Coin Current in Ireland* (Dublin, 1729).

5. [Jonathan Swift], *The Intelligencer* 19 (1728), in *The Prose Writings of Jonathan Swift*. Volume 12, *Irish Tracts 1728–1733*, ed. Herbert Davis (Oxford: Blackwell, 1971), 57.

6. Joseph Johnston, "Irish Currency in the Eighteenth Century," in *Berkeley's* "Querist," ed. Johnston, 52–71.

7. Revenue commissioners to Edward Hopkins, Aug. 7, 1722, SP63/380/110, Nat. Arch.; James Maculla, *Ireland's Consternation in the Losing of Two Hundred Thousand Pounds of their Gold and Silver for Brass Money* (Dublin, 1723).

8. For the best recent account, see Patrick McNally, "Wood's Halfpence, Carteret and the Government of Ireland," *Irish Historical Studies* 30, no. 119 (May 1997): 354–76.

9. In the period when the lord lieutenant was not resident in Ireland three lords justices were appointed to take care of the day-to-day government of Ireland. Hugh Boulter, archbishop of Armagh, to John, Lord Carteret, July 11, 1728; same to Sir Robert Walpole, Sept. 14, 1728, in *Letters Written by His Excellency Hugh Boulter D.D. Lord Primate of All Ireland to Several Ministers of State in England, and Some Others. Containing an Account of the Most Interesting Transactions which Passed in Ireland from 1724 to 1738*, 2 vols. (Dublin, 1770), 1:250–55.

10. [Thomas Maples], *A Vindication of the Intended Alteration of the Values of the Several Coins Now Current in the Kingdom* (Dublin, 1730), 4.

11. Boulter to Thomas Pelham-Holles, duke of Newcastle, Oct. 23, 1729, SP 63/391/184, Nat. Arch.

12. [Maples] *Vindication*, 5.

13. E. M. Johnston-Liik, *The History of the Irish Parliament, 1692–1800: Commons, Constituencies and Statutes*, 6 vols. (Belfast: Ulster Historical Foundation, 2002), 3:180–82

14. David Bindon, *A Political Essay Upon Commerce Written in French by Monsieur M[elon]* (Dublin, 1738).

15. Boulter to Carteret, May 13, 1729, in *Letters Written by His Excellency Hugh Boulter*, 1:243–46.

16. Bindon, *Essay*, 6, 14–15, 17.

17. Patrick Kelly, ed., *Locke on Money*, 2 vols. (Oxford: Clarendon, 1991); Patrick Kelly, "Perceptions of Locke in Ireland in the Eighteenth Century," *Proceedings of the Royal Irish Academy* 89, section C (1989): 17–35.

18. Bindon, *Essay*, 11.

19. Thomas Prior, *Observations on Coin in General* (Dublin, 1729), 299.

20. Bindon, *Essay*, 12.

21. Berkeley, *Querist*, in *Berkeley's* "Querist," ed. Johnston, 473.

22. [Jonathan Swift], *A Modest Proposal for Preventing the Children of Poor People in Ireland, from Being a Burden to their Parents or Country; and For Making Them Beneficial to the Publick* (Dublin, 1729), in *The Prose Writings of Jonathan Swift.* Volume 12, *Irish Tracts, 1728–1733*, ed. Herbert Davis (Oxford: Blackwell, 1971), 109–18.

23. James Kelly, "Jonathan Swift and the Irish Economy in the 1720s," *Eighteenth-Century Ireland* 6 (1991): 27–28.

24. Prior, *Observations on Coin*; Bindon, *Essay*, 14–15.

25. Michael Ryder, "The Bank of Ireland, 1721: Land, Credit and Dependency," *Historical Journal* 25, no. 3 (Sept. 1982): 557–82.

26. *Letter to an MP Touching the Late Intended Bank* (Dublin, 1721), 8.

27. Hercules Rowley, *An Answer to a Book, Intitl'd, Reasons Offer'd for Erecting a Bank in Ireland. In a Letter to Henry Maxwell, Esq.* (Dublin, 1721), 21–22.

28. Henry Maxwell, *Reasons Offered for Erecting a Bank in Ireland* (Dublin, 1721), 11.

29. L. M. Cullen, "Landlords, Merchants and Bankers: The Early Irish Banking World, 1700–1820," *Hermathena* 135 (1983): 25–44; L. M. Cullen, "The Exchange Business of Irish Banks in the Eighteenth Century," *Economica* 25, no. 100 (Nov. 1958): 326–38.

30. This does not compare badly with England, which had twenty banks in London in 1750 with another twelve country banks as well as the Bank of England.

31. Constantine George Caffentzis, *Exciting the Industry of Mankind: George Berkeley's Philosophy of Money* (Dordrecht: Kluwer, 2000); Antoin E. Murphy, *Richard Cantillon: Entrepreneur and Economist* (Oxford: Clarendon, 1986).

32. *Dublin Evening Post,* June 23, 1733.

33. Johnston-Liik, *History of the Irish Parliament,* 3:317.

34. Walter Cary to Charles Delafaye, Jan. 27, 1734, SP 63/397/34, Nat. Arch.

35. F. G. Hall, *The Bank of Ireland, 1783–1946* (Dublin: Hodges Figgis & Co., 1949), 7.

36. Marmaduke Coghill to Edward Southwell, July 7, 1733, f. 44, Add. MS 21123, B.L.

37. Boulter to Walpole, Mar. 28, 1734, in *Letters Written by His Excellency Hugh Boulter,* 2:119.

38. *The Case of Oswald Edwards* (Dublin, 1740). There was a further spat among the trustees and the agent of the creditors, Robert Roberts, in 1751–52 with more pamphlets and newspaper coverage. Three bills were needed to settle the bank's affairs (1734, 1751, and 1803) and quarrels about the claims of creditors appear to have been still rumbling on in the 1820s. See A. P. W. Malcomson, *Nathaniel Clements: Government and the Governing Elite in Ireland, 1725–75* (Dublin: Four Courts Press, 2005), 384.

39. David Dickson, *New Foundations: Ireland, 1660–1800* (Dublin: Irish Academic Press, 2000), 115.

40. *A Proposal for the Relief of Ireland, by a Coinage of Monies, of Gold, and Silver and Establishing a National Bank* (Dublin, 1734).

41. *Proposal for the Relief of Ireland,* i.

42. Berkeley, *Querist,* 148.

43. *Proposal for the Relief of Ireland,* 14.

44. Ibid., 19.

45. Webb, *Enquiry,* 17.

46. Ibid., 30.

47. [George Berkeley], *The Plan or Sketch of a National Bank,* in *Berkeley's* "Querist," ed. Johnston, 208.

48. Benjamin Rand, ed., *Berkeley and Percival* (Cambridge: Cambridge University Press, 1914), 180–85.

49. Kelly, "Politics of Political Economy," 123; Berkeley, *Querist,* 146.

50. Berkeley, *Querist,* 145.

51. Ibid., 134, 135, 151.

52. Ibid., 133, 195.

53. [Berkeley], *Plan or Sketch,* 205–7.

54. [George Berkeley], *Queries Relating to a National Bank, Extracted from "The Querist"* (Dublin, 1737). These select queries are marked in Joseph Johnston's 1970 edition of *The Querist* for easier access.

55. A. A. Luce, *A Life of George Berkeley* (Edinburgh: Thomas Nelson, 1949), 192.

56. Constantine George Caffentzis, "Why did Berkeley's Bank Fail? Money and Libertinism in Eighteenth-century Ireland," *Eighteenth-Century Ireland* 12 (1997): 100–15.

57. Luce, *Life of Berkeley*, 176.

58. Boulter to Walpole, May 25, 1736, in *Letters Written by His Excellency Hugh Boulter*, 2:148. But see note 69.

59. *Pue's Occurrences*, April 20, 27, 1736.

60. Ibid., April 27, May 1, 1736.

61. *Thoughts on the Gold Coins* (Dublin, 1736), 12; *Dublin Daily Advertiser*, March 21, 1737; Boulter to Walter Cary, April 8, 1737, SP 63/400/257, Nat. Arch.

62. Robert E. Burns, *Irish Parliamentary Politics in the Eighteenth Century*, 2 vols. (Washington, D.C.: Catholic University of America Press, 1989), 2:37–39; Irvin Ehrenpreis, *Swift: The Man, His Works and The Age*. Volume 3, *Dean Swift* (London: Methuen, 1983), 858–62; Lord George Sackville to Lionel Cranfield Sackville, duke of Dorset, Oct. 9, 1737, in H.M.C., *Stopford-Sackville MSS*, 1:166–68.

63. *A Short Answer to Short Reasons Why Our Gold Money in Ireland Should Not be Lowered* (Dublin, 1737), 2.

64. *An Unprejudiced Enquiry into the Nature and Consequences of the Reduction of Our Gold* (Dublin, 1737), 5.

65. *Some Reflections Concerning Lowering the Value of the Gold Coin* (Dublin, 1737), 4, 9; Kelly, "Swift and the Irish Economy," 26–27. This point about Swift and lowering gold coins is true although his views on small coins were consistent as he believed these should be minted in an Irish mint.

66. [Bryan Robinson], *A Short Essay upon Coin* (Dublin, 1737).

67. *Queries Relative to the New Half-pence and Lowering the Coin* (Dublin, 1737), 5–6; *A Reply to the Principal Arguments for the Reduction of the Gold Coin* (Dublin, 1737), 2.

68. Kelly, "Politics of Political Economy," 113.

69. Bindon, *Essay*, 192; Bindon, *Political Essay upon Commerce*, xxx; Berkeley, *Querist*, 151, 162.

70. Kelly, "Politics of Political Economy," 119.

71. John Boyle, Lord Orrery, to Edward Barry, Apr. 16, 1750, in Emily Charlotte, Countess of Cork and Orrery, ed., *The Orrery Papers* (London: Duckworth, 1903), 76–77; instructions of the Irish Revenue Board, Oct. 23, 1750, CUST 1/49, Nat. Arch.

72. Robert Jocelyn, Baron Newport, to Philip Yorke, earl of Hardwicke, Oct. 6, 1750, f. 126, Add MS 35591, B.L.; James Belcher to Thomas Waite, Sept. 29, 1750, T/3019/1254, Public Record Office of Northern Ireland.

73. George Stone, archbishop of Armagh, to Sackville, July 10, 1751, in H.M.C., *Stopford-Sackville MSS*, 1:173–74; Cullen, "Exchange Business," 333.

74. H.M.C., *Stopford-Sackville MSS*, 1:174.

75. Stone to Sackville, May 20, 1750; Henry Pelham to Sackville, Nov. 21, 1751, in H.M.C., *Stopford-Sackville MSS*, 1:171, 178; Thomas Waite to Sir Robert Wilmot, Apr. 23, 1752, T/3019/1273, Public Record Office of Northern Ireland.

76. *Belfast News-Letter*, May 28, 1753.

77. See Joseph Johnston, "Introductory and Biographical," in *Berkeley's "Querist,"* ed. Johnston, 1–9.

78. Cullen, "Landlords, Bankers and Merchants," 29.

Bibliography

The bibliography contained herein includes all texts referred to in the essays that constitute this book; also included are published works known to have been consulted by one or more authors during the writing of this book. Manuscripts used in the writing of the essays are fully cited in the end notes of the appropriate essay. Capitalization has been standardized for this bibliography. Spellings are as they appear on the title page of each work.

Allen, Robert. *An Essay on the Nature and Methods of Carrying on a Trade to the South-Sea.* London, 1712.

Anderson, Matthew S. *War and Society in Europe of the Old Regime, 1618–1789.* Guernsey: Sutton, 1998.

Andrews, J. H. "Land and People, c.1780." In *A New History of Ireland.* Volume 4, *Eighteenth Century Ireland, 1691–1800,* eds. T. W. Moody and W. E. Vaughan, 236–64. Oxford: Oxford University Press, 1986.

Angliæ Tutamen: Or, the Safety of England. Being an Account of the Banks, Lotteries, Mines, Diving, Draining, Lifting, and Other Engines, and Many Pernicious Projects Now on Foot, Tending to the Destruction of Trade. By a Person of Honour. London, 1695.

Arkell, Tom. "Assessing the Reliability of the Warwickshire Hearth Tax Returns of 1662–74." *Warwickshire History* 6, no. 6 (Winter 1986/87): 183–97.

———. "Cornwall's Hearth Tax Lists, 1662–67." *Cornwall Association of Local Historians* 28 (Autumn 1994): 13–18.

———. "The Incidence of Poverty in England in the Later Seventeenth Century." *Social History* 12 (1987): 29–38.

———. Rev. of *The Scope of Local History* by Margaret Spufford. *English Historical Review* 117 (Sept. 2002): 917–20.

Armitage, David. "The Fifty Years' Rift: Intellectual History and International Relations." *Modern Intellectual History* 1, no. 1 (April 2004): 97–109.

———. *The Ideological Origins of the British Empire.* Cambridge: Cambridge University Press, 2000.

Asgill, John. *The Freeholder's Answer to Mr. John Briscoe's Proposals for a National Bank: Shewing the Reasons Why They Will Rather Borrow Money of the Land-Bank Already Establish'd, than Subscribe to his Proposals.* [London], 1695.

[———]. *A List of the Names of the Subscribers to the Land-Bank.* [London], 1695.

[———]. *A Proposal for a Subscription to Raise One Hundred Thousand Pounds for Circulating the Credit of a Land-Bank.* [London], 1695.

[———]. *The Settlement of the Land-Bank, Established anno dom. 1695.* [London], 1695.

[Asgill, John, and Nicholas Barbon]. *An Account of the Land-Bank, Shewing the Design and Manner of the Settlement, the Profits to the Subscribers, the Advantage to the Borrowers, the Conveniency to the Lenders, that it Will be the Support of the Nobility and Gentry of England, and a Public Good to the Whole Nation.* London, 1695.

[———]. *Several Assertions Proved in Order to Create Another Species of Money than Gold and Silver.* [London], 1696.

[Asgill, John, Nicholas Barbon, and John Briscoe]. *Proposals Made to the Honourable House of Commons, by the Land-Bank United, for Raising Two Millions or More.* [London], 1696.

[Atwood, William]. *A Safe and Easy Method for Supplying the Want of Coin, and Raising as Many Millions as the Occasions of the Publick May Require.* [London], 1695.

Aveling, J. H. *The Chamberlens and the Midwifery Forceps: Memorials of the Family and an Essay on the Invention of the Instrument.* London, 1882.

Aydelotte, J. E. "The Duke of Ormond and the English Government of Ireland, 1677–85." Unpub. Diss., University of Iowa, 1975.

Backscheider, Paula. *Daniel Defoe: Ambition & Innovation.* Lexington: University Presses of Kentucky, 1986.

———. *Daniel Defoe: His Life.* Baltimore: Johns Hopkins University Press, 1989.

———. *Spectacular Politics: Theatrical Power and Mass Culture in Early Modern England.* Baltimore: Johns Hopkins University Press, 1993.

Baltes, Sabine. *The Pamphlet Controversy About Wood's Halfpence (1722–25) and the Tradition of Irish Constitutional Nationalism.* Frankfurt: Peter Lang, 2002.

Barnard, T. C. *Cromwellian Ireland: English Government and Reform in Ireland, 1649–1660.* Oxford: Oxford University Press, 1975.

———. "'Grand Metropolis' or 'The Anus of the World'? The Cultural Life of Eighteenth-Century Dublin." In *Two Capitals: London and Dublin, 1500–1840,* eds. Peter Clark and Raymond Gillespie, 185–210. Oxford: Oxford University Press, 2001.

———. *A New Anatomy of Ireland: The Irish Protestants, 1649–1770.* New Haven: Yale University Press, 2003.

———. "Reforming Irish Manners: The Religious Societies in Dublin During the 1690s." In *Irish Protestant Ascents and Descents, 1641–1770,* ed. T. C. Barnard, 143–79. Dublin: Four Courts Press, 2004.

Baston, Thomas. *Thoughts on Trade, and a Publick Spirit. Consider'd Under the Following Heads, viz. I. Companies in Trade. II. Stock-jobbers. III. Projectors. IV. Corruptions in the Law and Public Offices. V. Of a Public Spirit. Humbly Dedicated to all Lovers of their Country.* London, then Dublin, 1716.

Bayly, C. A. *Imperial Meridian: The British Empire and the World, 1780–1830.* Harlow: Pearson, 1989.

Beckett, J. C. *The Making of Modern Ireland 1603–1923.* London: Faber, 1969.

Beckett, J. V. "Land Tax or Excise: The Levying of Taxation in Seventeenth- and Eighteenth-Century England." *English Historical Review* 100, no. 395 (April 1985): 285–308.

Berkeley, George. *The Plan or Sketch of a National Bank.* In *Bishop Berkeley's* "Querist" *in Historical Perspective,* ed. Joseph Johnston, 205–8. Dundalk: Dundalgan, 1970.

[———]. *Queries Relating to a National Bank, Extracted from "The Querist."* Dublin, 1737.

———. *The Querist.* In *Bishop Berkeley's* "Querist" *in Historical Perspective,* ed. Joseph Johnston, 124–204. Dundalk: Dundalgan, 1970.

Bialuschewski, Arne. "Pirates, Slavers, and the Indigenous Population in Madagascar, *c.* 1690–1715." *International Journal of African Historical Studies* 38, no. 2 (2005): 401–25.

Bibliotheca Lindesiana (Volumes V and VI): A Bibliography of Royal Proclamations of the Tudor and Stuart Sovereigns, and of Others Published Under Authority, 1485–1714. Volume 1, *England and Wales,* ed. James Ludovic Lindsay, 26th earl of Crawford and 9th earl of Balcarres. Oxford: Clarendon, 1910.

Bindon, David. *An Essay on the Gold and Silver Coin Current in Ireland.* Dublin, 1729.

———. *A Political Essay Upon Commerce Written in French by Monsieur M[elon].* Dublin, 1738.

———. *Some Considerations on the Attempts Made to Pass Mr. Wood's Brass-Money in Ireland. By a Lover of his Country.* Dublin, 1724.

Blackwell, John. *An Essay Towards Carrying on the Present War Against France.* London, 1695.

Blaug, Mark. *Economic Theory in Retrospect.* 4th ed. Cambridge: Cambridge University Press, 1985.

Bolingbroke, Henry St John, Viscount. *Some Reflections on the Present State of the Nation, Principally with Regard to Her Taxes and Her Debts, and on the Causes and Consequences of Them.* In *The Works of Lord Bolingbroke,* 2:439–61. Repr. of 1844 repr. of 1753 ed. 4 vols. London: Frank Cass, 1967

Bonney, Margaret, and Mark W. Ormrod. "Crises, Revolutions and Self-Sustained Growth: Towards a Conceptual Model of Change in Fiscal History." In *Essays in European Fiscal History, 1130–1830,* ed. W. M. Ormrod, R. J. Bonney, and M. Bonney, 1–21. Stamford: Shaun Tyas, 1999.

Bonney, Richard, ed. *Economic Systems and State Finance.* Oxford: Clarendon, 1995.

———, ed. *The Rise of the Fiscal State in Europe, c. 1200–1815.* Oxford: Oxford University Press, 1999.

Boulter, Hugh. *Letters Written by His Excellency Hugh Boulter D.D. Lord Primate of All Ireland to Several Ministers of State in England, and Some Others. Containing an Account of the Most Interesting Transactions which Passed in Ireland from 1724 to 1738.* 2 vols. Dublin, 1770.

Braddick, Michael J. *The Nerves of State: Taxation and the Financing of the English State, 1558–1714.* Manchester: Manchester University Press, 1996.

———. *Parliamentary Taxation in Seventeenth-Century England: Local Administration and Response.* Woodbridge: Royal Historical Society, 1994.

———. *State Formation in Early Modern England, c. 1550–1700.* Cambridge: Cambridge University Press, 2000.

Brantlinger, Patrick. *Fictions of State: Culture and Credit in Britain, 1694–1994.* Ithaca, NY: Cornell University Press, 1996.

Brewer, John. *The Sinews of Power: War, Money and the English State, 1688–1783.* London: Unwin Hyman, 1989.

B[riscoe], J[ohn]. *A Discourse on the Late Funds of the Million-Act, Lottery-Act, and Bank of England. Shewing, that They Are Injurious to the Nobility and Gentry, and Ruinous to the Trade of the Nation.* London, 1694.

———. *An Account of the Value of the Estates in the Several Counties Subscribed Towards the Fund for a National Land-Bank, from Thursday the 11th of June, to Saturday the 13th of July, 1695.* London, 1695.

———. *An Account of the Value of the Estates in the Several Counties Subscribed Towards the Fund for a National Land-Bank, from Thursday the 11th of June, to Saturday the 3d of August, 1695.* London, 1695.

Briscoe, John. *An Abstract of the Discourse on the Late Funds of the Million-Act, Lottery-Act, and Bank of England.* London, 1694.

———. *An Account of the National Land-Bank.* London, 1695.

———. *Advertisement. I Have Been Desired by Some Gentlemen, Who are Well-Wishers to the Intended Land-Bank to Publish my Answer to the Following Queries, Propounded by Several Who Have Read My Proposals.* London, 1695.

———. *Advice to the Free-Holder.* Repr. in *To the Lords Spiritual and Temporal and Commons in Parliament Assembled,* 2–4. London, 1695.

———. *The Following Proposals for, and Accounts of, a National Land-Bank Having Been Printed at London. Its Proveable Many Gentlemen Who Would Have Subscribed Thereto, by Reason of the Distance of their Dwelling from Thence, Have Heard Nothing, or Had but an Imperfect Account of it; for Informing Whom, True Copies of Several of Mr Brisco's Papers are Herewith Reprinted, in Order to be Dispersed in Several Counties.* Edinburgh, 1695.

———. *The Freehold Estates of England, or England It Self the Best Fund or Security.* London, 1695.

[———]. *Mr. B—coe's Reply to the Almanack, Being Land and Money United: or, B—coe & the B—k of E—nd Joined.* [London, 1696].

———. *Mr. Briscoe's Reply to a Pamphlet Intitled,* "The Freeholders Answer to Mr. John Briscoe's 'Proposals for a National Land Bank.'" London, 1695.

———. *Mr. John Asgill His Plagiarism Detected; and His* "Several Assertions," *of Which He Pretends to Be the Author, Proved to Be Taken Out of Mr. Briscoe's* "Discourse on the Late Funds." London, 1696.

———. *To the Honourable the Knights, Citizens and Burgesses in Parliament Assembled.* London, 1695.

———. *The Humble Offer of the National Land-Bank.* London, 1696.

———. *To the Knights, Citizens and Burgesses in Parliament Assembled.* London, 1696.

———. *To the Lords Spiritual and Temporal and Commons in Parliament Assembled.* London, 1695.

———. *Proposals for Raising Money for the National Land-Bank.* London, 1695.

———. *Reasons Humbly Offered for the Establishment of the National Land-Bank.* [London], 1696.

Brock, Leslie V. "The Colonial Currency, Prices, and Exchange Rates." *Essays in History* 34 (1992), Charlottesville: Corcoran Department of History, University of Virginia: <http://etext.virginia.edu/journals/EH/EH34/brock34.htm>.

Burnet, Gilbert. *The Expedition of His Highness the Prince of Orange for England.* In *A Collection of Scarce and Valuable Tracts [Somers' Tracts]*, ed. Walter Scott, 9:276–80. London, 1813.

———. *History of His Own Time: With Notes by the Earls of Dartmouth and Hardwicke, Speaker Onslow, and Dean Swift: To Which are Added Other Annotations*, ed. Martin J. Routh. 2nd, enlarged ed. Oxford, 1833.

Burns, R. E. *Irish Parliamentary Politics in the Eighteenth Century.* 2 vols. Washington, D.C.: Catholic University of America Press, 1989–90.

C. J. *Proposals for Regulating the Silver Coyne, Bearing the Charge of it, Producing a Circulation, and Securing it to the Kingdom.* [London], 1695.

Caffentzis, C. George. "Why Did Berkeley's Bank Fail? Money and Libertinism in Eighteenth-Century Ireland." *Eighteenth-Century Ireland* 12 (1997), 100–15.

———. *Exciting the Industry of Mankind: George Berkeley's Philosophy of Money.* Dordrecht: Kluwer, 2000.

Carruthers, Bruce G. *City of Capital: Politics and Markets in the English Financial Revolution.* Princeton: Princeton University Press, 1996.

———. "Homo Economicus and Homo Politicus: Non-economic Rationality in the Early Eighteenth-Century London Stock Market." *Acta Sociologica* 37 (1994): 165–94.

Cary, John. *An Essay on the State of England in Relation to its Trade, its Poor, and its Taxes, for Carrying on the Present War Against France.* Bristol, 1695.

Case, Arthur E. *Four Essays on* "Gulliver's Travels." Princeton: Princeton University Press, 1945.

The Case of Oswald Edwards. Dublin, 1740.

The Case of the Royal African Company and of the Plantations. London, 1714.

The Case of the Sufferers of Nevis and St. Christophers. London, 1714.

[Chalmers, George]. *Arrangements with Ireland Considered.* London, 1785.

———. *Considerations on Commerce, Bullion and Coin, Circulation and Exchanges; With a View to our Present Circumstances.* London, 1811.

———. *An Estimate of the Comparative Strength of Great-Britain, During the Present and Four Preceding Reigns; And of the Losses of her Trade from Every War Since the Revolution. A New Edition, Corrected, and Improved; With A Dedication to Dr. James Currie, The Reputed Author of "Jasper Wilson's Letter."* Repr. of 1794 ed. New York: A. M. Kelley 1969.

[———]. *The Life of Thomas Paine, With a Review of his Writings; Particularly of* "Rights of Man," *Parts First and Second. By Francis Oldys, A.M. of the University of Philadelphia.* 5th ed. London, 1792.

[Chamberlen, Hugh]. *A Brief Narrative of the Nature & Advantages of the Land-Bank, as Proposed by Dr. Hugh Chamberlen, the First Author of Founding a Bank on an Annual Revenue.* London, 1695.

———. *A Collection of Some Papers Writ upon Several Occasions, Concerning Clipt and Counterfeit Money, and Trade, so Far as it Relates to the Exportation of Bullion.* London, 1696.

[———]. *The Constitution of the Office of Land-Credit Declared in a Deed by Hugh Chamberlen Senior, M.D. and Others, Joynt Undertakers and Managers Thereof: Inrolled in Chancery, anno dom. 1696.* London, 1696.

———. *Dr. Chamberlen's Petition and Proposals for a Land Bank to Increase Trade* [London], 1693.

———. *Dr. Hugh Chamberlen's Proposal to Make England Rich and Happy.* London, 1690.

[———]. *An Humble Proposal to the Honourable the House of Commons.* [London], 1690.

———. *Mr. J. Briscoe, Director in the National Land-Bank, his Defence of Dr. Hugh Chamberlen's Bank or Office of Land-Credit: In a Letter to the Doctor.* London, 1696.

[———]. *The Office of Land-Credit: Encouragement to Mony'd Men.* [London], 1696.

———. *Papers, Relating to a Bank of Credit, upon Land-Security; Proposed to the Parliament of Scotland.* Edinburgh, 1693.

———. *A Proposal and Considerations Relating to an Office of Credit upon Land Security: Proposed to their Excellencies the Lords Justices: And to the Lords of the Privy Council; And the Parliament of Ireland.* London, 1697.

———. *A Proposal by Dr. Hugh Chamberlen in Essex-Street for a Bank of Secure Current Credit to be Founded upon Land.* London, 1695.

[———]. *The Several Articles or Parts of the Proposal upon Land-Credit Rationally Explained.* London, 1695.

———. *A Short Abstract of Doctor H. Chamberlen's Proposal to the Honourable House of Commons the Last Sessions. And Also of Mr. John Briscoe's Present Printed Proposal Compared Together, Whereby the Benefits of Each to the Nation, and Every Freeholder Concern'd, May Plainly Appear.* [London], 1694.

———. *Some Reflections on the* "Brief Account of the Intended Bank of England," *Whose Author's Name is Supposed to be Mr. Jerry Squirt.* [London], 1694.

[———]. *Some Useful Reflections upon a Pamphlet called* "A Brief Account of the Intended Bank of England." [London], 1694.

———. *The Tunnage Bank Compared with Dr. Chamberlen's Land-Fund of Credit.* London, 1694.

Chamberlen, Hugh, and Thomas Dalby. *A Proposal for Encouraging of Persons, to Subscribe Towards a Common Stock of [———] for the Erecting and Managing of a Trade by a General Fishery to be with All Possible Moral Security of a Great Gain to the Adventurers, and of No Less Honour and Advantage to the Publick, and is a Benefit not to be Attained by Any Other Methods, as is Strongly Presumed from Arguments that Have All the Appearing Force of Demonstration.* [London], 1691.

———. *A Supplement to the Proposal for a General Fishery, Explaining the Nature and Benefit of the Fund Proposed for the Same.* [London], 1691.

Chandaman, C. D. *The English Public Revenue, 1660–1688.* Oxford: Clarendon, 1975.

Clarendon, R. V. *A Sketch of the Revenue and Finances of Ireland and of the Appropriated Funds, Loans and Debt of the Nation from their Commencement.* Dublin, 1791.

Clarke, Aidan. *Prelude to Restoration in Ireland: The End of the Commonwealth, 1659–1660.* Cambridge: Cambridge University Press, 1999.

Cokayne, G. E. *The Complete Peerage of England, Scotland, Ireland, Great Britain and the United Kingdom.* Rev. Vicary Gibbs, Geoffrey White, and R. S. Lea. 12 vols. London: St Catherine, 1910–59.

Coleman, D. C., ed. *Revisions in Mercantilism.* London: Methuen, 1969.

Colley, Linda. *Britons: Forging the Nation, 1707–1837.* New Haven, CT: Yale University Press, 1992.

The Commission for Taking Subscriptions for 1200000l. Pursuant to the Act of Parliament. [London], 1694.

The Commission for Taking Subscriptions to the National Land-Bank. [London], 1696.

Common Sense: In a Letter to a Friend. To Which is Prefixed an Explanatory Preface. By the Author of Ireland in Tears. London, 1755.

Connolly, S. J. "Precedent and Principle: The Patriots and their Critics." In *Political Ideas in Eighteenth-Century Ireland,* ed. S. J. Connolly, 130–58. Dublin: Four Courts Press, 2000.

———. "Varieties of Britishness: Ireland, Scotland and Wales in the Hanoverian State." In *Uniting the Kingdom? The Making of British History,* ed. Alexander Grant and Keith Stringer, 193–207. London: Routledge, 1995.

The Considerable Advantages of a South Sea Trade to Our English Nation. London, 1711.

A Copy of the Papers Which Were Prepared by The Court of Directors, and Read in a General Court of The South Sea Company. London, 1713.

Cork and Orrery, Emily Charlotte, Countess of. *The Orrery Papers.* London: Duckworth, 1903.

Coxe, William. *Memoirs of the Life and Administration of Sir Robert Walpole, Earl of Orford.* 2 vols. London: 1798.

Craig, Maurice. *Dublin, 1660–1860.* London: Cresset, 1952.

Crawfurd, George. *Peerage of Scotland.* Edinburgh, 1716.

Cruickshanks, Eveline, Stuart Handley, and D. W. Hayton, eds. *The History of Parliament: The House of Commons, 1690–1715.* 5 vols. Cambridge: Cambridge University Press, 2002.

Cullen, L. M. *An Economic History of Ireland since 1660.* 2nd ed. London: Batsford, 1987.

———. "The Exchange Business of Irish Banks in the Eighteenth Century." *Economica* 25, no. 100 (Nov. 1958): 326–38.

———. "Landlords, Merchants, and Bankers: The Early Irish Banking World, 1700–1820." *Hermathena* 135 (1983): 25–44.

———. "Problems in the Interpretation and Revision of Eighteenth-Century Irish Economic History." *Transactions of the Royal Historical Society* 5th series, 17 (1967): 1–22.

———. "The Value of Contemporary Printed Sources for Irish Economic History in the Eighteenth Century." *Irish Historical Studies* 14, no. 54 (Sept. 1964): 142–55.

Curtis, Edmund, and R. B. McDowell, eds. *Irish Historical Documents, 1172–1922.* London: Methuen, 1943.

Dalton, Charles. *English Army Lists and Commission Registers, 1661–1714.* 6 vols. London: Francis Edwards, 1960.

Daston, Lorraine. *Classical Probability in the Enlightenment.* Princeton: Princeton University Press, 1988.

Davenant, Charles. *Essays on the National Constitution, Bank Credit, and Trade.* London, 1717

———. *A Report to the Honourable the Commissioners for Putting in Execution the Act, Intitled, An Act, for the Taking, Examining, and Stating the Publick Accounts of the Kingdom.* London, 1712.

[———]. *The True Picture of a Modern Whig.* [London], 1701.

Davenport-Hines, R .P. T. and Jonathan Liebenau, eds. *Business in the Age of Reason.* London: Cass, 1987.

The Declaration of His Highness William Henry, By the Grace of God Prince of Orange, &c. of the Reasons Inducing Him, to Appear in Armes in the Kingdome of England, for Preserving of the Protestant Religion, and for Restoring the Lawes and Liberties of England, Scotland and Ireland. The Hague, 1688.

Defoe, Daniel. "The Anatomy of Exchange Alley." In *Political and Economic Writings of Daniel Defoe.* Volume 6, *Finance,* ed. John McVeagh, 127–56. London: Pickering & Chatto, 2000.

[———]. *Augusta Triumphans.* In *Political and Economic Writings of Daniel Defoe.* Volume 8, *Social Reform,* ed. W. R. Owens, 257–87. London: Pickering & Chatto, 2000.

[———]. *The Complete English Tradesman.* New York: B. Franklin, 1970.

[———]. *Defoe's Review: Reproduced from the Original Editions,* ed. Arthur Secord. New York: Columbia University Press, 1938.

[———]. *The Director Numb. XV* (Nov. 21, 1720). In *Political and Economic Writings of Daniel Defoe.* Volume 6, *Finance,* ed. John McVeagh, 248–51. London: Pickering & Chatto, 2000.

[———]. *An Essay upon Loans.* In *Political and Economic Writings of Daniel Defoe.* Volume 6, *Finance,* ed. John McVeagh, 63–76. London: Pickering & Chatto, 2000.

[———]. *An Essay upon Projects.* In *Political and Economic Writings of Daniel Defoe.* Volume 8, *Social Reform,* ed. W. R. Owens, 27–142. London: Pickering & Chatto, 2000.

[———]. *An Essay upon Publick Credit.* In *Political and Economic Writings of Daniel Defoe.* Volume 6, *Finance,* ed. John McVeagh, 49–62. London: Pickering & Chatto, 2000.

[———]. *Every-Body's Business is Nobody's Business.* In *Political and Economic Writings of Daniel Defoe.* Volume 8, *Social Reform,* ed. W. R. Owens, 217–35. London: Pickering & Chatto, 2000.

[———]. "An Explanatory Preface." *A True Collection of the Writings of the Author of the True Born Englishman.* In *The Earlier Life and The Chief Earlier Works of Daniel Defoe,* ed. Henry Morley, 177–81. London, 1889.

[———]. *Giving Alms No Charity.* In *Political and Economic Writings of Daniel Defoe.* Volume 8, *Social Reform,* ed. W. R. Owens, 167–91. London: Pickering & Chatto, 2000.

[———]. *A Humble Proposal to the People of England, for the Increase of Their Trade, and Encouragement of their Manufactures, Whether the Present Uncertainty of Affairs Issues in Peace or War*. In *The Complete English Tradesman*. In *The Novels and Miscellaneous Works of Daniel Defoe*, ed. Sir G. C. Lewis, 20 vols. 17: np. Oxford, 1841.

[———]. *A Journal of the Plague Year: Being Observations or Memorials of the Most Remarkable Occurrences, as Well Public as Private, Which Happened in London During the Last Great Visitation in 1665*, ed. Christopher Bristow. London: Penguin, 1966.

[———]. *The Life and Strange Surprising Adventures of Robinson Crusoe, of York, Mariner*. Dover thrift edition. Mineola: Dover, 1998.

[———]. *A Plan of the English Commerce*. In *Political and Economic Writings of Daniel Defoe*. Volume 7, *Trade*, ed. John McVeagh, 115–341. London: Pickering & Chatto, 2000.

[———]. *The Protestant Monastery*. In *Political and Economic Writings of Daniel Defoe*. Volume 8, *Social Reform*, ed. W. R. Owens, 237–55. London: Pickering & Chatto, 2000.

[———]. *A Review of the Affairs of France* (Jan. 6, 1705). In *Defoe's Review*, ed. Arthur Secord, 1: np. New York: Columbia University Press for the Facsimile Text Society, 1938.

[———]. *A Review of the Affairs of France* (Mar. 20, 1705). In *Defoe's Review*, ed. Arthur Secord, 2: np. New York: Columbia University Press for the Facsimile Text Society, 1938.

[———]. *A Review of the State of the British Nation* (Jan. 27, 1709). In *Defoe's Review*, ed. Arthur Secord, 5: np. New York: Columbia University Press for the Facsimile Text Society, 1938.

[———]. *A Review of the State of the British Nation* (June 14, 1709). In *Defoe's Review*, ed. Arthur Secord, 6: np. New York: Columbia University Press for the Facsimile Text Society, 1938.

[———] *A Review of the State of the British Nation* (March 1, 1711). In *Defoe's Review*, ed. Arthur Secord, 7: np. New York: Columbia University Press for the Facsimile Text Society, 1938.

[———]. *A Review of the State of the British Nation* (Sept. 29, 1711). In *Defoe's Review*, ed. Arthur Secord, 8: np. New York: Columbia University Press for the Facsimile Text Society, 1938.

[———]. "The True-Born Englishman." In *The Earlier Life and The Chief Earlier Works of Daniel Defoe*, ed. Henry Morley, 182–218. London, 1889.

[———]. *The Villainy of Stock-Jobbers Detected, and the Causes of the Late Run on the Bank and Bankers Discovered and Considered*. In *Political and Economic Writings of Daniel Defoe*. Volume 6, *Finance*, ed. John Mcveagh, 33–47. London: Pickering & Chatto, 2000.

Devine, T. M. *Scotland's Empire, 1600–1815*. London: Allen Lane, 2003.

Dharwadker, A. "Nation, Race, and the Ideology of Commerce in Defoe." *Eighteenth-Century Theory and Interpretation* 39, no. 1 (Spring 1998): 63–84.

Dickinson, H. T., ed. *The Letters of Henry St John to the Earl of Orrery, 1709–1711. Camden Miscellany* 26. Camden: Camden Soc. 4th series, 14 (1975).

Dickson, David. *New Foundations: Ireland, 1660–1800*. Dublin: Helicon, 1987.

———. *New Foundations: Ireland, 1660–1800*. 2nd ed. Dublin: Irish Academic Press, 2000.

Dickson, P. G. M. *The Financial Revolution in England. A Study in the Development of Public Credit, 1688–1756.* London: Macmillan, 1967.

Donnan, Elizabeth. *Documents Illustrative of the History of "The Early Days of the South Sea Company."* Repr. of 1930 ed. 2 vols. New York: Octagon, 1969.

———. "The Early Days of the South Sea Company, 1711–1718." *Journal of Economic and Business History* 3 (1930): 419–50.

Donnelly, A. J. "The Administration of Customs and Excise in Ireland." Typescript lecture delivered to the Civics Institute of Ireland, Nov. 1950. Dublin, National Library of Ireland.

Dottin, Paul. *The Life and Strange and Surprising Adventures of Daniel Defoe.* Trans. Louise Ragan. London: Stanley Paul, 1928.

Downie, J. A. "The Commission of Public Accounts and the Formation of the Country Party." *English Historical Review* 91, no. 358 (Jan. 1976): 33–51.

———. "The Myth of the Bourgeois Public Sphere." In *The Concise Blackwell Companion to the Restoration and Eighteenth Century,* ed. Cynthia Wall, 58–79. Oxford: Blackwell, 2005.

———. "Public Opinion and the Political Pamphlet." In *The Cambridge History of English Literature, 1660–1780,* ed. John Richetti, 549–71. Cambridge: Cambridge University Press, 2005.

———. *The World of Defoe.* New York: Atheneum, 1977.

Earle, Peter. *The Treasure of the* "Concepción": *The Wreck of the Almiranta.* New York: Viking, 1980. [First published as *The Wreck of the* "Almiranta"—*Sir William Phips and The Hispaniola Treasure.* London: Macmillan, 1979.]

Edgar, William. *A Collection of Several Statutes and Clauses of Acts Made and Passed in This Kingdom, and in Great Britain, Relating to His Majesty's Revenue of Ireland.* Dublin, 1720.

Egan, Seán. "Finance and the Government of Ireland, 1660–85." 2 vols. Unpub. Diss., University of Dublin, 1983.

Ehrenpreis, Irvin. *Swift: The Man, His Works, and the Age.* 3 vols. Cambridge, MA: Harvard University Press, 1962–83.

Ehrman, John. *The Navy in the War of William III, 1689–1697: Its State and Direction.* Cambridge: Cambridge University Press, 1953.

Ernst, Joseph Albert. *Money and Politics in America, 1755–1775: A Study in the Currency Act of 1764 and the Political Economy of Revolution.* Chapel Hill: University of North Carolina Press for the Institute of Early American History and Culture, 1973.

Fauske, Christopher J., ed. *Archbishop William King and the Anglican Irish Context, 1688–1729.* Dublin: Four Courts Press, 2003.

———. *Jonathan Swift and the Church of Ireland, 1710–1724.* Dublin: Irish Academic Press, 2002.

Fennelly, Teddy. *Thomas Prior: His Life, Times and Legacy.* Portlaoise: Royal Dublin Society, 2001.

Ferguson, Niall. *The Cash Nexus: Money and Power in the Modern World, 1700–2000.* London: Allen Lane, 2001.

Ferguson, Oliver. *Swift and Ireland.* Urbana: University of Illinois Press, 1962.

Fleming, James. *A Collection of all the Irish and English Statutes Now in Force and Use, Relating to His Majesty's Revenue in Ireland.* Dublin, 1749.

Forbes, Duncan. *Hume's Philosophical Politics.* Cambridge: Cambridge University Press, 1975.

Ford, R. *A Further Attempt Towards the Reformation of the Coin.* London, 1696.

Glassey, Lionel K. J. "Politics, Finance, and Government." In *The Reigns of Charles II and James VII & II,* ed. Lionel K. J. Glassey, 36–70. Problems in Focus Series. Basingstoke: Palgrave, 1997.

Goldie, Mark. "The Unacknowledged Republic: Officeholding in Early Modern England." In *The Politics of the Excluded, c. 1500–1850,* ed. Tim Harris, 153–94. Themes in Focus Series. New York: Palgrave, 2001.

Goldsmith, M. M. *Private Vices, Public Benefits: Bernard Mandeville's Social and Political Thought,* Cambridge: Cambridge University Press, 1985.

———. " 'The Treacherous Arts of Mankind': Bernard Mandeville and Female Virtue.' *History of Political Thought* 7, no. 1 (Spring 1986): 93–114.

Goodwin, Albert. "Wood's Halfpence." *English Historical Review* 51, no. 204 (Oct. 1936): 647–74.

Goose, N. "How Accurately Do the Hearth Tax Returns Reflect Wealth? A Discussion of Some Urban Evidence." *Local Population Studies* 67 (Autumn 2001): 44–63.

Graham, B. J., and L. J. Proudfoot. *Urban Improvement in Provincial Ireland, 1700–1840.* Irish Settlement Studies 4. Athlone: The Group for the Study of Irish Historic Settlement, 1994.

Green, David. *Queen Anne.* New York: Charles Scribner's, 1970.

Grey, Anchitell, ed. *Debates of the House of Commons from the Year 1667 to the Year 1694.* 10 vols. London, 1763.

Griffin, Joseph. "Parliamentary Politics in Ireland During the Reign of George I." Unpub. MA thesis, University College Dublin, 1977.

Griffin, Patrick. *The People with No Name: Ireland's Ulster Scots, America's Scots Irish, and the Creation of a British Atlantic World, 1689–1764.* Princeton: Princeton University Press, 2001.

Gunn, J. A. W. "Public Opinion." In *Political Innovation and Conceptual Change,* eds. Terence Ball, James Farr, Russell L. Hanson, 247–65. Ideas in Context. Cambridge: Cambridge University Press, 1989.

Guy, Alan. J., "The Irish Military Establishment, 1660–1776." In *A Military History of Ireland,* eds. Thomas Bartlett and Keith Jeffrey, 211–30. Cambridge: Cambridge University Press, 1996.

Habermas, Jürgen. *The Structural Transformation of the Public Sphere: An Inquiry into a Category of Bourgeois Society.* Trans. Thomas Burger. Cambridge: Polity Press; MIT Press, 1989.

Hall, F. G. *The Bank of Ireland, 1783–1946.* Dublin: Hodges Figgis, 1949.

Hamilton, Alexander Henry Abercromby. *Quarter Sessions from Queen Elizabeth to Queen Anne.* London: Sampson Low, Marston, Searle, and Rivington, 1878.

Hammond, Bray. *Banks and Politics in America from the Revolution to the Civil War.* Princeton: Princeton University Press, 1957.

Hancock, David. *Citizens of the World: London Merchants and the Integration of the British Atlantic Community, 1735–1785.* Cambridge: Cambridge University Press, 1995.

Hanson, J. W. *Contemporary Printed Sources for British and Irish Economic History.* Cambridge: Cambridge University Press, 1963.

Harris, Bob. *Politics and the Nation: Britain in the Mid-Eighteenth Century.* Oxford: Oxford University Press, 2002.

Harris, Joseph. *An Essay upon Money and Coins.* London, 1758.

H[aynes], T[homas]. *A Proposal to Make Good the Coyn of this Kingdom, Without Diminishing the Species Thereof.* [London], 1696.

Hayton, D. W. "The 'Country' Interest and the Party System, 1689–*c.*1720." In *Party and Management in Parliament, 1660–1784,* ed. Clyve Jones, 37–85. Leicester: Leicester University Press, 1984.

———. "A Debate in the Irish House of Commons in 1703: A Whiff of Tory Grapeshot," *Parliamentary History* 10, no. 1 (1991): 156–59.

———. "Introduction: The Long Apprenticeship," *Parliamentary History* 20, no. 1 (2001): 1–26.

———, ed. *The Letters of Marmaduke Coghill, 1722–1738.* Dublin: Irish Manuscripts Commission, 2005.

———. *Ruling Ireland, 1685–1742: Politics, Politicians and Parties.* Woodbridge: Boydell and Brewer, 2004.

Hayton, D. W. and Clyve Jones, eds. *A Register of Parliamentary Lists, 1660–1761.* Leicester: University of Leicester History Department, 1979.

———. "The Stanhope/Sunderland Ministry and the Repudiation of Irish Parliamentary Independence." *English Historical Review* 113, no. 452 (June 1998): 610–36.

Healey, George Harris, ed. *The Letters of Daniel Defoe.* Oxford: Clarendon, 1955.

Heckscher, Eli F. *Mercantilism.* Trans. Mendel Shapiro. 2 vols. London: Allen & Unwin, 1935.

———. *Mercantilism.* Tr. Mendel Shapiro. Rev. ed., ed. E. F. Soderlund. 2 vols. London: Unwin, 1955.

Henning, Basil Duke, ed. *The History of Parliament: The House of Commons, 1660–1690.* 3 vols. London: Secker and Warburg, 1983.

Hill, Jacqueline. "Ireland Without Union: Molyneux and His Legacy." In *A Union for Empire: Political Thought and the British Union of 1707,* ed. John Robertson, 271–96. Cambridge: Cambridge University Press, 1995.

Hodges, James. *Considerations and Proposals for Supplying the Present Scarcity of Money, and Advancing Trade.* Edinburgh, 1705.

Hoffman, Philip T., and Kathryn Norberg, eds. *Fiscal Crises, Liberty, and Representative Government, 1450–1789.* Stanford, CA: Stanford University Press, 1994.

Holmes, Geoffrey. *British Politics in the Age of Anne.* Rev. ed. London: Hambledon Press, 1987.

———. "Gregory King and the Social Structure of Pre-industrial England." *Transactions of the Royal Historical Society* 5th series, 27 (1977): 41–68.

Hoppitt, Julian. "Attitudes to Credit in Britain, 1680–1790." *Historical Journal* 33, no. 2 (1990): 305–22.

———. *A Land of Liberty? England, 1689–1727.* Oxford: Clarendon, 2000.

Horne, T. A. *The Social Thought of Bernard Mandeville: Virtue and Commerce in Eighteenth-Century England.* London: Macmillan 1978.

Horsefield, J. Keith. *British Monetary Experiments, 1650–1710.* Cambridge, MA: Harvard University Press, 1960.

Horwitz, Henry. *Parliament, Policy and Politics in the Reign of William III.* Manchester: Manchester University Press, 1977.

Hoskins, W. G. ed. *Exeter in the Seventeenth Century: Tax and Rate Assessments, 1602–1699.* Exeter: Devon and Cornwall Record Society (n. s., no. 2), 1957.

———. *Industry, Trade, and People in Exeter, 1688–1800.* 2nd ed. Exeter: Exeter University Press, 1968.

———. *The Midland Peasant: The Economic and Social History of a Leicestershire Village—Wigston Magna.* London: Macmillan, 1957.

———. "The Rebuilding of Rural England, 1570–1640." *Past and Present* 4 (Nov. 1953): 44–59.

Hume, David. *Essays, Moral, Political and Literary.* London: G. Richards,1903.

———. "Of Public Credit." In *David Hume: Political Essays,* ed. Knud Haakonssen, 166–78. Cambridge: Cambridge University Press, 1994.

Hundert E. G. *The Enlightenment's Fable: Bernard Mandeville and the Discovery of Society.* Cambridge: Cambridge University Press, 1994.

Husbands, C. "Hearths, Wealth, and Occupations: An Exploration of the Hearth Tax in the Later Seventeenth Century." In *Surveying the People: The Interpretation and Use of Document Sources for the Study of Population in the Later Seventeenth Century,* eds. Kevin Schurer and Tom Arkell, 65–77. A Local Population Studies Supplement. Oxford: Leopard's Head Press for Local Population Studies, 1992.

Hutchison, Terence. *Before Adam Smith: The Emergence of Political Economy, 1662–1776.* Oxford: Blackwell, 1988.

"Instructions to the Officers." In Tom Arkell, "Printed Instructions for Administering the Hearth Tax." In *Surveying the People: The Interpretation and Use of Document Sources for the Study of Population in the Later Seventeenth Century,* eds. Kevin Schurer and Tom Arkell, 56–64. A Local Population Studies Supplement. Oxford: Leopard's Head Press for Local Population Studies, 1992.

[Irwin, John]. *The Phoenix or a New Scheme for Establishing Credit.* Dublin, 1721.

James, F. G. *Ireland in the Empire 1688–1770.* Cambridge, MA: Harvard University Press, 1973.

Jenkins, Alexander. *The History of the City of Exeter.* London, 1806.

Johnston, Joseph. "Berkeley and the Abortive Bank Project of 1720–21." In *Bishop Berkeley's "Querist" in Historical Perspective,* ed. Joseph Johnston, 44–51. Dundalk: Dundalgan Press, 1970.

———, ed. *George Berkeley's "Querist" in Historical Perspective.* Dundalk: Dundalgan, 1970.

———. "Irish Currency in the Eighteenth Century." In *Bishop Berkeley's "Querist" in Historical Perspective,* ed. Joseph Johnston, 52–71. Dundalk: Dundalgan Press, 1970.

Johnston-Liik, Edith Mary. *The History of the Irish Parliament, 1692–1800: Commons, Constituencies and Statutes.* 6 vols. Belfast: Ulster Historical Society, 2002.

Jones, D. W. "London Merchants and the Crisis of the 1690s." In *Crisis and Order in English Towns, 1500–1700,* eds. Peter Clark and Paul Slack, 311–55. London: Routledge & Kegan Paul, 1972.

———. *War and Economy in the Age of William III and Marlborough.* Oxford: Blackwell, 1988.

Jones, J. R. "Fiscal Policies, Liberties, and Representative Government During the Reigns of the Last Stuarts." In *Fiscal Crises, Liberty, and Representative Government, 1450–1789,* eds. Philip Hoffman and Kathryn Norberg, 67–95. Stanford, CA: Stanford University Press, 1994.

———. *Marlborough.* Cambridge: Cambridge University Press, 1993.

Jordan, Louis. "Chronological Listing of Documents and Events Relating to the Massachusetts Mint." July 7, 2005 <http://www.coins.nd.edu/ColCoin/ColCoinIntros/MAMintDocs.chron.html>.

Keay, John. *The Honourable Company: A History of the English East India Company* London: HarperCollins, 1991.

Kelly, James. "Harvests and Hardship: Famine and Scarcity in Ireland in the late 1720s." *Studia Hibernica* 26 (1992): 65–105.

———. "Jonathan Swift and the Irish Economy in the 1720s." *Eighteenth-Century Ireland* 6 (1991): 7–36.

Kelly, Patrick. " 'Conclusions By No Means Calculated for the Circumstances and Condition of Ireland': Swift, Berkeley and the Solution to Ireland's Economic Problems." In *Locating Swift: Essays from Dublin on the 250th Anniversary of the Death of Jonathan Swift, 1667–1745,* eds. Aileen Douglas, Patrick Kelly and Ian Campbell Ross, 47–59. Dublin: Four Courts Press, 1998.

———. "Ireland and the Critique of Mercantilism in Berkeley's *Querist.*" *Hermathena* 139 (1985): 101–16.

———. *Locke on Money.* 2 vols. Oxford: Clarendon, 1991.

———. "Perceptions of Locke in Ireland in the Eighteenth Century." *Proceedings of the Royal Irish Academy* 89, section C (1989): 17–35.

———. "The Politics of Political Economy in Mid-Eighteenth-Century Ireland." In *Political Ideas in Eighteenth-Century Ireland,* ed. S. J. Connolly, 105–29. Dublin: Four Courts Press, 2000.

Kennedy, William. *English Taxation, 1640–1799.* London: London School of Economics, 1913.

Kiernan, T. J. *A History of the Financial Administration of Ireland to 1817.* London: P. S. King, 1930.

Killigrew, William. *A Proposal Shewing How This Nation May Be Vast Gainers by All the Sums of Money Given to the Crown Without Lessening the Prerogative: Humbly Offer'd to the King's Most Excellent Majesty, the Lords Spiritual and Temporal, and to the Knights, Citizens and Burgesses Assembled in Parliament.* [London], 1696.

———. *To the King and Queen's Most Excellent Majesties, the Lords Spiritual and Temporal, and to the Knights, Citizens, and Burgesses Assembled in Parliament: An Humble Proposal Shewing How This Nation May be Vast Gainers by All Sums of Mony Given to the Crown Without Lessening the Prerogative.* [London], 1690.

King, William. *The State of the Protestants of Ireland Under the Late King James's Government in Which their Carriage Towards Him is Justified, and the Absolute Necessity of Their Endeavouring to be Freed From His Government, and of Submitting to Their Present Majesties is Demonstrated.* London, 1691.

Koehn, Nancy F. *The Power of Commerce: Economy and Governance in the First British Empire.* Ithaca, NY: Cornell University Press, 1995.

Lawrence, Richard. *The Interest of Ireland in its Trade and Wealth Stated. In Two Parts.* Dublin, 1682.

Lawton, Charlwood. *A Short State of Our Condition, with Relation to the Present Parliament* London, 1693.

Lee, William. *Daniel Defoe: His Life and Recently Discovered Writings.* London, 1869.

Leersen, Joep. *Remembrance and Imagination: Patterns in the Historical and Literary Representation of Ireland in the Nineteenth Century.* Notre Dame, IN: University of Notre Dame Press, 1997.

Lein, Clayton. "Jonathan Swift and the Population of Ireland." *Eighteenth-Century Studies* 8, no. 4 (Summer 1975): 431–53.

A Letter from an Exchange Broker to a Country Gentleman Concerning Peace and South Sea Stock. London, 1711.

A Letter to a Member of Parliament, on the Settling of a Trade to the South-Sea of America. London, 1711.

Letter to an MP Touching the Late Intended Bank. Dublin, 1721.

A List of the Names of the Subscribers of Land and Money Towards a Fund for the National Land-Bank. [London], 1695.

Lock, F. P. *The Politics of* "Gulliver's Travels." Oxford: Oxford University Press, 1980.

———. *Swift's Tory Politics.* Newark, DE: University of Delaware Press, 1983.

Locke, John. *Further Considerations Concerning Raising the Value of Money: Wherein Mr. Lowndes's Arguments for it in his Late* "Report Containing an Essay for the Amendment of the Silver Coins," *are Particularly Examined.* London, 1695.

———. *Second Treatise of Government,* ed. C. B. Macpherson. Indianapolis: Hackett, 1980.

———. *Some Considerations of the Consequences of the Lowering of Interest and Raising the Value of Money in a Letter to a Member of Parliament.* In *Locke on Money,* ed. Patrick Kelly, 1: 203–342. Oxford: Clarendon, 1994.

Lowndes, William. *A Report Containing an Essay for the Amendment of the Silver Coins.* London, 1695.

Luce, A. A. *A Life of George Berkeley.* Edinburgh: Thomas Nelson, 1949.

Luttrell, Narcissus. *A Brief Historical Relation of State Affairs from September 1678 to April 1714.* Repr. ed. 6 vols. Westmead: Gregg International, 1969.

———. *The Parliamentary Diary of Narcissus Luttrell, 1691–1693*, ed. Henry Horwitz. Oxford: Clarendon, 1972.

MacLeod, Christine. "The 1690s Patents Boom: Invention or Stock-Jobbing?" *Economic History Review* 2nd series, 39, no. 4 (Nov. 1986): 549–71.

Maculla, James. *Ireland's Consternation in the Losing of Two Hundred Thousand Pounds of their Gold and Silver for Brass Money.* Dublin, 1723.

Madden, Samuel. *Reflections and Resolutions Proper for the Gentlemen of Ireland, as to Their Conduct for the Service of Their Country, as Landlords, Masters of Families, as Protestants, as Descended from British Ancestors, as Country Gentlemen and Farmers, as Justices of the Peace, as Merchants, as Members of Parliament.* Dublin, 1738.

Magennis, Eoin. "Coal, Corn and Canals: Parliament and the Dispersal of Public Moneys, 1695–1772." *Parliamentary History* 20, no. 1 (2001): 71–86.

———. *The Irish Political System, 1745–1765: The Golden Age of the Undertakers.* Dublin: Four Courts Press, 2000.

Malcomson, A. P. W. *Nathaniel Clements: Government and the Governing Elite in Ireland, 1725–1775.* Dublin: Four Courts Press, 2005.

Mandeville, Bernard. *Fable of the Bees*, ed. F.B. Kaye. 2 vols. Indianapolis: Liberty, 1988.

[Maples, Thomas]. *A Vindication of the Intended Alteration of the Values of the Several Coins Now Current in the Kingdom.* Dublin, 1730.

Markley, Robert. " 'So Inexhaustable a Treasure of Gold': Defoe, Capitalism, and the Romance of the South Seas." *Eighteenth-Century Life* 18 (1994): 148–67.

Marshall, Lydia. "The Levying of the Hearth Tax, 1662–1688." *English Historical Review* 51, no. 204 (Oct. 1936): 628–46.

Massie, Joseph. *Observations Relating to the Coin of Great Britain; Consisting Partly of Extracts from Mr Locke's Treatise Concerning Money, but Chiefly of Such Additions Thereto, as are Thought to be Very Necessary at this Juncture, not only for Remedying the Present Great Scarcity of Silver, but for Putting a Stop to Those Losses which this Nation Suffers by the Over-Valuing of Gold-Money, and by Prohibiting both the Melting and Exporting of British Coin. Whereunto is Annexed, Sir William Petty's* "Quantulumcunque" *Concerning Money, Reprinted from an Edition that was Printed for Private use in the year 1695, and Corrected by a Manuscript Copy of Very Good Authority.* London, 1760.

Maxwell, Henry. *Reasons Offered for Erecting a Bank in Ireland.* Dublin, 1721.

McCavitt, John. *Sir Arthur Chichester: Lord Deputy of Ireland, 1605–16.* Belfast: Institute of Irish Studies, 1998.

McCusker, John J. *Money and Exchange in Europe and America, 1600–1775: A Handbook.* Chapel Hill: The University of North Carolina Press, 1978.

McGrath, Charles Ivar. "Central Aspects of the Eighteenth-Century Constitutional Framework in Ireland: The Government Supply Bill and Biennial Parliamentary Sessions, 1715–82." *Eighteenth-Century Ireland* 16 (2001): 9–34.

———. "English Ministers, Irish Politicians and the Making of a Parliamentary Settlement in Ireland, 1692–95." *English Historical Review* 119, no. 482 (June 2004): 584–613.

———. "The Irish Revenue System: Government and Administration, 1689–1702." Unpub. Diss., University of London, 1997.

———. *The Making of the Eighteenth-Century Irish Constitution: Government, Parliament and the Revenue, 1692–1714.* Dublin: Four Courts Press, 2000.

———. "Parliamentary Additional Supply: The Development and Use of Regular Short-Term Taxation in the Irish Parliament, 1692–1716." *Parliamentary History* 20, no 1 (2001): 27–54.

———. "Review Article: Parliament, People and Other Possibilities." *Eighteenth-Century Ireland* 17 (2002): 157–66.

———. " 'The Public Wealth is the Sinew, the Life, of Every Public Measure': The Creation and Maintenance of a National Debt in Ireland, 1716–45." In *The Empire of Credit: The Financial Revolution in the British Atlantic World, 1700–1800,* ed. Daniel Carey and Christopher Finlay. Dublin: Irish Academic Press, 2008.

———. "Securing the Protestant Interest: The Origins and Purpose of the Penal Laws of 1695." *Irish Historical Studies* 30, no. 117 (May 1996): 25–46.

McGuire, James. "The Irish Parliament of 1692." In *Penal Era and Golden Age. Essays in Irish History, 1690–1800,* eds. Thomas Bartlett and D. W. Hayton, 1–31. Belfast: Ulster Historical Foundation, 1979.

McNally, Patrick. *Parties, Patriots and Undertakers: Parliamentary Politics in Early Hanoverian Ireland.* Dublin: Four Courts Press, 1997.

———. "Wood's Halfpence, Carteret, and the Government of Ireland, 1723–26." *Irish Historical Studies* 30, 119 (May 1997): 354–76.

McVeagh, John, ed. *Political and Economic Writings of Daniel Defoe.* Volume 6, *Finance.* London: Pickering & Chatto, 2000.

Meekings, C. A. F. "Analysis of Hearth Tax Accounts, 1662–1665." List and Index Society, vol. 153 (1979): 39–45.

———. "Analysis of Hearth Tax Accounts, 1666–1699." List and Index Society, vol. 163 (1980): 27–29.

Meier, Keith Thomas. *Defoe and the Defense of Commerce.* English Literary Studies Monograph 38. Victoria, B.C.: University of Victoria Press, 1987.

Mill, John Stuart. *Autobiography of John Stuart Mill.* In *Essential Works of John Stuart Mill,* ed. Max Lerner, 1–182. New York: Bantam, 1961.

The Mint and Exchequer United: Being a Method to Furnish his Majesty with Two, Three or Four Millions Immediately, at the Present Charge but of One Million or Less, and Supply the Want of Coin, till New Money Can be Had. [London], [1695].

Minto, William. *Daniel Defoe.* New York: Harper, 1901.

[Molesworth, Robert]. *An Account of Denmark, as it Was in the Year 1692.* London, 1694.

———. *Some Considerations for the Promoting of Agriculture and Employing the Poor.* Dublin, 1723.

Moody, T. W., F. X. Martin, and F. J. Byrne, eds. *A New History of Ireland.* Volume 9, *Maps, Genealogies, Lists.* Oxford: Oxford University Press, 1984.

——— "Daniel Defoe and Modern Economic Theory." *Indiana University Studies* 104 (June 1934): 3–28.

Moore John Robert. *A Checklist of the Writings of Daniel Defoe.* 2nd ed. Hamden: Archon, 1971.

Morgan, William. *The Origins of the South Sea Company*. New York: Academy of Political Science, 1929.

Mossner, E. C., Ian Simpson Ross, eds. *The Correspondence of Adam Smith*. Oxford: Oxford University Press, 1987.

Muldrew, Craig. "Credit and the Courts: Debt Litigation in a Seventeenth-Century Urban Community." *Economic History Review* 46, no. 1 (Feb. 1993): 23–38.

———. *The Economy of Obligation: The Culture of Credit and Social Relations in Early Modern England*. New York: St. Martin's, 1998.

Munck, Thomas. *The Enlightenment: A Comparative Social History*. London: Arnold, 2000.

Murdoch, A. *British History, 1660–1832: National Identity and Local Culture*. Basingstoke: Macmillan, 1998.

Murphy, Antoin E. *Richard Cantillon: Entrepreneur and Economist*. Oxford: Clarendon, 1986.

Murray, A. E. *A History of the Commercial and Financial Relations Between England and Ireland from the Period of the Restoration* London: P. S. King, 1903.

Murray, Robert. *A Proposal for the More Easie Advancing to the Crown Any Fixed Sum of Mony, to Carry on the War against France, and Payment of the Debts Contracted Thereby*. [London], 1696.

Neal, Larry. *The Rise of Financial Capitalism: International Capital Markets in the Age of Reason*. Cambridge: Cambridge University Press, 1990.

Neale, Thomas. *The National Land-Bank, Together with Money: So Composed, as not Only to be Easie Understood and Easily Practiced, but More Capable also of Supplying the Government with Any Sum of Money in Proportion to what Fund Shall be Settled: As Likewise, the Free-Holder with Money at a More Moderate Interest, than if Such a Bank did Consist of Money Alone without Land*. [London], 1696.

[———]. *A Proposal for Raising a Million on a Fund of Interest by Setling One Hundred Thousand Pounds Yearly to Pay 8 per cent. For One Million Two Hundred Thousand Pounds, of Which the King to have a Million*. [London], 1694.

———. *A Way How to Supply the King's Occasions with Two Millions of Money on a Fund of 120000l. Yearly, Which is at 6 Only Per Cent. Without Any Prejudice to His Majesty's Present Revenue, or Compulsion to Those that Shall Receive it, but Rather a Convenience to Both*. [London], 1694.

Newton, Isaac, Sir. "A Copy of the *Report* Made by *Sir Isaac Newton, Edw Southwel,* and *John Scroope,* Esqs; of the *Assay* made of Mr *Wood's Copper Money*." In *The Prose Works of Jonathan Swift*. Volume 10, *The Drapier's Letters and Other Works,* ed. Herbert Davis, 187–88. Rev. ed. Oxford: Blackwell, 1959.

Nicholson, Colin. *Writing and the Rise of Finance: Capital Satires of the Early Eighteenth Century*. Cambridge: Cambridge University Press, 1994.

North, Douglas and Barry Weingast. "Constitutions and Commitment: The Evolution of Institutions Governing Public Choice in Seventeenth-Century England." *Journal of Economic History* 49, no. 4 (Dec. 1989): 802–32.

Novak, Maximillian. *Daniel Defoe: Master of Fictions*. Oxford: Oxford University Press, 2001.

———. *Economics and the Fiction of Daniel Defoe.* Berkeley: University of California Press, 1962.

O'Brien, Patrick K. "England, 1485–1815." In *The Rise of the Fiscal State in Europe c. 1200–1815*, ed. Richard Bonney, 53–100. Oxford: Oxford University Press, 1999.

———. "Excises and the Rise of a Fiscal State in England, 1586–1688." In *Crises, Revolutions and Self-Sustained Growth: Essays in European Fiscal History, 1130–1830*, eds. Mark Ormrod, Margaret Bonney and Richard Bonney, 198–223. Stamford: Shaun Tyas, 1999.

———. "Fiscal Exceptionalism: Great Britain and its European Rivals from Civil War to Triumph at Trafalgar and Waterloo." In *The Political Economy of British Historical Experience, 1688–1914*, eds. Patrick K. O'Brien and Donald Winch, 245–66. Oxford: Oxford University Press / British Academy, 2002.

———. *"Inseparable Connections: Trade, Economy, Fiscal State, and the Expansion of Empire, 1688–1815."* In *The Oxford History of the British Empire.* Volume 2, The Eighteenth Century, ed. P. J. Marshall, 53–77. Oxford: Oxford University Press, 1998.

———. "The Political Economy of British Taxation, 1660–1815." *Economic History Review* 41, no. 1 (Feb. 1988): 1–32.

———. 'Public Finance in the Wars with France, 1793–1815." In *Britain and the French Revolution, 1789–1815*, ed. H. T. Dickinson, 165–87. Basingstoke: Macmillan, 1989.

O'Brien, Patrick K., and P. A. Hunt. "The Emergence and Consolidation of Excises in the English Fiscal System before the Glorious Revolution." *British Tax Review* no. 1 (1997): 35–58.

———. "The Rise of a Fiscal State in England 1485–1815." *Historical Research* 66, no. 160 (June 1993): 129–76.

O'Donovan, Declan. "The Money Bill Dispute of 1753." In *Penal Era and Golden Age. Essays in Irish History, 1690–1800*, eds. Thomas Bartlett and D. W. Hayton, 55–87. Belfast: Ulster Historical Foundation, 1979.

Oldmixon, John. *The History of England during the Reigns of King William and Queen Mary, Queen Anne, King George I.* London, 1735.

The Only Way to Have the Rents of England Well Paid, and also Help Trade and Supply the Government. London, 1696.

O'Regan, Philip. "Accountability and Financial Control as 'Patriotic' Strategies: Accomptants and the Public Accounts Committee in Late Seventeenth- and Early Eighteenth-Century Ireland." *Accounting Historians Journal* 30, no. 2 (Dec. 2003): 105–31.

———. *Archbishop William King of Dublin (1650–1729) and the Constitution in Church and State.* Dublin: Four Courts Press, 2000.

Ormrod, W. Mark, Margaret Bonney and Richard Bonney, eds. *Crises, Revolutions and Self-Sustained Growth: Essays in European Fiscal History, 1130–1830.* Stamford: Shaun Tyas, 1999.

[Paterson, William]. *A Brief Account of the Intended Bank of England.* [London], 1694.

[———]. *Some Account of the Transactions of Mr. William Paterson in Relation to the Bank of England and the Orphans Fund: In a Letter to a Friend.* London, 1695.

Payne, William Lytton. *Mr. Review: Daniel Defoe as Author of The Review.* New York: King's Crown Press, 1947.

Pearson, J. B. "Six Assessments of Devon." *Transcripts of the Devon Association* 22 (1890): 143–65.

Phillips, Mark S. *Society and Sentiment: Genres of Historical Writing in Britain, 1740–1820.* Princeton: Princeton University Press, 2000.

Philp, Mark, ed. *Thomas Paine:* "Rights of Man," "Common Sense," *and Other Political Writings.* World's Classics. Oxford: Oxford University Press, 1998.

Pincus, Steven, and Alan Houston, eds. *A Nation Transformed: England after the Restoration.* Cambridge: Cambridge University Press, 2001.

Pocock, J. G. A. "Cambridge Paradigms and Scotch Philosophers." In *Wealth & Virtue: The Shaping of Scottish Political Economy in the Scottish Enlightenment,* eds. Istvan Hont and Michael Ignatieff, 235–52. Cambridge: Cambridge University Press, 1983.

———, ed. *Edmund Burke:* "Reflections on the Revolution in France." Indianapolis: Hackett, 1987.

———. "Machiavelli, Harrington, and English Political Ideologies in the Eighteenth Century." *William and Mary Quarterly* 22, no. 4 (Oct. 1965): 549–83.

———. *The Machiavellian Moment: Florentine Political Thought and the Atlantic Republican Tradition.* Princeton: Princeton University Press, 1975.

———. *Virtue, Commerce, and History: Essays on Political Thought and History, Chiefly in the Eighteenth Century.* Cambridge: Cambridge University Press, 1985.

Prior, Thomas. *A List of the Absentees of Ireland and an Estimate of the Yearly Value of Their Estates and Incomes Spent Abroad: With Observations on the Trade and Manufactures of Ireland, and the Means to Encourage, Improve, and Extend them; With Some Reasons why Great-Britain Should be More Indulgent to Ireland, in Particular Points of Trade: Also Some Reasons and Observations why Absentees Should be Obliged to Contribute to the Support and Welfare of the Country They Derive Their Honours, Estates, and Incomes from: Humbly Submitted to the Consideration of the Legislature of Ireland.* Dublin, 1729.

———. *Observations on Coin in General With Some Proposals for Regulating the Value of Coin in Ireland* (Dublin, 1729). In "Old and Scarce Tracts on Money." *Photographed from the Original Volume Printed for the Political Economy Club, 1856,* ed. J. R. McCulloch, 291–338. London: P.S. King, 1933.

A Proposal for an Equal Land-Tere: Humbly Submitted to Consultation. London, 1691.

A Proposal for the Relief of Ireland, by a Coinage of Monies, of Gold, and Silver and Establishing a National Bank. Dublin, 1734.

Proposals Humbly Offered to the Honourable House of Commons for Calling the Coyn of England and Preventing Clipping. [London], 1695.

Proposals Humbly Offered to the Parliament Concerning the Coyn. [London], 1695.

Proposals Humbly Offer'd to the Parliament for Regulating the Coyn of this Kingdom. [London], 1695.

Proposals Humbly Offered to the Parliament for the Supplying of the King with Present Money Without Interest. [London], 1694.

Publick Securities: Or, the Parliamentary Funds Established for Paying the Annuities, or Other Interests Granted to Private Persons or Communities for Moneys at Several Times Advanc'd to the Public Service, Extracted from all the Acts of Parliament Relating Thereunto. London, 1712.

Queries Relative to the New Half-Pence and Lowering the Coin. Dublin, 1737.

Quinn, Stephen. "Tallies or Reserves? Sir Francis Child's Balance between Capital Reserves and Extending Credit to the Crown, 1685–1695." *Business and Economic History* 23, no. 1 (1994): 39–51.

R. L. *A Proposal for Supplying his Majesty with Twelve Hundred Thousand Pounds, by Mending the Coin, and Yet Preserve the Ancient Standard of the Kingdom.* London, 1695.

Rand, Benjamin, ed. *Berkeley and Percival.* Cambridge: Cambridge University Press, 1914.

Rashid, Salim. "The Irish School of Economic Development, 1720–1750." *The Manchester School of Economic and Social Studies* 54 (1988): 345–69.

Real, Hermann J., and Heinz J. Vienken. "The Structure of *Gulliver's Travels.*" In *Proceedings of the First Münster Symposium on Jonathan Swift,* eds. Hermann J. Real and Heinz J. Vienken, 216–31. Munich: Wilhelm Fink, 1985.

Réamonn, Seán. *History of the Revenue Commissioners.* Dublin: Institute of Public Administration, 1981.

Reasons for Regulating the Coin, and Reducing the Interest; With a Scheme for Paying Part of the National Debt Without Burthening Ireland. [Dublin], 1731.

Reflections on the National Debt; With Reasons for Reducing the Legal Interest; And Against a Publick Loan. With some Advice to the Electors of Members of Parliament. [Dublin?], 1731.

Remarks upon the Bank of England, with Regard More Especially to Our Trade and Government. Occasion'd by the Present Discourse Concerning the Intended Prolongation of the Bank. London, 1706.

A Reply to the Principal Arguments for the Reduction of the Gold Coin. Dublin, 1737.

Richards, R. D. *The Early History of Banking in England.* Repr. of 1929 ed. New York: A. M Kelley, 1965.

Ries, Paul. "Robert Molesworth's *Account of Denmark*: A Study in the Art of Political Publishing and Bookselling in England and on the Continent Before 1700." *Scandinavica* 7 (1968): 108–25.

Ritchie Robert C. *Captain Kidd and the War Against the Pirates.* Cambridge, MA: Harvard University Press, 1986.

Roberts, Stephen K. *Recovery and Restoration in an English County: Devon Local Administration, 1646–1670.* Exeter: Exeter University Press, 1985.

[Robinson, Bryan]. *A Short Essay upon Coin.* Dublin, 1737.

Roseveare, Henry. Rev. of Ormrod, W. Mark, Margaret Bonney, and Richard Bonney, eds. *Crises, Revolutions and Self-Sustained Growth: Essays in European Fiscal History, 1130–1830. Economic History Review* 54, no. 2 (May 2002): 391–92.

———. *The Financial Revolution, 1660–1760.* London: Longman, 1991.

———. *The Treasury 1660–1870: The Foundation of Control.* London: Allen and Unwin, 1973.

———. *The Treasury: The Evolution of an Institution.* London: Allen Lane, 1969.

Rotwein, Eugene, ed. *David Hume's Writings on Economics.* Madison: University of Wisconsin Press, 1955.

Rousseau, Jean-Jacques. *Emile, or Education.* Trans. Barbara Foxley. New York: Dutton, 1911.

Rowley, Hercules. *An Answer to a Book, Intitl'd, Reasons Offer'd for Erecting a Bank in Ireland. In a Letter to Henry Maxwell, Esq.* Dublin, 1721.

Rubini, Dennis. "Politics and the Battle for the Banks, 1688–1697." *English Historical Review* 85, no. 337 (Oct. 1970): 693–714.

Ryder, Michael, "The Bank of Ireland, 1721: Land, Credit and Dependency." *Historical Journal* 25, no. 3 (Sept. 1982): 557–82.

Saville, Richard. *Bank of Scotland: A History, 1695–1995.* Edinburgh: Edinburgh University Press, 1996.

A Scheme, with Reasons for Settling the South Sea Trade. London, 1711.

Schumpter, Joseph. *History of Economic Analysis.* New York: Oxford University Press, 1954.

Schwoerer, Lois. *No Standing Armies! The Anti-Army Ideology in the Seventeenth Century.* Baltimore: Johns Hopkins University Press, 1975.

A Second Discourse About Banks: Between a Brigadier, a Lawyer, a Merchant and a Goldsmith. [London], [1696].

The Several Acts of Parliament Made for Establishing, Ordering and Collecting of His Majesties Revenue Arising by Hearth-Money: Abstracted also in an Index, and Margented Accordingly, for the Benefit of Such Persons as Are or May Be Concerned Therein. London, 1668. Repr. ed. 1678 and 1681.

Shelton, George. *Dean Tucker and his Eighteenth-Century Economic and Political Thought.* New York: St. Martin's, 1981.

Sherman, Sandra. "Credit, Simulation, and the Ideology of Contract in the Early Eighteenth Century." *Eighteenth-Century Life* 19, no. 3 (Nov. 1995): 86–102.

———. *Finance and Fictionality in the Early Eighteenth Century: Accounting for Defoe.* Cambridge: Cambridge University Press, 1996.

———. *History of the Public Revenue of the British Empire.* Repr. of 1803–4 3rd ed. New York: A. M. Kelley, 1970.

Sinclair, John. *Hints; Addressed to the Public. Calculated to Dispel the Gloomy Ideas which have been Lately Entertained of the State of our Finances.* London, 1783.

Simmel, Georg. *The Philosophy of Money,* ed. David Frisby. Trans. Tom Bottomore and David Frisby. London: Routledge, 1990.

Simms, J. G. *Jacobite Ireland, 1685–91.* London: Routledge & K. Paul, 1969. Repr. ed. Dublin: Four Courts Press, 2000.

A Short Answer to Short Reasons Why Our Gold Money in Ireland Should Not be Lowered. Dublin, 1737.

Simon, James. *An Essay Towards an Historical Account of Irish Coins and of the Currency of Foreign Monies in Ireland: With an Appendix Containing Several Statutes, Proclamations, Patents, Acts of State and Letters Relating to the Same.* Dublin, 1749.

Smith, Adam. *An Inquiry into the Nature and Causes of The Wealth of Nations,* ed. Edwin Cannan. Chicago: University of Chicago Press, 1976.

———. "Of Public Debts." In *An Inquiry into the Nature and Causes of the Wealth of Nations,* ed. Edwin Cannan, 441–86. Chicago: University of Chicago Press, 1976.

———. *The Wealth of Nations,* ed. Andrew S. Skinner. Harmondsworth: Pelican, 1979.

———. *The Wealth of Nations.* Intro. Robert Reich. Ed. Edward Canaan. Repr. of 1776 ed. New York: Modern Library, 2000.

Some Observations by Way of Answer to a Pamphlet Called "England's Glory or the Royal Bank." London, 1695.

Some Observations upon a Late Pamphlet, Intitled, A Modest Representation of the Past and Present State of Great Britain, Occasion'd by the Late Change in the Administration. By Eubulus. London, 1711.

Some Queries, which Being Nicely Answered May Tend Very Much to the Encouragement of the South-Sea Company, and to Forwarding that Laudable Undertaking to Our Greater Satisfaction. [London], 1711.

Some Reflections Concerning Lowering the Value of the Gold Coin. Dublin, 1737.

The South Sea Scheme Examin'd and the Reasonableness Thereof Demonstrated. London, 1720.

The South Sea Whim, to the Tune of "To You Fair Ladies Now at Land, &c." London, 1711.

Sperling, John. *The South Sea Company: An Historical Essay and Bibliographical Finding List.* Cambridge, MA: Baker Library, 1962.

Spufford, Margaret. "The Scope of Local History and the Potential of the Hearth Tax Returns." *The Local Historian* 30, no. 4 (Nov. 2000): 202–21.

———. "The Significance of the Cambridgeshire Hearth Tax." *Proceedings of the Cambridge Antiquarian Society* 55 (1962): 53–64.

Starkey, David J. *British Privateering Enterprise in the Eighteenth Century.* Exeter: University of Exeter Press, 1990.

Stasavage, David. *Public Credit and the Birth of the Democratic State: France and Great Britain, 1688–1789.* Cambridge: Cambridge University Press, 2003.

Steuart, James. *An Inquiry into the Principles of Political Œconomy. Being an Essay on the Science of Domestic Policy in Free Nations.* London, 1767.

Stoate, T. L., ed. *Cornwall Hearth and Poll Taxation, 1660–1664: Direct Taxation in Cornwall in the Reign of Charles II.* Almondsbury: Arapacana, 1981.

[Swift, Jonathan]. *The Conduct of the Allies, and of the Late Ministry, in Beginning and Carrying on the Present War* (London, 1711). In *The Prose Works of Jonathan Swift.* Volume 6, *Political Tracts, 1711–13,* ed. Herbert Davis, 1–66. Oxford: Blackwell, 1951.

———. *The Correspondence of Jonathan Swift,* ed. Harold Williams. 5 vols. Oxford: Clarendon, 1963–65.

———. *The Correspondence of Jonathan Swift, D.D.*, ed. David Woolley. 5 vols. Frankfurt: Peter Lang, 1999–.

[———]. *The Examiner.* In *The Prose Works of Jonathan Swift.* Volume 3, *Contributions to* "The Examiner" *and Other Pieces Written in 1710–11,* ed. Herbert Davis, 1–173. Oxford: Blackwell, 1957.

[———]. *Gulliver's Travels* (Dublin, 1726). In *The Prose Works of Jonathan Swift.* Volume 11, *Gulliver's Travels,* ed. Herbert Davis. Oxford: Blackwell, 1959.

[———]. *The History of the Four Last Years of the Queen* (Dublin, 1758). In *The Prose Works of Jonathan Swift.* Volume 7, *The History of the Four Last Years of the Queen,* ed. Herbert Davis. Oxford: Blackwell, 1951.

[———]. "*Intelligencer* Papers." In *The Prose Works of Jonathan Swift.* Volume 12, *Irish Tracts 1728–1733,* ed. Herbert Davis, 27–62. Oxford: Blackwell, 1971.

———. "A Letter *from Dr* Swift *to Mr* Pope 1721." In *The Prose Works of Jonathan Swift.* Volume 9, *Tracts Relating to Ireland, 1720–1723,* ed. Herbert Davis, 23–34. Oxford: Blackwell, 1948.

[———]. *A Letter from a Member of the House of Commons in Ireland to a Member of the House of Commons in England Concerning the Sacramental Test* (London, 1708). In *The Prose Works of Jonathan Swift.* Volume 2, *Bickerstaff Papers and Pamphlets on the Church,* ed. Herbert Davis, 109–26. Oxford: Blackwell, 1957.

[———]. *A Letter to the Shop-keepers, Tradesmen, Farmers, and Common-People in General, of the Kingdom of Ireland* (Dublin, 1724). In *The Prose Works of Jonathan Swift.* Volume 10, *The Drapier's Letters and Other Works, 1724–1725,* ed. Herbert Davis, 1–12. Rev. ed. Oxford: Blackwell, 1959.

[———]. *A Modest Proposal for Preventing the Children of Poor People in Ireland, from Being a Burden to their Parents or Country; and for Making them Beneficial to the Publick* (Dublin, 1729). In *The Prose Works of Jonathan Swift.* Volume 12, *Irish Tracts, 1728–1733,* ed. Herbert Davis, 109–18. Oxford: Blackwell, 1971.

[———]. *A Proposal for Giving Badges to Beggars* (London, 1737). In *The Prose Works of Jonathan Swift.* Volume 13, *Directions to Servants and Miscellaneous Pieces, 1733–1742,* ed. Herbert Davis, 127–41. Oxford: Blackwell, 1959.

[———]. *A Proposal for the Universal Use of Irish Manufacture in Cloaths and Furniture of Houses, &c., Utterly Rejecting and Renouncing Every Thing Wearable that Comes from England* (Dublin, 1720). In *The Prose Works of Jonathan Swift.* Volume 9, *Tracts Relating to Ireland, 1720–1723,* ed. Herbert Davis, 13–22. Oxford: Blackwell, 1948.

[———]. *Reasons Why We Should Not Lower the Coins Now Current in this Kingdom. Occasioned by a Paper Entitled, Remarks on the Coins Current in this Kingdom. To Which is Added The Rev. Dean Swift's Opinion* (Dublin, 1736). In *The Prose Works of Jonathan Swift.* Volume 13, *Directions to Servants and Miscellaneous Pieces, 1733–1742,* ed. Herbert Davis, 115–20. Oxford: Blackwell, 1973.

[———]. *A Short View of the State of Ireland* (Dublin, 1728). In *The Prose Works of Jonathan Swift.* Volume 12, *Irish Tracts, 1728–1733,* ed. Herbert Davis, 1–12. Oxford: Blackwell, 1971.

[———]. *Some Arguments Against Enlarging the Powers of the Bishops in Letting of Leases with Remarks on Some Queries Lately Published* (Dublin, 1723). In *The Prose Works of Jonathan Swift.* Volume 9, *Irish Tracts, 1720–1723,* ed. Herbert Davis, 43–60. Oxford: Blackwell, 1948.

Taylor, Jonathan. *A Journey to Edenborough in Scotland.* Edinburgh, 1893.

Thompson, James. *Models of Value: Eighteenth-Century Political Economy and the Novel.* Durham, NC: Duke University Press, 1996.

Thoughts on the Gold Coins. Dublin, 1736.

To the Nobility, Gentry and Commonalty of this Kingdom of Ireland. Dublin, 1720.

The Trade Granted to the South-Sea-Company Considered with Relation to Jamaica in a Letter to One of the Directors of the South-Sea-Company by a Gentleman who has Resided Several Years in Jamaica. London, 1714.

Treadwell, Victor. "The Irish Customs Administration in the Sixteenth Century." *Irish Historical Studies* 20, no. 80 (Sept. 1977): 384–417.

A True Account of the Design and Advantage of the South Sea Trade: With Answers to all the Objections Rais'd Against it. London, 1711.

Trenchard, John, and Thomas Gordon. *Cato's Letters,* ed. Ronald Hamowy. 2 vols. Indianapolis: Liberty Fund, 1995.

Trenchard, John, and Walter Moyle. *An Argument Shewing, that a Standing Army is Inconsistent with a Free Government, and Absolutely Destructive to the Constitution of the English Monarchy.* London, 1697.

Tuck, Richard. *Natural Rights Theories: Their Origins and Development,* Cambridge: Cambridge University Press, 1979.

———. *Philosophy and Government, 1572–1651.* Cambridge: Cambridge University Press, 1993.

Two Letters to a Member of Parliament Concerning the Publick Debts as They Were Printed and Delivered to the Members of the House of Commons, on Occasion of His Majesty's Speech Concerning the Reduction of the Publick Debts: To Which is Added, The Present State of the Coin and Credit of the Kingdom, as it was Published and Delivered to the Members of the House of Commons. London, 1718.

An Unprejudiced Enquiry into the Nature and Consequences of the Reduction of Our Gold. Dublin, 1737.

Vaughn, Karen Iversen. "The Economic Background to John Locke's *Two Treatises of Government.*" In *John Locke's* "Two Treatises of Government": *New Interpretations,* ed. Edward J. Harpham, 118–47. Lawrence: University Press of Kansas, 1992.

Vickers, Douglas. *Studies in the Theory of Money, 1690–1776.* New York: A. M. Kelley, 1959.

Victory, Isolde. "The Making of the 1720 Declaratory Act." In *Parliament, Politics and People: Essays in Eighteenth-Century Irish History,* ed. Gerard O'Brien, 9–29. Dublin: Irish Academic Press, 1989.

Von Broeck, Adrian. *The Life and Adventures of Capt. John Avery, the Famous English Pirate (Rais'd from a Cabbin-Boy, to a King) Now in Possession of Madagascar* London, 1709

Von Ranke, Leopold. *A History of England Principally in the Seventeenth Century.* Oxford, 1875.

W. E. *A Speedy Way to Supply their Majesties Occasions.* London, 1691.

Wagner, Henry R. *Irish Economics, 1700–1783: A Bibliography with Notes.* New York: A. M. Kelley, 1969.

Webb, Daniel. *An Enquiry into the Reasons of the Decay of Credit, Trade, and Manufactures of Ireland.* Dublin, 1738.

Wennerlind, Carl. "Credit-Money as the Philosopher's Stone: Alchemy and the Coinage Problem in Seventeenth-Century England." *History of Political Economy* 35, Supplement (2003): 235–62.

———. "The Link Between David Hume's *Treaties of Human Nature* and his Fiduciary Theory of Money." *History of Political Economy* 33, no. 1 (2001): 139–60.

Whatley, Christopher A. *Bought and Sold for English Gold? Explaining the Union of 1700.* East Linton: Tuckwell, 2001.

W[hately], T[homas]. *Now is the Time: Or, the Proposal of the Loan-Bank Seasonable.* London, 1696.

Whately, Thomas. *An Advantageous Method of Extricating the Nation Out of its Present Difficulties.* London, 1696.

———. *A Double Proposal Concerning Guineas.* London, 1696.

———. *The Loan-Office: Or, An Advantageous Method of Extricating the Nation Out of its Present Difficulties.* London, 1696.

Williams, Glynwr. *The Great South Sea: English Voyages and Encounters, 1570–1750.* New Haven: Yale University Press, 1997.

Woolley, James, ed. *Jonathan Swift and Thomas Sheridan:* "The Intelligencer." Oxford: Clarendon, 1992.

Young, Arthur. *The Example of France a Warning to Britain.* London, 1793.

Contributors

ARNE BIALUSCHEWSKI is assistant professor of history at Trent University in Peterborough, Ontario. His research interests include early modern piracy, cross-cultural relations, overseas migrations, and the English publishing business in the age of Defoe.

J. ALAN DOWNIE is professor of English at Goldsmiths' College, University of London. He is the author of a number of books and essays on the long eighteenth century, including *Robert Harley and the Press: Propaganda and Public Opinion in the Age of Swift and Defoe* and *Jonathan Swift, Political Writer.* He is currently writing a political biography of Henry Fielding.

CHRIS FAUSKE is the interim dean in the school of arts and sciences at Salem State College in Massachusetts. He is the author, most recently, of *"Side by Side in a Small Country": John Frederick MacNeice and the Church of Ireland,* and the translator from Norwegian of *Skipper Worse* by Alexander Lange Kielland.

JAMES E. HARTLEY is a professor of economics at Mount Holyoke College and is currently the director of the first-year seminar program.

RICHARD KLEER has taught in the department of economics at the University of Regina in Saskatchewan since 1990. Earlier work on Adam Smith gradually awakened an interest in early-modern British monetary policy, and he is currently studying the Great Recoinage of 1696 and the South Sea Bubble of 1720.

EOIN MAGENNIS is policy research manager with InterTradeIreland, the all-island agency for trade and business development in Ireland. The research on which his chapter is based is part of a larger study of economic thought and practice in Ireland between 1690 and 1780.

CHARLES IVAR MCGRATH is a lecturer in the school of history and archives, University College Dublin. He is the author of *The Making of the Eighteenth-Century Irish Constitution: Government, Parliament and the Revenue, 1692–1714,* of articles in *The English Historical Review, Irish Historical Studies, Parliamentary History, Eighteenth-Century Ireland,* and in several edited collections and reference works. He is the coeditor of *Converts and Conversion in Ireland, 1650–1850.*

STEPHEN A. TIMMONS received a doctorate from the University of North Carolina at Chapel Hill in 1999 and currently serves as an adjunct professor at Columbus State Community College, Ohio. He has published articles relating to late seventeenth-century west country studies in *Historical Research, The Mariner's Mirror, The Historian* (Phi Alpha Theta), and *The Journal of Early Modern History.*

Index

Where an individual is known by more than one name (usually by virtue of possessing a title), the entry can be found under that person's family name.